NEW

CUTTING EDGE

UPPER INTERMEDIATE

TEACHER'S RESOURCE BOOK

photocopiable resources by Chris Redston

david albery

with sarah cunningham   peter moor

Longman

Contents

Introduction

New Cutting Edge Upper Intermediate at a glance

New Cutting Edge Upper Intermediate is aimed at young adults studying general English at an upper intermediate level and provides material for approximately 120 hours of teaching. It is suitable for students studying in either a monolingual or multilingual classroom situation.

STUDENTS' BOOK **CLASS CDS/CASSETTES**	*New Cutting Edge Upper Intermediate Students' Book* is divided into twelve modules, each consisting of approximately ten hours of classroom material. Each module contains some or all of the following: • **reading** and/or **listening** and/or **vocabulary** – an introduction to the topic of the module, and incorporates speaking • **grammar** – input/revision in two *Language focus* sections with practice activities and integrated pronunciation work • **vocabulary** – includes a *Wordspot* section which focuses on common words (*have, get, take*, etc.) • **task preparation** – a stimulus or model for the task (often listening or reading) and *Useful language* for the task • **task** – extended speaking, often with an optional writing component • a **Real life** section – language needed in more complex real-life situations, usually including listening and speaking • **writing skills** • a **Study ... Practise ... Remember!** section – to develop study skills, with practice activities and a self-assessment section for students to monitor their progress. At the back of the *Students' Book* you will find: • a **Mini-dictionary** which contains definitions, pronunciations and examples of key words and phrases from the *Students' Book* • a detailed **Language summary** covering the grammar in each module • **Tapescripts** for material on the Class CDs/Cassettes.
WORKBOOK **STUDENTS' CD/CASSETTE**	*New Cutting Edge Upper Intermediate Workbook* is divided into twelve modules, which consist of: • **grammar** – consolidation of the main language points covered in the *Students' Book* • **vocabulary** – additional practice and input • **skills work** – *Improve your writing* and *Listen and read* sections • **pronunciation** – focus on problem sounds and word stress. The optional **Students' CD/Cassette** features exercises on grammar and pronunciation. There are two versions of the *Workbook*, one with and the other without an **Answer key**.

TEACHER'S RESOURCE BOOK	*New Cutting Edge Upper Intermediate Teacher's Resource Book* consists of three sections:
	
	• **Introduction** and **Teacher's tips** on:
	  • using a discovery approach in the teaching of grammar
	  • using the *Study ... Practise ... Remember!* and *Mini-check* sections
	  • working with lexis
	  • responding to learners' individual language needs
	  • making the most of the *Mini-dictionary*
	  • making tasks work
	• **Step-by-step teacher's notes** for each module, including alternative suggestions for different teaching situations (particularly for tasks), detailed language notes and integrated answer keys
	• photocopiable **Resource bank**, including learner-training worksheets, communicative grammar practice activities and vocabulary extension activities.
	
	The teacher's notes section is **cross-referenced** to the *Resource bank* and the *Workbook*.

The thinking behind *New Cutting Edge Upper Intermediate*

Overview

New Cutting Edge Upper Intermediate has a multilayered, topic-based syllabus which includes thorough and comprehensive work on grammar, vocabulary, pronunciation and the skills of listening, reading, speaking and writing. Structured speaking tasks form a central part of each module. *New Cutting Edge Upper Intermediate* gives special emphasis to:

- communication
- the use of phrases and collocation
- active learning and study skills
- revision and recycling.

Topics and content

We aim to motivate learners by basing modules around up-to-date topics of international interest. Students are encouraged to learn more about the world and other cultures through the medium of English, and personalisation is strongly emphasised. The differing needs of monocultural and multicultural classes have been kept in mind throughout.

Approach to grammar

Learners are encouraged to take an active, systematic approach to developing their knowledge of grammar, and the opportunity to use new language is provided in a natural, communicative way. There are two *Language focus* sections in each module, in which grammar is presented using reading or listening texts. Each *Language focus* has an *Analysis* box focusing on the main language points, in which learners are encouraged to work out rules for themselves. This is followed up thoroughly through:

- a wide range of communicative and written practice exercises in the *Students' Book*
- the opportunity to use new grammar naturally in the speaking tasks (see below)
- the *Study ... Practise ... Remember!* and *Mini-check* sections, in which learners are encouraged to assess their progress and work on any remaining problems
- the *Language summary* section at the back of the *Students' Book*
- further practice in the *Workbook*.

(See *Teacher's tips: using a discovery approach in the teaching of grammar* on page 8, and *Using the* Study ... Practise ... Remember! *and* Mini-check *sections* on page 9.)

Approach to vocabulary

A wide vocabulary is vital to communicative success, so new lexis is introduced and practised at every stage in the course. Particular attention has been paid to the selection of high-frequency, internationally useful words and phrases, drawing on information from the British National Corpus.

Vocabulary input is closely related to the topics and tasks in the modules, allowing for plenty of natural recycling. Further practice is provided in the *Study ... Practise ... Remember!* section at the end of each module and in the Workbook.

In order to communicate, fluent speakers make extensive use of 'prefabricated chunks' of language. For this reason, *New Cutting Edge Upper Intermediate* gives particular emphasis

to collocations and fixed phrases. These are integrated through:

- *Wordspot* sections, which focus on high-frequency words such as *get*, *have* and *think*
- the *Useful language* boxes in the speaking tasks
- *Real life* sections, which focus on phrases used in common everyday situations such as telephoning or making arrangements
- topic-based vocabulary lessons.

(See *Teacher's tips: working with lexis* on pages 9–10.)
In addition, more straightforward single-item vocabulary is also extended through the *Vocabulary booster* sections of the *Workbook*.

'Useful' vocabulary is partly individual to the learner. With this in mind, the speaking tasks in *New Cutting Edge Upper Intermediate* provide the opportunity for students to ask the teacher for the words and phrases they need.
(See *Teacher's tips: responding to learners' individual language needs* on pages 11–12.)

To encourage learner independence, *New Cutting Edge Upper Intermediate* has a *Mini-dictionary* which includes entries for words and phrases appropriate to the level of the learner. Learners are encouraged to refer to the *Mini-dictionary* throughout the course, and there are study tips to help them to do this more effectively. (See *Teacher's tips: making the most of the Mini-dictionary* on pages 12–13.)

The speaking tasks

New Cutting Edge Upper Intermediate aims to integrate elements of a task-based approach into its overall methodology. There are structured speaking tasks in each module which include interviews, mini-talks, problem-solving and story-telling. Here the primary focus is on achieving a particular outcome or product, rather than on practising specific language. Learners are encouraged to find the language they need in order to express their own ideas.

The frequent performance of such tasks is regarded in this course as a central element in learners' progress. They provide the opportunity for realistic and extended communication, and because learners are striving to express what they want to say, they are more likely to absorb the language that they are learning. Much of the grammar and vocabulary input in each module is therefore integrated around these tasks, which in turn provide a valuable opportunity for the teacher to revisit and recycle what has been studied.

In order to make the tasks work effectively in the classroom:

- they are graded carefully in terms of difficulty
- a model/stimulus is provided for what the student is expected to do
- useful language is provided to help students to express themselves
- thinking and planning time is included.

(See *Teacher's tips: making tasks work* on pages 13–14, and *Responding to learners' individual language needs* on pages 11–12.)

In addition to the tasks, *New Cutting Edge Upper Intermediate* offers many other opportunities for speaking. For example, through the discussion of texts, communicative practice exercises, and the wide range of games and activities in the photocopiable *Resource bank* in the *Teacher's Resource Book*.

Other important elements in *New Cutting Edge Upper Intermediate*

Listening

New Cutting Edge Upper Intermediate places strong emphasis on listening. Listening material consists of:

- short extracts and mini-dialogues to introduce and practise new language
- words and sentences for close listening and to model pronunciation
- longer texts (interviews, stories and conversations), many of which are authentic, often in the *Preparation* section as a model or stimulus for the task
- regular *Listen and read* sections in the *Workbook* to further develop students' confidence in this area.

Speaking

There is also a strong emphasis on speaking, as follows.

- The tasks provide a regular opportunity for extended and prepared speaking based around realistic topics and situations (see page 6).
- Much of the practice of grammar and lexis is through oral exercises and activities.
- The topics and reading texts in each module provide opportunities for follow-up discussion.
- There is regular integrated work on pronunciation.
- Most of the photocopiable activities in the *Resource bank* are oral.

Reading

There is a wide range of reading material in the *Students' Book*, including newspaper articles, factual/scientific texts, stories, quizzes, forms, notes and letters. These texts are integrated in a number of different ways:

- extended texts specifically to develop reading skills
- texts which lead into grammar work and language analysis
- texts which provide a model or stimulus for tasks and models for writing activities.

Note: for classes who do not have a lot of time to do reading in class, there are suggestions in the teacher's notes section on how to avoid this where appropriate.

Writing

Systematic work on writing skills is developed in *New Cutting Edge Upper Intermediate* through:

- regular writing sections in the *Students' Book*, which focus on writing e-mails and letters, writing narratives and reviews, drafting and redrafting, use of linkers, etc.
- *Improve your writing* sections in the *Workbook*, which expand on the areas covered in the *Students' Book*
- written follow-up sections to many of the speaking tasks.

Pronunciation

Pronunciation work in *New Cutting Edge Upper Intermediate* is integrated with grammar and lexis, and in the *Real life* sections in special pronunciation boxes. The focus in the *Students' Book*

is mainly on stress, weak forms and intonation, while the *Workbook* focuses on problem sounds and word stress. A range of activity types are used in the *Students' Book*, including discrimination exercises and dictation, and an equal emphasis is placed on understanding and reproducing. In addition, there are *Pronunciation spots* in the *Study ... Practise ... Remember!* sections, which focus on problem sounds. These activities are intended as quick warmers and fillers, and can be omitted if not required.

Learning skills

New Cutting Edge Upper Intermediate develops learning skills in a number of ways, as follows.

- The discovery approach to grammar encourages learners to experiment with language and to work out rules for themselves.
- The task-based approach encourages learners to take a proactive role in their learning.
- Looking words and phrases up in the *Mini-dictionary* gives students constant practice of a range of dictionary skills.
- The *Study ...* sections of *Study ... Practise ... Remember!* focus on useful learning strategies, such as keeping notes and revision techniques. Learners are encouraged to share ideas about the most effective ways to learn.
- The *Resource bank* includes five learner-training worksheets aimed at developing students' awareness of the importance of taking an active role in the learning process.

Revision and recycling

Recycling is a key feature of *New Cutting Edge Upper Intermediate*. New language is explicitly recycled through:

- extra practice exercises in the *Study ... Practise ... Remember!* sections. These are designed to cover all the main grammar and vocabulary areas in the module. After trying the exercises, learners are encouraged to return to any parts of the module that they still feel unsure about to assess what they have (and have not) remembered from the module.

(See *Teacher's tips: using the* Study ... Practise ... Remember! *and* Mini-check *sections on page 9.*)

- *Consolidation* spreads after Modules 4, 8 and 12. These combine grammar and vocabulary exercises with listening and speaking activities, recycling material from the previous four modules.
- three photocopiable tests in the *Resource bank* for use after Modules 4, 8 and 12.

In addition, the speaking tasks offer constant opportunities for learners to use what they have studied in a natural way, and for teachers to assess their progress and remind them of important points.

Teacher's tips

Using a discovery approach in the teaching of grammar

New Cutting Edge Upper Intermediate uses a 'discovery' approach to grammar, because students at this level will already have some knowledge of the given language area which they can use to work out further rules for themselves. This often takes the form of 'test-teach' introductory material, and *Analysis* boxes consisting of questions to guide students towards forming hypotheses about the language and working out the rules themselves.

This approach is used because we believe that learners absorb rules better this way, and we hope that this will provide them with a useful skill to deploy outside the classroom.

❶ *Get to know the material available*

Every module of *New Cutting Edge Upper Intermediate* has two *Language focus* sections, which include:
*   a short text or 'test-teach' type introductory material
*   an *Analysis* box focusing students on the main language points
*   a *Language summary* section at the back of the *Students' Book* providing more detailed information about what is covered in the *Analysis* boxes
*   oral and/or written practice exercises.
These language areas are recycled through:
*   the *Study ... Practise ... Remember!* sections at the end of each module.
*   the *Consolidation* spreads after Modules 4, 8 and 12.
In addition to this, the *Workbook* includes additional practice material.

In the *Resource bank* of this *Teacher's Resource Book*, there are some games and other activities designed to further consolidate the grammar areas covered.

❷ *Use a global approach to grammar*

The approach in *New Cutting Edge Upper Intermediate* is to look at broad ideas of grammar (such as continuous aspect, or hypothesising about the past), enabling students to see general patterns and rules, rather than a number of details which do not appear to form any overall picture. The practice excercises that follow often focus more on individual points, however, and this approach is taken further in the *Workbook*.

❸ *Be prepared to modify your approach*

It is unlikely that you will discover that all students are using the target language perfectly and need no further work on it. However, you may realise that they only need brief revision, or that you can omit certain sections of the *Analysis* or go through some or all of it very quickly. Alternatively, you may decide to omit some of the practice activities, or set them for homework.

On the other hand, you may discover that many students know less than you would normally expect at this level. In this case, spend more time on the basic points, providing extra examples as necessary, and leave more complex issues for another day.

❹ *Encourage students to share what they know and to make guesses*

As different students will know different things, they can share what they know by working in pairs and groups. If students are not used to this approach, it is worth explaining the reasons to them, and you should allow time for them to get used to it. On the other hand, if students are getting frustrated because they want to be told the answer, there is no harm in answering individual queries. Answers can be compared as a class at the end.

❺ *Use the* Workbook *to deal with your students' individual problems*

If you have students in your group whose knowledge is lower than it should be, or if specific points in the *Students' Book* need special practice, you will find that most of the grammar exercises in the *Workbook* cover much narrower areas than the *Language focus* sections in the *Students' Book*. If your students are preparing for exams, you will find many typical exam-type exercises in the *Workbook*, designed to help here.

❻ *Include revision and recycling*

There are lots of opportunities to revise and recycle new language in this course. You can use the games and activities in the *Resource bank* for consolidation as well as the activities in the *Study ... Practise ... Remember!* sections.

Using the *Study ... Practise ... Remember!* and *Mini-check* sections

These sections are a fresh component in *New Cutting Edge Upper Intermediate*, replacing and extending the old *Do you remember?* sections. They occur at the end of each module except Modules 4, 8 and 12, where there is a more extensive *Consolidation* section.

The *Study ... Practise ... Remember!* and *Mini-check* sections have the following main aims:

- to ensure systematic consolidation of new language before learners move on to the next module
- to encourage learners to take responsibility for and assess their own progress
- to cover problem sounds which are not covered elsewhere.

❶ *Use the activities as warmers and fillers*

The activities in the *Study ... Practise ... Remember!* sections are not intended to be used all together. They can be used as warmers or fillers when you have time to spare. For example, you could do the *Study ...* section at the end of one lesson, use the *Pronunciation spot* as a warmer in another lesson and use the exercises in the *Practise ...* section either as warmers or fillers in other lessons. The *Mini-check* could be done as a short slot in the final lesson before you move on to the next module.

❷ *Encourage learners to discuss the best ways to learn and to set targets*

The *Study ...* sections draw learners' attention to a number of important study skills such as using a monolingual dictionary, revision techniques, taking notes, etc. Learners often look at a list of suggestions and discuss which ideas they feel would work best for them. They are also asked to contribute ideas of their own. This should be an open discussion, but at the end it would be useful to pin down a particular suggestion or suggestions that the learner is going to try (for example, to speak more during pair and group work). You could get them to stick a note on the front of their *Students' Book* reminding them of this target. It is very useful to return to these targets a few weeks later to discuss how well they are getting on.

❸ *Set homework based on these sections*

If you are short of time in class, the *Practise ...* section could easily be set as homework. If you do this, draw learners' attention to the *Need to check?* rubric at the end of each exercise. It might be useful to explain in class where students should look (for example, in the *Language summary*) if they need to do further revision.

❹ *Set aside time for students' questions*

If you set the *Practise ...* section for homework, in the next lesson set aside some time for students to ask any questions they have, and to complete the *Remember!* self-assessment section, before getting students to do the *Mini-check*.

❺ *Encourage students to take responsibility for their own progress*

The approach throughout the *Study ... Practise ... Remember!* section is intended to encourage learner independence and personal responsibility for progress, and the *Mini-checks* should be presented to students in this light. Of course, it would be possible for learners to cheat and prepare beforehand (which in itself might be perfectly valid revision!) but explain to learners that these checks are for their own benefit and that if they cheat, they are cheating themselves. Of course, it is also a good opportunity for you to check informally how well they are progressing.

❻ *Select the* Pronunciation spots *that are useful for your learners*

More than any other part of these sections, the *Pronunciation spots* are intended to stand alone. They can be used at any time as a warmer or filler. Some areas covered may not be a problem for your learners, in which case they can easily be omitted.

Working with lexis

❶ *Become more aware of phrases and collocations yourself*

Until recently, relatively little attention was given to the thousands of phrases and collocations that make up the lexis in English, along with the traditional one-word items. If necessary, spend some time looking at the following list of phrase types and start noticing how common these 'prefabricated chunks' are in all types of English. They go far beyond areas traditionally dealt with in English-language courses – phrasal verbs, functional exponents and the occasional idiom – although of course they incorporate all of these too.

---

a **collocations** – common word combinations – including:
- verbs + nouns (*work long hours, have a drink*)
- adjectives + nouns (*old friends, good news*)
- verbs + adverbs (*work hard, will probably*)
- verbs + prepositions/particles, including phrasal verbs (*think about, grow up*)
- adjectives + prepositions (*famous for, jealous of*)
- other combinations of the above (*go out for a meal, get to know*)

b **fixed phrases** (*Never mind! On the other hand ...*, *If I were you ..., Someone I know*)

c **semi-fixed phrases** – phrases with variations (*a friend of mine/hers/my brother's, both of us/them/my parents, the second/third/tenth biggest in the world*)

d **whole sentences which act as phrases** (*How are you? He's gone home. I'll give you a hand. I agree to some extent.*)

Such phrases blur the boundaries between 'vocabulary' and 'grammar'. In teaching these phrases you will find that you are helping students with many problematic areas that are traditionally considered to be grammar, from the use of articles and prepositions, to the use of the passive and the Present perfect. Many common examples of these structures are in fact fixed or semi-fixed phrases. A 'lexical approach' should not replace the traditional grammatical approach to such verb forms, but it is a useful supplement.

❷ Make your students aware of phrases and collocations

Students should also know about the importance of such phrases. They may look at a phrase such as *leave home* and assume that they know it (because the two constituent words look 'easy'), although in fact they are unable to produce the phrase for themselves when appropriate. *Learner-training worksheet 4* on pages 108–109 of the *Resource bank* aims to develop students' awareness of such collocations.

❸ Keep an eye on usefulness and be aware of overloading students

It is easy to 'go overboard' with collocations and phrases as there are so many of them. Also, perhaps because they often consist of such common words, they can be more difficult for students to retain, so limit your input to high-frequency, useful phrases as much as possible. As you teach lexis, ask yourself questions such as: *How often would I use this phrase myself? How often do I hear other people using it? Can I imagine my students needing it? Is it too idiomatic, culturally specific or complex to bother with?*

❹ Feed in phrases on a 'little but often' basis

To avoid overloading students and ensure that your lexical input is useful, teach a few phrases relating to particular activities as you go along. For example, in a grammar practice activity, instead of simple answers such as *Yes, I do* or *No, I haven't*, feed in phrases such as *It depends, I don't really care, I would probably …, I've never tried it*. The same is true of discussions about reading/listening texts and writing activities.

❺ Introduce phrases in context, but drill them as short chunks

Phrases can be difficult to understand and specific to certain situations, so it is important that they are introduced in context. However, students may retain them better if you drill just the phrase (for example, *badly damaged, go for a walk*) rather than a full sentence with problems which might distract from the phrase itself. Alternatively, use a very minimal sentence (*It's worth visiting* rather than *The National Gallery is worth visiting*). The drilling of such phrases can be a valuable opportunity to focus on pronunciation features such as weak forms and linking.

❻ Point out patterns in phrases

Pointing out patterns will help students to remember phrases. Many do not fit into patterns, but you can often show similar phrases with the same construction, like this:

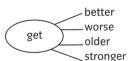

❼ Keep written records of phrases

One simple way to make your students more aware of collocation is to get into the habit of writing word combinations on the board wherever appropriate, rather than just individual words. The more students see these words together, the more likely they are to remember them as a unit. Rather than just writing up *housework* or *crime*, write up *do the housework* or *commit a crime*. In sentences, collocations can be highlighted in colour or underlined – this is particularly important when the associated words are not actually next to each other in the sentence. Remind students to write down the collocations too, even if they 'know' the constituent words.

❽ Reinforce and recycle phrases

This is particularly important with phrases which, for the reasons given above, can be hard to remember. Most revision games and activities that teachers do with single items of vocabulary can be adapted and used with phrases. You may find the following useful in addition.

- **Make wall posters:** many of the diagrams in the *Wordspot* sections in the *Students' Book* could be made into a wall poster. Seeing the phrases on the wall like this every lesson can provide valuable reinforcement. There are many other areas for which wall posters would be effective, for example, common passive phrases, or common offers with *I'll*. Always write the full phrase on the poster (*get married* not just *married*) and remove the old posters regularly as they will lose impact if there are too many.
- **Make a phrase bank:** copy new words and phrases from the lesson onto slips of card or paper (large enough for students to read if you hold them up at the front of the room) and keep them in a box or bag. This is a good record for you, as well as the students, of the phrases that the class has studied – you can get them out whenever there are a few spare moments at the beginning or end of a lesson for some quick revision. Hold them up, and as appropriate, ask students to give you:
  - an explanation of the phrase
  - a translation of the phrase
  - synonyms
  - opposites
  - the pronunciation
  - situations where they might say this
  - a sentence including the phrase
  - the missing word that you are holding your hand over (for example, *on* in the phrase *get on well with*)
  - the phrase itself, based on a definition or translation that you have given them.

Responding to learners' individual language needs

At appropriate points throughout the *Students' Book*, during the tasks and speaking activities, students are instructed to ask their teacher about any words or phrases they need. The ability to respond to students' individual language needs is central to a task-based approach, and you may find yourself doing this during pair/group/individual work and during preparation stages. The following suggestions are designed to help teachers who may feel daunted by the idea of unplanned, unpredictable input.

❶ *Encourage students to ask about language*

Students who take an active approach to their own learning are far more likely to succeed than those who sit back and expect the teacher to do it all for them. It is important to make students aware of this (see *Learner-training worksheet 1* on page 104 of the *Resource bank*), and to convey to them your willingness to deal with their queries. Circulate during pair and individual work, making it clear that you are available to answer questions. Even if you cannot answer a query on the spot, let students know that you are happy to deal with it.

❷ *Be responsive, but do not get sidetracked*

One danger of this approach is that a teacher may get sidetracked by dominant students who want all their attention, leading to frustration and irritation among others. If you feel that this is happening, tell these students that you will answer their questions later, and move quickly on. Make sure that you keep moving round during pair/group/individual work. Keep a 'bird's-eye' view of the class, moving in to help students if they need it rather than spending too much time with one pair/group/individual.

❸ *Encourage students to use what they already know*

There is also a danger that students will become overdependent on you, perhaps asking you to translate large chunks for them, which they are very unlikely to retain. Always encourage students to use what they know first, only asking you if they really have no idea.

❹ *Have strategies for dealing with questions you cannot answer*

Have at least one bilingual dictionary in the classroom (especially for specialised/technical vocabulary) for students to refer to, although you may still need to check that they have found the right translation. If students ask for idioms and expressions, make sure you keep it simple – in most cases you will be able to come up with an adequate phrase even if it is not precisely the phrase the student wanted. Finally, if all else fails, promise to find out for the next lesson!

❺ *Note down important language points to be dealt with later*

Note down any important language points that come up during tasks and discussions, and build in time slots to go over these later on. Write the errors on the board, and invite students to correct them / think of a better word, etc. Remember that it is also motivating (and can be just as instructive) to include examples of good language used as well as errors. Feedback slots can either be at the end of the lesson, or, if time is a problem, at the beginning of the next.

Students are more likely to retain a few well-chosen points in these correction slots than a long list of miscellaneous language points. The following are useful things to bear in mind:

- **Usefulness:** many items may only be of interest to individual students – only bring up general language with the whole class.
- **Quantity/Variety:** try to combine one or two more general points with a number of more specific/minor ones, including a mixture of grammar, vocabulary and pronunciation as far as possible.
- **Level:** be careful not to present students with points above their level or which are too complex to deal with in a few minutes.
- **Problems induced by students' mother tongue:** correction slots are an excellent opportunity to deal with L1-specific errors (false friends, pronunciation, etc.) not usually mentioned in general English courses.
- **Revision:** the correction slots are a very good opportunity to increase students' knowledge of complex language covered previously, as well as to remind them of smaller language points.

❻ *Don't worry if you cannot think of 'creative' practice on the spot*

If students encounter a genuine need for the language as they try to achieve a particular goal, it is more likely to be remembered than if it is introduced 'cold' by the teacher. In many cases, elaborate practice may be unnecessary – what is important is that you are dealing with the language at the moment it is most likely to be retained by the student. With lexis and small points of pronunciation, it may be enough to get students to repeat the word a few times and write an example on the board, highlighting problems.

❼ *Try some simple 'on the spot' practice activities*

If you feel more work is needed, the box opposite includes some well-known activities which are relatively easy to adapt 'on the spot' (you can always provide a more substantial exercise later). A few examples should be enough for students to see how the structure is formed, and to increase awareness of it. These activities are also useful for practising phrases in the *Useful language* boxes in the tasks.

a **Choral and individual drilling**

b **Questions and answers:** ask questions prompting students to use the language item in the answer. For example, to practise the phrase *famous for*, ask questions such as:

What's Monte Carlo famous for? > *It's famous for its casinos.*

What's Loch Ness famous for? > *It's famous for the Loch Ness Monster.*

Alternatively, give an example, then prompt students to ask questions to each other, like this:

Monica, ask Henri about Venice. > *What's Venice famous for, Henri?*

c **Forming sentences/phrases from prompts:** for example, to practise the construction *it's worth … -ing* provide the example *The National Gallery is worth visiting*, then give prompts like this:

ROYAL PALACE / SEE > *The Royal Palace is worth seeing.*

THIS DICTIONARY / BUY > *This dictionary is worth buying.*

d **Substitutions:** give an example phrase/sentence, then provide prompts which can easily be substituted into the original. For example, to practise the non-use of the article, start with *I hate cats*, then prompt as follows:

LOVE > *I love cats.*

BABIES > *I love babies.*

DON'T LIKE > *I don't like babies.*

e **Transformations:** these are useful if there is another construction with almost the same meaning. Give one construction and ask students to say the same thing using another. For example, to practise *although*:

He's rich, but he's very mean. > *Although he's rich, he's very mean.*

She's over eighty, but she's very active. > *Although she's over eighty, she's very active.*

f **Combining shorter sentences/phrases:** give two short sentences and ask students to combine them with a more complex construction. For example, to practise *too … to*:

She's very young. She can't do this job. > *She's too young to do this job.*

He's too old. He can't drive. > *He's too old to drive a car.*

g **Dictating sentences for students to complete:** dictate a few incomplete sentences including the phrase or structure, which students complete themselves, then compare with other students. For example, to practise *it takes … to*, dictate:

It takes about three hours to get to …, It only takes a few minutes to …, It took me ages to …

Making the most of the *Mini-dictionary*

❶ Build up students' confidence with monolingual dictionaries

Some students may have never used a monolingual dictionary before. *New Cutting Edge Upper Intermediate Mini-dictionary* is designed to help students make the transition from bilingual to monolingual dictionaries. The explanations are graded to upper intermediate level, and the dictionary focuses on the meanings of words as they are used in the *Students' Book*, so students should have little difficulty in finding the information they are looking for. If students lack confidence, the following ideas may help.

- Discuss with them the value of using a monolingual dictionary. Point out that they will avoid misleading translations, that it may help them to 'think in English' and that they will be increasing their exposure to English.
- Look up words together at first, reading out and discussing the explanations as a class. Use the *Mini-dictionary* 'little and often' for limited but varied tasks (for example, for finding the word stress or dependent preposition of a new item of vocabulary).
- Encourage students to use the *Mini-dictionary* in pairs and groups as well as individually so that they can help each other to understand the explanations and examples. Circulate, making sure that they understand definitions.

❷ Explain the different features of the Mini-dictionary

Many students do not realise how much information they can find in a dictionary, so point out all the features given, such as parts of speech, phonemic script, irregular verb forms, etc. *Learner-training worksheets 2* and *3* on pages 105–107 of the *Resource bank* introduce students to these areas.

❸ Discourage overuse of the Mini-dictionary

There are many other important strategies for improving vocabulary as well as dictionary skills, such as guessing meaning from context, sharing information with other students and listening to the teacher. Encourage your students to use a balance of approaches.

Discourage overuse of the *Mini-dictionary* during reading activities, by focusing students' attention initially on 'key' words in the text, rather than anything they don't understand. If students are really keen to look up other words, you can allow time for this at the end.

❹ Vary your approach

If you always use the *Mini-dictionary* in the same way, students may get tired of it before long. Try using the *Mini-dictionary* in the following ways instead for a change.

a **Matching words to definitions on a handout:** make a worksheet with the new words in column A and their definitions from the *Mini-dictionary* mixed up in column B. Students match the words with the definitions.

b **Matching words to definitions on cards:** the same idea can be used giving each group two small sets of cards with definitions and words to match.

c ***I know it / I can guess it / I need to check it:*** write the list of new words on the board, and tell students to copy it down marking the words ✔✔ if they already know it, ✔ if they can guess what it means (either from context, or because it is similar in their own language) and ✖ if they need to look it up. They then compare answers in pairs to see if they can help each other, before looking up any words that neither of them know.

d **Student–student teaching:** write out (either on the board or on a handout) the list of words you want to introduce, and allocate one to each student. Tell students to look up the word and find the meaning, the pronunciation and a good example of how it is used to help other students to understand it. Circulate, helping individuals, particularly with pronunciation problems. Students then mingle and find out the meaning and pronunciation of other words on the list they did not know. Go through any problems/questions at the end.

e **Look up the five words you most need to know:** instead of pre-teaching the vocabulary in a reading text, set the first (gist-type) comprehension activity straightaway, instructing students not to refer to their *Mini-dictionary* at this point. Check answers or establish that students cannot answer without some work on vocabulary. Tell them that they are only allowed to look up five words from the text – they have to choose the five that are most important to understanding the text. Demonstrate the difference between a 'key' unknown word in the text and one that can easily be ignored. Put students into pairs to select their five words, emphasising that they must not start using their *Mini-dictionary* until they have completed their list of five. After they have finished, compare the lists of words that different pairs chose and discuss how important they are to the text, before continuing with more detailed comprehension work.

f ***True/False*** **statements based on information in the *Mini-dictionary*:** write a list of statements about the target words on the board, then ask students to look them up to see if they are true or false, for example: *The phrase ... is very informal – true or false?*
... means ... – true or false?

Making tasks work

❶ *Treat tasks primarily as an opportunity for communication*

Some of the tasks in this course may be familiar; the difference is in how they are treated. The main objective is for students to use the language that they know (and, if necessary, learn new language) in order to achieve a particular communicative goal, not to 'practise' specific language. Although it is virtually impossible to perform some of the tasks without using the language introduced in the module, in others students may choose to use this language only once or twice, or not at all. Do not try to 'force-feed' it. Of course, if learners are seeking this language but have forgotten it, this is the ideal moment to remind them!

❷ *Make the task suit your class*

Students using this course will vary in age, background, interests and ability. All these students need to find the tasks motivating and 'doable', yet challenging at the same time. Do not be afraid to adapt the tasks to suit your class if this helps. The teacher's notes contain suggestions on how to adapt certain tasks for monolingual and multilingual groups, students of different ages and interests, large classes, and weaker or stronger groups. There are also ideas for shortening tasks, or dividing them over two shorter lessons. We hope these suggestions will give you other ideas of your own on how to adapt the tasks.

❸ *Personalise it!*

The tasks in *New Cutting Edge Upper Intermediate* have a model or stimulus to introduce them. Sometimes these are recordings of people talking about something personal, such as their life story or what makes them happy. However, finding out about you, their teacher, and your opinions, may be more motivating for some students, so you could try providing a personalised model instead. If you do this, remember to:
- plan what you are going to say, but do not write it out word for word, as this may sound unnatural
- bring in any photos or illustrations you can to bring your talk alive
- either pre-teach or explain as you go along any problematic vocabulary
- give students a comprehension task to do as they are listening.

This approach may take a little courage at first, but students are likely to appreciate the variety it provides.

❹ *Set the final objective clearly*

Do not assume that students will work out where their preparations are leading if you do not tell them! Knowing, for example, that their film review will be recorded for a class radio programme may make a big difference to how carefully they prepare it.

❺ Give students time to think and plan

Planning time is very important if students are to produce the best language that they are capable of. It is particularly useful for building up the confidence of students who are normally reluctant to speak in class. The time needed will vary from task to task, from about five to twenty minutes.

This planning time will sometimes mean a period of silence in class, something that teachers used to noisy, communicative classrooms can find unnerving. Remember that just because you cannot hear anything, it does not mean that nothing is happening!

It may help to relieve any feelings of tension at this stage by playing some background music, or, if practical in your school, suggesting that students go somewhere else to prepare – another classroom if one is available.

Students may well find the idea of 'time to plan' strange at first, but, as with many other teaching and learning techniques, it is very much a question of training.

Once students have planned, discourage them from reading from notes. Give them time to look at their notes, then ask them to close their notebooks. With certain students this may have to be a gradual process.

❻ Respond to students' language needs and feed in useful language

As students are preparing, it is important that they are able to ask you about language queries, so that when they perform the task they can say what they personally want to say. Although the task should not be seen as an opportunity to 'practise' discrete items, there may be specific language that would be useful in order to perform the task successfully. Each task is accompanied by a *Useful language* box containing phrases which can be adapted by individual students to express different ideas and opinions. Sometimes the *Useful language* boxes include structures which have not yet been covered in the grammar syllabus. However, the examples used can be taught simply as phrases – it is not intended that you should embark on a major grammatical presentation here!

The phrases in the *Useful language* boxes can be dealt with at different points in the lesson:
- before students start the *Preparation* stage
- during the *Preparation* stage on an individual basis
- after *Task: speaking* in the feedback stage.

(See *Teacher's tips: responding to learners' individual language needs* on pages 11–12.)

❼ Give students time to 'rehearse'

For more complicated tasks, or with less confident students, this makes a big difference. It helps fluency, encourages students to be more ambitious with their language and irons out some errors. This rehearsal stage can take various forms.
- Students tell their story, etc. in pairs before telling it in groups or to the whole class.
- Students discuss issues in groups before discussing them as a class.
- Students go over what they are going to say 'silently' in their heads (either during the lesson, or at home if the task is split over two lessons).

❽ Insist that students use English!

It may not be realistic to prevent students from using their own language completely in the classroom, but they should understand that during the performance of the task (if not in the planning stage, where they may need their mother tongue to ask for new language) they must use English. At the beginning of the course, it may be useful to discuss the importance of this, and the best ways of implementing it. Students will be more tempted to use their own language if they find the task daunting, so do not be afraid to shorten or simplify tasks if necessary. However, planning and rehearsal time will make students less inclined to use their first language.

❾ Increase the 'pressure' on students

A teacher's first priority is to improve students' confidence with the language. At the beginning of the course, this may mean putting students under as little pressure as possible (for example, by doing tasks in groups rather than in front of the whole class). As time goes on, however, a certain amount of pressure can sometimes improve the quality of language students produce. This can be done:
- by getting students to give their talk, report, etc. standing up in front of the whole class
- by recording or videoing their performance of the task and replaying it to them later
- by making it clear that you will be correcting any errors they make at the end of the task.

❿ Make notes for further input

Before or during the performance of the task, you may notice errors and gaps in students' knowledge that you want to look at. It is usually best not to interrupt the flow of the task, but to make a note of points to cover later on.

(See *Teacher's tips: responding to learners' individual language needs* on pages 11–12.)

⓫ Relate the task to the Language focus sections

As you monitor the students during the task, it would be useful to make a note of any important errors or problems relating to the language areas covered in the module. These may help you to decide how much time to spend on the *Language focus* areas, and which points to pay particular attention to. After the analysis section you can write up relevant errors your class made, for more personalised, and perhaps more meaningful, reinforcement. Of course, even if you did not notice any related errors during the performance of the task, you may well decide that the *Language focus* sections are still worth doing.

⓬ Use the follow-up writing task

A number of the tasks have a written follow-up which could either be done in class or set for homework. These offer students the opportunity to repeat or carry out a similar task in written form, enabling them to consolidate what they have learnt, and put into practice any suggestions and corrections that you have discussed. Encourage students to think about how they can incorporate what they have learnt during the performance of the oral task. It may help if you at least start the follow-up writing in class.

module 1

Past and present

Task: Talk about your life circles
(PAGES 6–7)

PREPARATION: LISTENING

1 As an introduction, ask students if they keep photos of important events. Explain that the photos on pages 6–7 show things that remind us of the past, and check that students understand *sentimental value*. Put students into small groups and give them five minutes to answer the questions. If necessary, do the first example as a class. Help students with any vocabulary they need during the activity, e.g. *confetti*, *gate*. Check answers with the class.

> **ANSWERS**
> a   a wedding; people throwing confetti, taking photos
> b   a group of children, perhaps on holiday
> c   a family group standing at the gate of a house
> d   a group of friends at college or university
> e   a group of friends, probably in their early teens
> f   a young couple standing in front of their car

2 **a** 📼 [1.1] Explain that students are going to listen to people talking about important names, dates and places in their lives. Give students time to read the list, and then tell them they need to write what each item (1–10) is. Play the recording and do the first example with them. Play the rest of the recording, pausing after each item if necessary. Get students to check their answers in pairs, and then check as a class.

> **ANSWERS**
> 1 grandparents' house
> 2 sports teacher
> 3 favourite day
> 4 parents' and cousin's birthday
> 5 place where most of family come from
> 6 very close friend
> 7 house number
> 8 wedding day
> 9 brother
> 10 place visited recently

b Put students into small groups. Tell them to look at the life circles on pages 6–7 and match each item (1–10) to a circle (1–12). Explain that some of the people talk about the same life circle. Play the recording again and check the answers.

> **ANSWERS**
> 1 circle 6   2 circle 5   3 circle 10   4 circle 8
> 5 circle 6   6 circle 3   7 circle 7   8 circle 2
> 9 circle 1   10 circle 4

3 Tell the students they will hear the recording again and they need to note more information. Explain that they

should write short notes, not full sentences. Play the recording, pausing after each speaker if necessary. Get the students to compare their answers in pairs. Check answers with the class and clarify any difficult vocabulary.

> **ANSWERS**
> 1 huge house, north of England, lovely gardens, kitchen with enormous table for family dinners
> 2 loathed her, can't forget her, very strict, short time for students to get dressed after swimming
> 3 likes going out then, naughty because work next day
> 4 both parents and one cousin born then
> 5 mother born there, family comes from there, visited as a child, house, every summer
> 6 college friend, moved to San Francisco, not seen for long time, like to see her again
> 7 born in this house, Buenos Aires, now pulled down, parents took number plate, now on fireplace
> 8 best day of their life, all people they know in one place at the same time
> 9 ten or eleven years older, no jealousy, good friend
> 10 interesting, completely divided by cold war

Task: speaking

1 **a** Explain that the circles on page 6 refer to students' past, and the ones on page 7 refer to their present. Students note key information, not full sentences. If necessary, refer them to *Preparation: listening*, exercise 3, as a guide for note-taking and for the type of information to include.

b Tell students that they are going to explain their life circles, and get them to look at *Useful language a* for phrases they can use. Give students a few minutes to think about what they are going to say, and tell them to ask you for any words and phrases they need.

2 In pairs, the students explain their life circles. Tell the listeners to ask questions and take notes because they will be presenting their partner's life circles later. Refer them to the question forms in *Useful language b* for examples. While they are talking, move around the classroom, providing language they need and noting examples of errors with tenses, which you could use for further revision of *Language focus 1* on pages 10–11. Give a time check halfway through the activity, so that students get equal speaking/listening time.

3 Give students a few minutes to decide which points to tell the others in the class. Set a time limit (e.g. one minute) for each student to speak.
   If you have a large class, to reduce this stage you can:
- get students to talk about only one thing from their partner's past and present
- choose only a few students to talk about their partners
- split the class into large groups and ask students to talk about their partner to the group.
   During the presentations, make notes of errors with tenses for further revision of *Language focus 1* on pages 10–11.

Reading (PAGES 8–9)

1 Explain any of the types of music students do not understand. If possible, play a sample or show pictures of famous singers in each category. Put students into pairs to answer the questions. Go through the questions with the class.

2 Ask students to look at the people in the photos on pages 8–9. If students do not know them, give them the answers and then tell them a few things about the people or groups. If students know who they are, ask them to tell you about the people, and what they all have in common.

> **ANSWERS**
> The Bee Gees   The Corrs   Oasis   BoomKat
> Ozzy and Kelly Osbourne
> The people in each photo are from the same family.

3 Ask students to read the questions before they read the text. If you think it's necessary, pre-teach *outlasted*, *decades*, *album*, *hit single*. Explain that question a is not answered in the text for all the people/groups. Set a time limit of two to four minutes and ask students to read the text quickly, just to answer the questions, and not to focus on difficult vocabulary. Ask them to check their answers in pairs or small groups, and then check the answers with the whole class.

> **ANSWERS**
> a   **The Bee Gees:** not given in the text
>   **The Corrs:** from Ireland
>   **Oasis:** from Manchester in northern England
>   **BoomKat:** from the USA
>   **Ozzy and Kelly Osbourne:** not given in the text.
>
> b   The Bee Gees were most successful in the 1970s, but have been successful for four decades (1970s–2003).
>   The Corrs were successful in the 1990s.
>   Oasis were successful in the 1990s.
>   BoomKat are successful now.
>   Ozzy Osbourne was previously successful with Black Sabbath, but he and Kelly are successful now.
>
> c   **The Bee Gees:** *Saturday Night Fever*
>   **The Corrs:** *In Blue*
>   **Oasis:** *What's the Story Morning Glory?*
>   **BoomKat:** *Boomkatalog 1*
>   **Ozzy and Kelly Osbourne:** *Changes*

4 Ask students to read the questions, and check that they understand *admit (that)*; *ceased to exist*; *bad behaviour*; *imply*; *express different views*; *grateful*; *ambitious*. Explain that more than one person/group could be the answer to some questions. Students should try to read the text once to answer the questions, rather than read the whole text to answer a, then read to answer b and so on. Put students into pairs to compare answers, and then check with the class.

> **ANSWERS**
> a   The Corrs   b   The Bee Gees   c   Oasis
> d   The Bee Gees   e   The Corrs   f   Kelly Osbourne
> g   BoomKat

5 As an introduction to the discussion, ask students if they think the family groups are happy working together. Put the students into small groups, set the questions and give a time limit of at least five minutes. Ask one student in each group briefly to tell the rest of the class what they decided.

ADDITIONAL PRACTICE

Workbook: Vocabulary: Types of music, page 4; Vocabulary booster: Instruments and musicians, page 4

Vocabulary (PAGE 9)

Past and present time phrases

1 Ask students to find the phrases highlighted in bold in the text. Students should answer the questions individually. Ask students to check their answers in pairs before checking as a class.

> **ANSWERS**
> *Back in the 1970s* (past)   *Over the last few years*
> *in those days* (past)   *(past)*
> *At one time* (past)   *nowadays* (present)
> *currently* (present)   *these days* (present)
> *During the 1990s* (past)   *latest* (present)
> *at that time* (past)   *now* (present)
>   *former* (past)

2 Ask students to look at the picture and tell you the name of the group and anything they know about them. Encourage them to complete the sentences without using dictionaries and to think about whether the sentences refer to the past, present or both. Check the answers with the class.

> **ANSWERS**
> a   back, that time   b   one time   c   those days
> d   during   e   the last few years   f   currently
> g   former, days   h   latest   i   now, nowadays

3 **a** Ask *who has a favourite group? What type of music do they play?* Set the activity and tell students to write notes. Encourage them to add further information.

b Give students time to think about what they are going to say, and ask them to look at the time words in exercise 2 on page 9. Put them into pairs and give a time check halfway through the exercise so that all students get equal time.

ADDITIONAL PRACTICE

Workbook: Vocabulary: Past and present time phrase page 4

Language focus 1 (PAGES 10–11)

Revision of verb forms

a Explain that the quiz is to find out what students know about English verbs. This will help decide what to focus on in later lessons. Students work individually. Move around the room while students are working to make sure they understand what to do. If you want to test students' knowledge, do not give them help with the answers.

b Students check their answers on page 138. Put them into pairs to compare ratings, and then to discuss the grammar. Check with the class and explain any difficulties.

PRACTICE

1 a Tell students to look at the picture on page 11, and ask/tell them what the picture shows (Keema, a British Asian woman and her daughter). Ask students what they think it's like growing up as part of two cultures. Students complete the exercise individually, then compare answers in pairs.

b 🖭 [1.2] Explain that the recording is just the correct verb forms. Play the recording so students can check their answers.

> **ANSWERS**
> See tapescript on page 161 of the *Students' Book*.

2 a Explain that students are going to write sentences similar to Keema's about themselves. They can use the ideas provided and add anything they want.

b As an example, give students one true and one false sentence about your childhood or family background. Ask them to guess which is false. Set the first part of the exercise and then put them into pairs to guess the false information. Show them the speech bubbles for language they can use.

ADDITIONAL PRACTICE

Workbook: Revision of verb forms, page 5; Present simple or continuous, page 6; Past simple or continuous, page 6; Present perfect or Past simple, page 7; Present perfect or Past perfect, page 7, All forms, page 7

Writing (PAGES 12–13)

Planning and drafting a biography

1 a This discussion should be brief but students should say what they do in their own language **and** in English.

b Explain that *Four steps to better writing* gives good ideas about drafting a piece of writing. Give time for students to read the advice, and help with any new vocabulary.

2 a Ask students to tell you who is in the photos and what they know about him. If students do not know him, give them a few facts. Then ask students quickly to read notes A and B. Put them into pairs to decide which of the four stages in exercise 1b the notes illustrate. Check answers with the class. Ask students if they have found any information they didn't know before about Rowan Atkinson from note A.

> **ANSWERS**
> A illustrates step 1; B illustrates step 2.

b Do an example with the students. Put them into pairs and ask them to discuss the question. Check the answers with the class.

> **ANSWERS**
> Paragraph 1: f, i, j   Paragraph 2: d, e, c
> Paragraph 3: g, h   Paragraph 4: b, a

3 Do an example with the class and tell them to use their dictionaries for the spelling mistakes, if necessary. Check the answers, then ask students in which 'steps' they should check their work like this. (Answer: Steps 3 and 4.) Tell them it is always very important to check their writing carefully.

> **ANSWERS AND LANGUAGE NOTE**
> *fourth* = correct
> *british* = wrong (*British*)
> *mr Bean* = wrong (*Mr Bean*) i.e. the capitalisation is wrong, even if the punctuation is correct. (Note that in US English Mr. Bean is the correct punctuation.)
> *preist* = wrong (*priest*)
> *'Four Weddings and a Funeral'* = correct
> *1955* = wrong (*1955,*)
> : = wrong (;)
> *studyed* = wrong (*studied*)
> *Newcastle University* = correct
> *countrys* = wrong (*countries*)
> *biggest-earning* = correct
> *giveing* = wrong (*giving*)
> *quietly* = correct
> .'/'. = wrong (.')

4 a Give students a few minutes to choose a person. As they work individually on the first two steps, go round and guide them as necessary. Allow five to ten minutes for each step, then get them to check step 2 in pairs.

b When they have completed step 3, ask them to check each other's drafts for spelling and punctuation first. Then get them to check for verb forms. Students write their final draft.

ADDITIONAL PRACTICE

Workbook: Improve your writing: Linking phrases for a personal profile, page 8

Wordspot (PAGE 13)

get

1 Introduce this *Wordspot* by asking students what *get* means in their language, to show them it has many meanings. Check that students understand the headings in the box (*catch*, *obtain/receive*, etc.). Tell them that the diagram on page 13 shows some examples with *get*, but the headings explaining the meanings are missing. Do an example of the exercise using *become*. Give students a few minutes to write the other headings in the diagram. Check answers with the class and give examples to show meaning if necessary.

> **ANSWERS**
> a become b understand c obtain/receive d arrive
> e catch f phrasal verbs

2 Give students a few minutes to put the phrases in the correct sections of the diagram. If necessary, give example sentences to help students with the meaning.

> **ANSWERS**
> a   get better/worse, get angry, get lost, get stuck
> b   I don't get what you mean
> c   get a better job, get €50,000 a year, get a shock
> d   get there
> e   get an early flight
> f   get on with your work, get into trouble

3 Put students into pairs and ask one to look at page 138 and the other to look at page 141. As an example, ask one student A to read out the first question from her/his card and get the partner, student B, to answer. Ask the pairs to do the same with all the other questions/answers on their cards.

4 Give students a few minutes to think about what they need to ask, e.g. *What time did you get home last night? / Did you get home late last night?* If your classroom is quite open, get students to move around the room asking their questions. If not, students can ask the others sitting near them. Finish by asking for the name of someone who got a really special present for his/her last birthday, rarely gets angry, etc.

ADDITIONAL PRACTICE

Workbook: Wordspot: *get*, page 9

Language focus 2 (PAGES 14–15)

Uses of auxiliaries

1 Set the question and get students to look at the women's facial expressions in particular. As students give their ideas, introduce the verb *gossip*.

2 a 🔊 [1.3] Set the question and play the recording without pausing. Check the answer as a whole class.

> **ANSWER**
> two friends who have recently split up

b 🔊 [1.3] Look at the dialogue and do the first example with the students. When students have finished, play the recording and pause after each answer to check.

> **ANSWERS**
> 1 Have they?   2 is it?   3 isn't   4 does   5 she has

c 🔊 [1.3] Set the question and, if necessary, play the recording again without pausing. Briefly check answers.

> **POSSIBLE ANSWERS**
> by asking questions / using tag questions / using intonation

Analysis

This is revision for many students. Either answer the questions with the class or put students into pairs and check their answers at the end.

> **ANSWERS AND LANGUAGE NOTES**
> a   4   *She does like going out more than him.*
>   (This is often used to add emphasis. Give more
>   examples, e.g. *I do like your dress.*)
> b   2   *It's not really surprising, is it?*
>   (Remind students: negative sentence = positive
>   tag question, positive sentence = negative tag
>   question. Give more examples if necessary.)
> c   1   *Have they?* (1)
>   (Remind students that the level of interest is
>   shown in the intonation. Here, the very high
>   rising tone shows great interest and surprise.)
> d   5   *Yes, she has.*
>   (Students will know this form.)
> e   3   *... but she isn't.* (3)
>   (Ask students to give you the complete sentence:
>   *... but she isn't into computers.* Give more
>   examples, e.g. *I'm not interested in football but my
>   friends are.*)
>
> Remind students that in 1–5 above the auxiliary must
> 'agree' with the main verb, e.g. *is – is*. This is also true
> of the affirmative forms of the Present and Past simple
> where we do not use the auxiliary in the main sentence:
> *She speaks five languages.*   *Does she?*
> *I started my new job yesterday.*   *Did you?*

PRACTICE

1 🔊 [1.4] Explain that students are going to hear ten short conversations, and that you are going to play the first half of each one. Students must then choose the correct response. Do the first one as an example and check answers. For the rest, play the first half, pause, give students time to answer and check in pairs, then play the second half to check their answers.

> **ANSWERS**
> a 2   b 1   c 3   d 1   e 2   f 3   g 2   h 1   i 1   j 3

Pronunciation

1 🔊 [1.5] Go through the information with students and play the recording. Play the recording again and pause after each example for students to repeat.

2 🔊 [1.6] Repeat the procedure used in exercise 1.

3 🔊 [1.4] Put students in pairs. Play the recording, pausing after each dialogue for students to practise. Correct the pronunciation of weak forms, contractions and stressed words.

2 a Students do this alone and then check in pairs. Refer to the *Language summary* on page 144 if necessary.

ANSWERS
1 do   2 didn't   3 do   4 haven't   5 did, didn't
6 didn't   7 can   8 aren't

b If necessary, have a dialogue already prepared as an example. With a very strong class, ask students to write notes instead of full sentences. If time is short, cut the number of dialogues.

c Tell students they are going to act out one dialogue for the class. Give five minutes for practice and, if necessary, correct pronunciation of auxiliaries. With a large class, divide students into groups or choose only a few pairs to act out their dialogues.

ADDITIONAL PRACTICE

Workbook: Auxiliary verbs, pages 9–10; Pronunciation: Weak forms, page 10

Real life (PAGES 15–16)

Making conversation

1 Look at the picture on page 15 and ask students where the people are and what they are doing. Put the students into pairs or small groups to discuss the questions.

2 a [1.7] Ask students to read the list, and explain any problem vocabulary, e.g. *purpose* and *details*. Play the conversation without stopping. Get students to check their answers in pairs, and then check as a whole class.

ANSWER
All 'Fiona' items should be ticked.

b Students discuss the question in pairs before checking with you. Ask why they think the speakers have different attitudes.

ANSWERS
Sean wants to talk; Fiona doesn't. Sean is more forthright; Fiona is more tentative.

3 [1.7] Ask students to read the questions, and then play the recording again. Get students to compare their answers. If necessary, play the end of the conversation again to give students help with question e. Check the answers as a class.

ANSWERS
a   *Hi, excuse me, I couldn't help overhearing …*
b   six
c   short factual sentences, which do not give much information or encourage Sean to ask more questions
d   none
e   *Well, if you'll excuse me, I have to er … / So, I must be getting on, really. / It's been nice talking to you.*

4 a Do the first example with the students. Students do this individually and then compare their answers with a partner. Check answers with the whole class.

ANSWERS
1 S   2 E   3 S   4 E   5 E   6 S   7 E   8 S   9 S   10 E

b [1.8] Explain that students are going to hear the sentences from exercise 4a, and that they should listen to the intonation.

ANSWERS
1 P   2 R   3 C   4 C   5 C   6 P   7 C   8 P   9 P   10 C

Pronunciation

1 [1.8] Go through the information with students and provide examples using your own voice. If necessary, play a few examples from the recording.

2 [1.8] Pause the recording after each phrase and ask students to repeat. Correct their intonation, if necessary.

5 Ask students to read the examples, and tell them that asking questions is a good way of maintaining a conversation. Put them into pairs for the rest of the exercise and give them time to decide on their questions before practising. Correct their pronunciation, if necessary.

POSSIBLE ANSWERS
a   Oh, really, what time did you arrive? Where did you come from?
b   What do you teach? What age group do you teach? Have you been teaching long?
c   Is that your first name? Do you have a nickname?
d   What are you going to see? What time does the film start?

6 a Put students into pairs and give them time to choose from the list. Check that they understand *acquaintances*.

b Give them time to discuss their roles in pairs. Then give them time individually to think about what they are going to say and how to use phrases and pronunciation from exercises 2–5. Put them back into pairs to act out the conversation. Make some notes so that you can give feedback.

ADDITIONAL PRACTICE

Workbook: Real life: Making conversations, page 11

Study … (PAGE 16)

Using the *Mini-dictionary*

Start by explaining that it will help students to use the *Mini-dictionary* and to improve their study skills. If they are able to use the dictionaries effectively, they will be able to study more efficiently. You can use the *Study …* section either at the end of the module or earlier, depending on your students' needs. Students can do it for homework, or in class time if they need teacher guidance. If your students are going to use the *Mini-dictionary* for the *Practise …* on page 17, suggest that they do the *Study …* section first. For more practice of *Mini-dictionary* use, refer to *Learner-training worksheet 2* in the *Resource bank*. For practice in using other monolingual dictionaries, use *Learner-training worksheet 3*.

To check that students have read and understood the information in this section, set some questions, for example:
1 *How does the* Mini-dictionary *show word stress*?
2 *How does the* Mini-dictionary *show meaning*?
3 *List three pieces of extra information the* Mini-dictionary *gives you*.

Practise ... (PAGE 17)

This section can be done independently by students, which will encourage them to monitor their own learning and achievement. However, you can also use this section for further practice of the language areas covered in Module 1, or as a test. If you are testing students, make sure they do not look at the *Language summaries* until they have finished.

1–5 For each exercise, make sure students read the instructions carefully. If students find exercises 1–5 difficult, refer them to the appropriate pages in the *Students' Book* for extra help. Provide the answers by checking as a class or giving students a copy from the *Teachers' Resource Book*.

ANSWERS AND LANGUAGE NOTES
1 Continuous forms
a The verb can be changed. The meaning is 'His work was more temporary.'
b The verb can be changed. The meaning is 'I haven't finished thinking about it yet.' / 'I haven't decided on the answer yet.'
c The verb can be changed. The meaning is 'Ben started looking at his magazine before I saw him and continued after I saw him.'
d The verb cannot be changed; *like* is a stative verb.
e The verb can be changed. The meaning is 'Susan is probably still having problems with her car.'
f The verb can be changed. There is little, if any, change in meaning.
g The verb can be changed. The meaning is 'This is Juliette's action/behaviour rather than her character.'
h The verb cannot be changed; *belong* is a stative verb.

2 Past and present verb forms
a We went to Spain once = F. We went to Spain more than once = T. We go to Spain now = F.
b My parents live nearby = F. My parents used to live nearby = NS. My parents don't live nearby now = T.
c When we arrived, they began eating = F. When we arrived, they were eating = T. When we arrived, the meal was finished = F.
d I'm a travel courier now = F. I used to be a travel courier = T. I was a travel courier at one time = T.

3 Auxiliary verbs
1 ..., *was it?* – to form a tag question
2 ..., *honestly I do! / I do honestly!* – to add emphasis
3 ..., *but she is now.* – to avoid repeating a phrase
4 '*Has he?*' – to show interest
5 '*Yes, I did.*' – to form a short answer

4 Time phrases
a in the 1980s b that time c during
d these e currently f former g now

5 Phrases with *get*
a become b understand c catch/take
d received e arrive

Pronunciation spot
Word stress

a 📼 [1.9] Start by humming or clapping stress pattern number 1. Ask students to identify the pattern and get them to do the same. Then ask which word fits that pattern. Put students into pairs to do numbers 2–5, and encourage them to hum or clap the pattern before choosing the word. Play the recording and check answers with the class, playing each word again if need be and asking students to repeat.

ANSWERS
1 global 2 supportive 3 traditional
4 success 5 nowadays

b Give students time to find more examples from the text on pages 8–9. For feedback, hum or clap each stress pattern and elicit words for that pattern. If necessary, write their words on the board and mark the stress patterns.

Remember! (PAGE 17)

Explain that ticking the boxes honestly will let students know which areas they might need more practice in. Give them a few minutes to tick the boxes, or ask them to do this at home if it is a personal record of achievement.

Mini-check (PAGE 158)

This can be done in class, or set for homework. For each exercise, tell students to read the instructions carefully. If you do not want students to feel you are testing them, set this as homework, provide the answers from the *Teachers' Resource Book* and ask students to keep their personal score. Encourage students to use their dictionaries. If you want to use the *Mini-check* as a more formal test or to introduce further work on the language areas, check answers as a class, providing more explanation and/or referring students to the *Language focus* sections in Module 1 or the relevant *Language summaries* on pages 144–145.

ANSWERS
1 is looking after 2 do you think 3 is 4 're having
5 Was it raining 6 was reading 7 had 8 used to play
9 lived 10 had started 11 saw 12 over 13 in
14 At 15 on 16 get back 17 during 18 These days
19 to 20 will you?

module 2

Life's ups and downs

Reading and vocabulary
(PAGES 18–19)

1 **a** Start by asking students to look at the picture on page 18, read the title of the article on page 19 and then tell you what they expect the article to be about. Make sure students understand that you will be talking about things that are good or bad for you both physically and psychologically. Put students into pairs and set the activity. Check answers as a whole class.

b Put students into small groups. Check that they understand that some items in the box could go on both lists (i.e. items that are good and bad for you). Encourage students to guess unknown words and only use their mini-dictionaries when necessary. When they have finished the activity, check answers as a whole class. If there is disagreement, ask students to say why they chose a particular answer.

> **POSSIBLE ANSWERS**
> **Good for you:** being single / being married, belonging to a community, doing absolutely nothing, drinking coffee/ tea, eating chocolate, gentle/strenuous exercise, a low-fat diet, playing computer games, watching soap operas
>
> **Bad for you:** being single / being married, belonging to a community, doing absolutely nothing, drinking coffee/tea, eating chocolate, feeling out of control, gentle/strenuous exercise, high blood pressure, a low-fat diet, low self-esteem, playing computer games, watching soap operas

2 Put students into pairs, tell them who is student A and who is student B and ask them to read only Part A or Part B of the article. As a first exercise, give students one minute to look through their part to find any of the items listed in exercises 1a and b. Do not check answers as a whole class at this stage.

Then give students five minutes to read their part again and to answer their questions by ticking the correct alternative(s). Encourage students to guess the meaning of the vocabulary in bold, but if necessary to use their mini-dictionaries. Tell them not to worry about vocabulary in the article itself. Walk round the class to make sure that students are answering the questions correctly, by looking at the ticks.

> **ANSWERS**
> **Part A**
> 1 After strenuous exercise, people are often **less** active for the rest of the day.
> 2 Doing nothing for a couple of hours every day is the best way to **increase your immunity.**
> 3 A low-fat diet will make you **slimmer but more aggressive.**

4 The chemicals in **tea** reduce the risk of heart disease.
5 The chemicals in **chocolate** protect you from coughs and colds.

> **Part B**
> 1 Children who play a lot of computer games have better **social skills** than children who don't.
> 2 **Married** men are happier than **single** men.
> 3 Married women with children and a job have **fewer** mental health problems than other groups.
> 4 The biggest cause of backache is **depression.**
> 5 People who watch soap operas **have** a sense of belonging to a community.

3 **a** Make sure that students are in A-and-B pairs and ask them to close their books. Give students a minute to think about what they're going to say and then time to summarise what they've learnt from the article. Give a time check halfway through the activity so that students get equal speaking and listening time.

b In the same A-and-B pairs, ask students to answer the questions, and encourage them to say why they find some information surprising and why they do not believe something from the article. Check ideas/opinions as a whole class.

4 Keep students in their A-and-B pairs, ask them to open their books and give them time to read the other part of the article. Encourage them to help each other with problem vocabulary from the questions. If time is short, get students to check problem vocabulary for homework. Tell them not to worry about vocabulary in the article itself. Then give a few minutes for them to discuss the questions in exercise 4. Check ideas/opinions with the whole class.

ADDITIONAL PRACTICE

Workbook: Vocabulary: Health quiz, page 12

Language focus 1 (PAGES 20–21)

Forming nouns and gerunds

a Students work in pairs. Emphasise that they must not look at the article on pages 18–19. Check that they understand the abbreviations in the definitions (*n*. = noun, *pl*. = plural, [U] = uncountable, [C] = countable). Give them time to complete the definitions and give help with any problem words. Refer students to the *Analysis* box on page 20 for help with forming the nouns. Ask students to compare their answers.

b Get students to check by referring to the article.

> **ANSWERS**
> 1 happiness   2 researcher   3 depression
> 4 employees   5 friendships   6 scientists
> 7 movement   8 evidence   9 society
> 10 criticism   11 feeling   12 behaviour

Analysis

Make sure students understand what suffixes and gerunds are by eliciting examples from *Language focus 1*. For each exercise in the *Analysis*, read through the explanation before eliciting answers. Go through the additional information in the language notes below. Refer students to *Language summaries A* and *B* on page 145 for extra help.

1 In pairs or individually, students write each noun (1–12) in the correct box. Check answers as a whole class.

ANSWERS AND LANGUAGE NOTES

-ness (*happiness*). Further examples: *kindness, sadness, madness*. This is probably the most common noun suffix in English, and one which English native speakers will add to almost anything to form a noun (often colloquially).
-ance/-ence (*evidence*). Further examples: *allowance; independence, patience*
-ship (*friendships*). Further examples: *relationship, membership, citizenship*
-ion/-sion/-tion (*depression*). Further examples: *religion, confusion, competition*
-our/-iour (*behaviour*). Further examples: *colour, saviour*
-ee (*employees*). Further examples: *interviewee, divorcee, licensee*
-ity/-iety/-y (*society*). Further examples: *curiosity, anxiety*
-ism (*criticism*). Further examples: *racism, communism, capitalism*
-er (*researcher*). Further examples: *teacher, driver, cleaner*
-ment (*movement*). Further examples: *unemployment, disappointment, improvement*
-ing (*feeling*). Further example: *doing*. Do not give too many other examples because students will be asked to do this for *Analysis*, exercise 3. If you do give more examples, make sure they are nouns and not adjectives, e.g. *I like **walking*** (behaves like a noun) but *this is **interesting*** (is an adjective).
-ist (*scientists*). Further examples: *psychologist, traditionalist, capitalist*
There are more suffixes in addition to those above. It is more difficult to try and find rules to tell you which suffix to use than simply to memorise which word takes which suffix.

2 Read through the information and elicit or give further examples, e.g. *increase, surprise, support.*

3 Use the examples given to show how a gerund acts like a noun. It is very common to put a gerund at the beginning of a sentence when we are talking in general. Put students into pairs to find and underline examples in the paragraph called *Exercise* on page 18. Check answers as a class.

ANSWERS

staying (slim), keeping (fit), walking, cycling, spending, building, prolonging, achieving, vegetating

Pronunciation

1 [recording] [2.1] Check that students understand the concept of stressed and weak forms in spoken English. You may need to ask them to write the list of nouns (1–12 in *Language focus 1*) again, so that they can mark the stress clearly. Write the words on the board. Use the example in the book to show students how to mark the stress. Play the first word (happiness) so that students can hear the first syllable is stressed. Then play the recording, pausing after each item. Students compare answers in pairs. Check answers as a class.

ANSWERS AND LANGUAGE NOTE

1 happiness 2 researcher 3 depression

4 employees 5 friendships 6 scientists

7 movement 8 evidence 9 society

10 criticism 11 feeling 12 behaviour

The only stressed suffix is *-ee* (*employees*). Show students how stress is marked in the *Mini-dictionary* so that they can check stressed syllables themselves.

2 Check students understand that schwa is a weak form and give a few examples, e.g.
/ə/ /ə/ /ə/   /ə/
America, about, yesterday.
Give students a short time to practise drawing the schwa symbol. In pairs, students mark the schwa syllable. If necessary, tell them not all the words will have a schwa, and if there is one it won't be on the stressed syllable.

3 [recording] [2.1] Play the recording, pausing after each word so that students can check their answers. Check answers after each item and mark the schwas on the board. Point out that native speakers will pronounce some of the words differently (see below). Give students time to read the words aloud to themselves, then play the recording, pausing after each word and asking the students to repeat. Correct pronunciation if necessary.

ANSWERS AND LANGUAGE NOTES
/ə/   /ə/
1 *happiness*   2 *researcher*
/ə/
3 *depression*   4 employees (no schwa)
5 *friendships* (no schwa)
/ə/   /ə/
6 *scientists*   7 *movement*
/ə/
8 *evidence*
/ə/   /ə/
9 *society* (some native speakers will pronounce *ciety* as a schwa, some will pronounce it /i/)
/ə/
10 *criticism* (some native speakers will pronounce *ticism* as a schwa, some will pronounce it /i/)
11 *feeling* (no schwa)
/ə/   /ə/
12 *behaviour* (some native speakers will pronounce *be* as a schwa, some will pronounce it /i/)

PRACTICE

To extend exercises 1–3 below, get them to mark the stressed syllables and/or any schwas on their answers after each activity. Then give them a few minutes to practise the pronunciation, and correct them if necessary.

1 a Put the students into pairs. If necessary, refer them to the *Analysis* on page 20 and *Language summary A* on page 145. Check answers as a whole class.

ANSWERS
activity   aggression   development   hostility   illness
membership   psychology   suffering   violence

b Put the students into pairs. Check that they understand they need to decide which noun forms are **different** from the verbs in the box. Check answers as a whole class and go through the language notes below.

ANSWERS AND LANGUAGE NOTES
The noun form of the verb *reduce* is different (*reduction*). Explain that the noun forms of *research* and *increase* are the same as the verb forms, but the stress is different:

research (verb)   *research* (noun)   *increase* (verb)

increase (noun)
Note, too, that the noun for the person who does research is *researcher*.

2 [2.2] Introduce the text by telling students it contains experts' opinions on how to be happy and healthy. Elicit from students what they expect the experts to mention. Then, put students into pairs and give them time to check their predictions and underline the correct alternative. If they need extra help, refer them to the *Analysis* on page 20 and *Language summaries A* and *B* on page 145. When students have finished, play the recording without pausing and then ask students to check answers in pairs. Finally, check answers as a class and ask if students found any of their predictions.

ANSWERS
See tapescript for recording 2 on page 162 of the *Students' Book*.

3 a Start by asking students to look at the pictures on page 21 and to say what each picture represents and whether each thing makes them feel good or bad. Put students into pairs and ask them to complete the noun/gerunds in the exercise. Explain that each underscore (_) represents one letter. Walk round the class and help students with vocabulary or ask them to use their mini-dictionaries. Check answers as a whole class and ask students to spell the words aloud.

ANSWERS
What makes you feel good?
security   success   being   sleeping
variety, excitement   spending   being, relationship
having   keeping   friendships   going   being
stimulation   spending   feeling

What makes you feel bad?
worries   feeling, pressure   sleeping   criticism
anxieties   confidence   eating   loneliness
relationship   feeling   boredom

b Students complete the sentences with items from exercise 3a. Check that they understand ... *doesn't bother me much* and give them about three minutes to do the exercise.

c Put the students into pairs and give them time for the discussion. Encourage them to say why they chose each item, and to ask each other questions. Tell them to note the biggest differences in their answers. Check answers with the class.

ADDITIONAL PRACTICE

RB **Resource bank:** 2B – Who am I? (gerunds and phrases to describe abstract ideas), page 117

Workbook: Forming nouns, page 12; Gerunds, page 13

Language focus 2 (PAGES 22–23)
Forming adjectives

Start by writing *inspirations.com* on the board and ask the whole class what they think this is. Students check their ideas by reading the introduction on page 22. Elicit the meaning of *life's ups and downs* by getting students to guess from the context. Ask them if they think such websites are useful. Then ask students quickly to read the text and to guess the blanked word. Tell them not to worry about problem vocabulary at this stage. Put students into pairs to compare their ideas before referring them to page 138 for the answer. In pairs or in open class, get students to discuss whether they agree with the text.

ANSWER
smile

Analysis 1 (PAGE 22)

Make sure that students understand what suffixes and prefixes are. Read through the explanation before eliciting the answers to the questions. Draw students' attention to the language notes below, and elicit or give further examples.

1 Suffixes

a Ask students to find *powerful* and *valuable* in the text they have just read, and to underline each suffix. Read the explanation in exercise 1a to check which part is the suffix. Ask students to underline any suffixes of the other adjectives. Tell them that not all the adjectives in bold have suffixes. Check answers as a class.

ANSWERS
benefic<u>ial</u>   wealth<u>y</u>   power<u>ful</u>   penni<u>less</u>
unhappy (no suffix)   *discourag<u>ed</u>   optimis<u>tic</u>   depress<u>ed</u>*
anx<u>ious</u>   insecure (no suffix)   *valu<u>able</u>   tir<u>ed</u>*

b Ask students to read the explanation, and then put them into pairs to answer the two questions. Check the answers with the class before getting students to think of more examples.

ANSWERS AND LANGUAGE NOTES

Depressed describes the way you feel; *depressing* describes the thing that makes you feel like this.

More examples are *excited/exciting, surprised/surprising, tired/tiring, discouraged/discouraging, terrified/terrifying, confused/confusing.*

Explain that not all *-ed* and *-ing* adjectives have both forms. For these and other suffixes, students need to learn and memorise them as they go along. Refer students to *Language summary C* on page 146.

2 Prefixes that mean 'the opposite of'

Ask students to find *unhappy* and *discouraged* in the text, and then read the explanation in exercise 2. Give students time to find another such prefix in the text. Check the answer as a class. Put students into pairs to think of at least three other such prefixes. Refer students to *Language summary D* on page 146.

ANSWERS AND LANGUAGE NOTES

Another prefix in the text is *in-*, which forms part of *insecure*.

Other examples are *dis-, il-, im-, un-*.

Highlight the following points about this class of prefixes.

- Dis- and un- can also be used with some verbs. For these and other prefixes, students need to learn and memorise them as they go along.
- The main stress is always on the word after the prefix, e.g. *un'married*, but there is generally a smaller (secondary) stress on the prefix, e.g. ˌun'married. For practice, get students to say some of the prefixed adjectives in *Language summary D* on page 146.

PRACTICE

1 Reintroduce *inspirations.com* by asking students to summarise what they know about it. Put students into pairs, set the exercise and give them time to complete the adjectives in bold. Refer them to *Analysis 1* and *Language summaries A, C* and *D* for more help. Encourage them to guess the meaning of vocabulary from the context, and to use their mini-dictionaries only if necessary. Check answers as a class, spelling the words on the board if necessary. Then put students into pairs and give them five minutes to discuss whether they agree or not with sentences a–h. Check ideas as a class.

ANSWERS
a effic<u>ient</u>, use<u>ful</u>
b excit<u>ing</u>, interest<u>ing</u>
c pessimis<u>tic</u>, optimis<u>tic</u>, disappoint<u>ed</u>
d wonder<u>ful</u>, unsolv<u>ed</u>
e success<u>ful</u>, talent<u>ed</u>, determin<u>ed</u>
f <u>un</u>popular, <u>dis</u>honest
g enthusias<u>tic</u>, persist<u>ent</u>, <u>im</u>possible
h posit<u>ive</u>, catch<u>ing</u>

2 **a** Individually, give students a few minutes to put the adjectives into two lists and to add more ideas. While students are writing, walk round and help.

ANSWERS

Adjectives describing a person's character: effective, efficient, useful, exciting, interesting, pessimistic, optimistic, disappointed, wonderful, successful, talented, determined, unpopular, dishonest, enthusiastic, persistent, positive

Positive adjectives: effective, efficient, useful, exciting, interesting, optimistic, wonderful, successful, talented, determined, enthusiastic, persistent, positive

Negative adjectives: pessimistic, disappointed, unpopular, dishonest

b Put students into pairs and give them time to discuss the questions. Encourage them to agree and/or disagree, and to give reasons for their choices. Check answers as a class.

Analysis 2

Reintroduce prefixes by asking students for a few examples from the previous activities. Read through the first two sentences of information in the *Analysis 2* box. Put the students into pairs, set the activity and do the first example as a whole class. Encourage them to guess the answers, but refer them to *Language summary E* on page 146 for help. Check answers as a whole class.

ANSWERS AND LANGUAGE NOTES

overpaid   underfed   non-stop   post-war
pre-arranged   self-confident
pro-American   anti-government

Highlight the following points about this class of prefixes.

- There are no absolute rules about whether a word containing a prefix should be written as a one-word, two-word or hyphenated form. Tell students to look in a dictionary if they have doubts.
- The prefix is usually given equal stress to the word after it, because it changes or adds meaning to this word, e.g. ˌanti-ˈgovernment.

3 **a** Students do this in pairs. Encourage them to guess meaning from what they have learnt in *Analysis 2* and from their knowledge of the word after each prefix. Refer them to *Language summary E* on page 146 for further help.

b Put the students into groups and give them time to compare their answers, ask questions, agree or disagree. Walk round the class and help if necessary. Check answers with the whole class by asking one person from each group to give an idea for each item. Answers will vary according to the students' culture and world view.

POSSIBLE ANSWERS
1 teaching, nursing, factory work
2 banking, professional football
3 nanny, childminder, nursery
4 library, plane, hospital
5 MBA (Master of Business Administration)
6 This will depend on the current government and the local context.
7 This will depend on students' own experience.
8 This will depend on students' own opinions.

ADDITIONAL PRACTICE

RB **Resource bank:** 2D Prefix and suffix dominoes (prefixes and suffixes with nouns and adjectives), pages 119–120

Workbook: Forming adjectives, page 14; Word building with nouns, verbs and adjectives, page 15; Prefixes, page 16

Real life (PAGE 23)

Responding sympathetically

1 Check that students understand *sympathetic* and do not confuse it with 'generally nice or kind'. For example, a sympathetic person is someone who will listen to you, try to understand your feelings and help you when you are upset. Put students into pairs to discuss the questions. Do not do class feedback as this may embarrass some students.

2 a 🔲 [2.3] Set the first question and tell students not to write sentences, only short notes. Play the recording without pausing. Check answers as a class.

ANSWERS
Conversation 1: not taken seriously by boss
Conversation 2: stuck in traffic – going to be late for something
Conversation 3: lost her cat, Tony

b 🔲 [2.3] Set the questions and check the meaning of *reasonably*. Tell students to write short notes. Play the recording, pausing after each conversation so students can write their answers. Put students into pairs to compare, and play the recording again. Check answers as a class.

ANSWERS
Conversation 1: listener = very sympathetic; suggestions = talk to boss or colleague
Conversation 2: listener = not very sympathetic; suggestions = calm down, don't get upset, will ring and explain
Conversation 3: listener = reasonably sympathetic; suggestions = look under bed, call his name, look in garden

3 a Do the first example with the class. Tell students not to worry about the meaning of individual words. Walk round the class while students are working in pairs and help with any problem phrases. Check answers as a class and draw students' attention to the language note below.

ANSWERS AND LANGUAGE NOTE
Calm down!*
Come on! Pull yourself together!*
Don't take any notice of him/her.**
Don't worry. It doesn't matter.**
How annoying!**
Just ignore him/her/it/them.**
Never mind.**
That sounds awful!***
There's no point in getting upset about it.*
Try not to worry about it.**

What a shame!**
You must be really worried.***

Before you elicit the answers, explain that the level of sympathy in each phrase might change with the situation and the intonation. For example, *calm down* could be sympathetic if said in a particular situation with the correct intonation. Tell students they will be practising this in the next activities. The answers are appropriate to conversations 1–3 in exercise 2.

b Put students into pairs and ask them to read through the situations. Check the meaning of *spilled, row, hairstyle*. Ask students if all the situations are equally serious. Explain that an appropriate response in one situation could sound unsympathetic or excessive in other situations. Elicit responses for the first situation as an example, then give students a few minutes to do the others. Check answers as a whole class and go through the language notes below.

ANSWERS AND LANGUAGE NOTES
1 *Don't worry. / It doesn't matter. / Never mind.* (non-serious situation)
2 *Don't take any notice of him/her. / Just ignore him/her/it/them.* (non-serious or a more serious situation)
3 *Try not to worry about it. / That sounds awful!* (non-serious or more serious situation)
4 *Come on! Pull yourself together! / There's no point in getting upset about it.* (first response: non-serious situation, second response: non-serious or a more serious situation)
5 *Try not to worry about it. / You must be really worried.* (serious situation)
6 *Don't take any notice of them. / Just ignore them.* (non-serious or a more serious situation)
7 *Come on! Pull yourself together. / Try not to worry about it.* (first response: non-serious situation, second response: more serious situation)

Pronunciation

1 🔲 [2.4] Start by saying one of the sentences sympathetically and then unsympathetically. Ask students to tell you which is which. If they have problems hearing the intonation, exaggerate it. Explain that you need to use the correct intonation and the correct sentence if you want to sound sympathetic. Ask students to write down the numbers 1–12 and to write 'U' for unsympathetic and 'S' for sympathetic next to each number. Play the recording without pausing. Students check in pairs. Check answers as a class.

ANSWERS
Sympathetic: 1, 2, 3, 4, 5, 6, 7, 9, 10, 12
Unsympathetic: 8, 11

2 🔲 [2.4] Put students into pairs and refer them to the tapescript for recording 4 on page 162. Play the recording, pausing after each sentence, and ask students to repeat. Tell students they will need to change the intonation of numbers 8 and 11. Correct if necessary. Ask students to practise the sentences in their pairs.

25

4 Put students into pairs and give them ten minutes to choose a situation from exercise 3b and to write a dialogue similar to the tapescript for recording 3. Walk round the class helping students with language and providing vocabulary. If students find this difficult, refer them to the tapescript on page 162 as a model. If some pairs finish early, get them to choose another situation and write a second conversation.

5 In pairs, ask students to practise their conversations, paying attention to intonation. After a few minutes, ask them to change roles so that everyone practises sounding sympathetic. Walk round the class, and correct if necessary. Then get each pair to act out their conversation for the class. With a large class, select a limited number of students to act out their conversations.

ADDITIONAL PRACTICE

Workbook: Real life: Responding sympathetically, page 16; Improve your writing: Responding sympathetically in writing, page 17

Task: List the things that make you feel ... (PAGES 24–25)

See *Teacher's tips: making tasks work* on pages 13–14.

Preparation: listening

1 [2.5] Introduce the task by asking students to look at the pictures on pages 24–25 and eliciting how the people are feeling and what could make them feel like this. Ask students to read questions a–h, and check they understand *depressed*, *detest*, *stressed* and *embarrassed*. Set the activity. Explain that some of the speakers may be answering more than one of the questions, and some of the questions are answered by more than one speaker. Tell students not to worry if they do not understand every word. If necessary, pre-teach *my big mouth*; *trotting down*; *chant*; *Buddhist chanting*; *an odd sense of humour*; *I haven't got the faintest idea*. Play the recording without pausing. Put students into pairs to compare answers, and then check answers with the whole class.

> **ANSWERS**
> a   speakers 5 and 9
> b   speaker 6 and possibly speaker 8
> c   speaker 3
> d   speaker 4
> e   speaker 8 and possibly speaker 3
> f   speaker 2
> g   speakers 1 and 10
> h   speaker 7

2 [2.5] Play the recording again, pausing after each speaker. Tell students to write short notes.

3 Put students into pairs to compare their notes and answer the question. Check answers as a whole class.

> **ANSWERS**
> See tapescript for recording 5 on pages 162–163 of the *Students' Book*.

4 [2.6] Explain that students are going to hear eight sentences taken from the recording in exercise 1. Play the recording, pausing after each sentence to give students time to write. Put students into pairs to compare their answers. Play the recording again and check answers as a whole class.

> **ANSWERS AND LANGUAGE NOTES**
> See tapescript for recording 6 on page 163 of the *Students' Book*.
>
> To focus students on language in the sentences, ask them to underline any useful or new phrases in the answers. Draw their attention to the following phrases: *One thing that always make me feel* + adjective; *... one thing that really* + verb + *me*; *It/He/She/They just send(s) me completely crazy*; *I find* + noun phrase + adjective; *The thing that* + verb me the most is + *-ing*; *It/He/She/They put(s) me in a good/bad mood*; *I know you shouldn't laugh, but*; *I can't stop myself from laughing/crying*.

Task: speaking

1 Tell students to look again at the questions on page 24. Give them time to make notes. For phrases that they could use, refer students to *Useful language a* on page 25 and to the phrases in exercise 4 on page 24. Walk round the class providing further words and phrases.

2 Put students into groups to compare, and give them time to discuss their ideas. Tell each group to keep a list of the most interesting ideas for each question they discuss. Refer students to *Useful language b* on page 25 for phrases they could use. While students are speaking, note errors for feedback at the end of the task. Listen specifically for errors in the language covered in *Language focus 1* (pages 20–21) and *Language focus 2* (pages 22–23).

3 If you have a small class, get students to explain their ideas to the whole class. If you have a large class, put them into pairs with a student from another group. Encourage them to explain their answers and ask each other questions. Finally, provide some comments and correction of the language you heard students use during the task.

Wordspot (PAGE 26)

life

1 **a** Put students into pairs and encourage them to guess the answers if they are unsure. If your students are weak, refer them to their dictionaries. Check answers as a class.

b Make sure students are underlining the phrases and not only single words. Check answers as a whole class.

> **ANSWERS**
> 1 a life of luxury   2 private life
> 3 life jacket   4 having the time of her life
> 5 was given a life sentence
> 6 lifeguard   7 the chance of a lifetime
> 8 is making life very difficult for us
> 9 had a very good social life
> 10 in real life   11 lifelike
> 12 that's life

2 Put students into pairs, and refer them to the previous activity for help if necessary. Check answers as a whole class and emphasise that students often need to learn the whole phrase, e.g. *make life difficult, have a good/bad social life*.

> **ANSWERS**
> a real life   b time of your life   c social life
> d life sentence   e lifelike   f That's life
> g life difficult   h life jacket   i private life
> j life of luxury   k lifeguard   l chance of a lifetime

3 Students work individually and then compare their sentences. Refer them to the example for help. Walk round the class to help individuals. Ask a few students to read some of their sentences to the class.

ADDITIONAL PRACTICE

Workbook: Wordspot: life, page 19

Study ...   (PAGE 26)

Word building with a dictionary

You can use the *Study* ... section at the end of the module or earlier, depending on your students' needs. Students can do it for homework, or in class time if they need teacher guidance. If your students are going to use a dictionary for the *Practise* ... on page 27, suggest that they do the *Study* ... section first.

1 If you do this in class, students work in pairs. Check that they understand *satisfy*, and give an example if necessary.

> **ANSWERS**
> • satisfied, satisfying, satisfies
> • satisfaction, dissatisfaction
> • satisfactory/unsatisfactory, satisfied/dissatisfied, satisfying/unsatisfying

2–3 Make sure students read the information and instructions carefully. Read through the instructions in exercise 2 with them and check answers as a whole class.

> **ANSWERS AND LANGUAGE NOTES**
> a   satisfying   b   satisfactory
> c   dissatisfaction   d   unsatisfactory
> e   dissatisfied

PRACTISE ... (PAGE 27)

This section can be done independently by students or you can use it for further practice of the language areas covered in Module 2, or as a test.

1—7 For each exercise, make sure students read the instructions carefully. For exercise 3, demonstrate *cross out*. If students find any of the exercises difficult, refer them to the appropriate pages in the *Students' Book* for help. Provide the answers either by checking as a whole class or giving students a copy from the *Teachers' Resource Book*.

> **ANSWERS**
> 1 Nouns
> a behaviour   b criticism   c depression
> d evidence   e friendship   f happiness
> g movement   h employee, employment   i society
> 2 Gerunds
> a going, doing   b joining, meeting
> c going, taking, spending, sitting
> 3 Suffixes
> a talent-   b pleas-   c disappoint-   d import-
> e imagine-
> 4 Prefixes to form opposites
> a in-   b il-   c dis-   d un-   e im-
> 5 Other prefixes which change meaning
> a against war   b without violence
> c too confident   d paid for before
> 6 Responding sympathetically
> a Never mind.   b What a shame!
> c There's no point in getting upset about it.
> d Don't take any notice of her.   e Calm down!
> 7 Phrases with *life*
> a lifelike   b time   c chance   d private   e lifeguard

Pronunciation spot

Stress within word families

a 📼 [2.7] Start by saying the words *record* (noun) and *record* (verb) and asking students which syllable is stressed. Read through the information on how stress is shown in a dictionary and then set the activity. Play the recording, pausing after each word. Put students into pairs to compare their answers. Check answers as a class.

> **ANSWERS**
> 1   i'magine, imagi'nation, i'maginary
> 2   'organise, 'organised, organi'sation
> 3   'politics, poli'tician, po'litical
> 4   psy'chology, psy'chologist, psycho'logical
> 5   'satisfy, satis'faction, satis'factory

b 📼 [2.7] Play the recording and ask them to repeat each word. Correct if necessary. If this is not difficult for them, put students into pairs to read the words aloud to each other. Walk round the room, and correct if necessary.

Remember! (PAGE 27)

Give students a few minutes to tick the boxes, or ask them to do this at home if it is a personal record of achievement.

Mini-check (PAGE 158)

This can be done in class, or set for homework. You can refer students to the *Language focus* sections in Module 2 or the relevant *Language summaries* on pages 145–146 for help.

> **ANSWERS**
> 1 happiness   2 criticism   3 healthy   4 patient
> 5 scientific   6 development   7 childhood   8 creativity
> 9 healthy   10 friendship   11 anxious   12 exciting
> 13 getting   14 depressed   15 not to   16 self   17 non
> 18 anti   19 over   20 post

module 3

Adventures and mishaps

Speaking and reading (PAGES 28–29)

1 Start by discussing what the people are doing in the pictures. Explain that this is a quiz to find out how adventurous they are. Put students into pairs to discuss their answers, and tell them to tick their partner's answers, and take notes.

2 Students read their partner's answers and prepare what they will say. Students present their ideas.

Vocabulary and listening (PAGE 29)

Mishaps

1 Students work in pairs to match the words in A and B. Check answers and ask what is happening in each picture.

ANSWERS

a	you spill	15	your drink over someone
b	you stumble	1	and fall over
c	you bang your	5	head/knee/elbow
d	you run out of	11	petrol
e	you lock yourself	10	out
f	you get	8	lost
g	you over	12	sleep
h	you get on the	13	wrong train
i	you're late	7	for school/work/an appointment
j	you miss	14	your plane
k	you leave something	3	at home
l	you lose	9	your ticket/bag/ID card
m	you slip	2	on some ice
n	you get stuck	6	in bad traffic
o	your car	4	breaks down

Picture a: you stumble and fall over, and you spill your drink over someone.
Picture b: you oversleep (and possibly: you're late for school/work/an appointment; you miss your plane).
Picture c: your car breaks down.
Picture d: you lose your ticket/ID card.

2 [3.1] Explain that students are going to hear four people describing a mishap that happened to them. Ask students to read the questions, and explain that they should answer the four questions for each speaker. Play the recording, pausing after each speaker. Get students to compare answers, and play the recording again if necessary. Check answers with the class.

ANSWERS
Speaker 1
a   at home in bed, on the morning of an exam
b   people taking the same exam
c   overslept and missed the start of the exam; still had pyjamas on during the exam
d   uncomfortable

Speaker 2
a   in Denmark, on holiday; in Copenhagen; later in Sweden
b   parents
c   got on the wrong train and went to Sweden
d   scared

Speaker 3
a   in a posh restaurant, on a first date
b   the date
c   spilled a drink over the date
d   embarrassed

Speaker 4
a   in their flat; had to go to grandmother's ninetieth birthday
b   their flatmate and the fire brigade
c   the flatmate locked them in the flat
d   calm, then in a state of panic

3 Give students time to think about their stories. Walk round the class helping with vocabulary. Put students into pairs to tell their stories. For feedback, ask students to tell the class the funniest story they heard.

ADDITIONAL PRACTICE

Workbook: Vocabulary: Mishaps, page 20

Reading and speaking (PAGES 30–31)

1 **a** Start by asking students to say what's happening in the pictures on page 30. Elicit *crime*; *anti-social behaviour*; *vandalism*; *graffiti*; *truancy*; *begging*. If your students are from the same country, they can do this exercise in pairs. If not, they can do it individually and then compare answers. Ask a few students to feed back to the class.

b Set the activity and check students understand *a matter for*; *deal with*; *be tough on something*. *Note:* answers will be mostly subjective and specific to the students' culture(s). However, some items are obviously more serious than others.

c Put students into groups and ask them to explain their answers. Get feedback from each group.

2 **a** Focus attention on the picture on page 31 and elicit what's happening. Introduce the text by telling them it was written by Bill Bryson, an American travel writer, in a book about his travels round Europe.

b Give students time to read the text quickly and choose the best interpretation. Check answers with the class.

3 Give students time to read the text again and answer the questions. Check answers as a class.

ANSWERS
a   Copenhagen
b   He saw a small crowd by the town hall.
c   He had fallen and hurt himself after taking drugs.
d   They were very gentle and sympathetic.
e   He will probably be in trouble with his father, but not with the police.

4   Students underline the words/phrases in the text as they answer each question. Check answers with the class.

ANSWERS
a   *were talking softly and with sympathy* (line 3)
b   *turns one's brain into an express elevator to Pluto. Disorientated by this sudden journey through the cosmos* (lines 5–7)
c   *stumbled and cracked his head; a trickle of blood ran from above his hairline to his cheek* (lines 8–9)
d   *They looked as if between them they could handle any emergency* (lines 11–13)
e   *The Danes are almost absurdly law-abiding* (lines 16–17)
f   *made to stand with my arms and legs spread against a wall and frisked* (lines 39–40)
g   *with the deepest admiration* (line 50)

5   In pairs, students guess all the words before using their mini-dictionaries to check. Check answers with the class.

ANSWERS
Below are the definitions from the *Mini-dictionary*.
a   *gorgeous*: very beautiful or attractive
b   *trickle*: a small amount of liquid flowing down a surface
c   *virulent*: a virulent problem or crime is very common and affects a lot of people
d   *involuntarily*: suddenly and without being able to control yourself
e   *frisked* (inf. *frisk*): to search someone's clothes and body for illegal things such as guns or drugs
f   *booked* (inf. *book*): if the police book someone, the record shows that person has committed a crime

6   Read the questions and check any problem vocabulary, e.g. *lenient* and *harsh*. Give students plenty of time to discuss the questions. Finally, choose one of the questions and ask groups to give their opinions in open class.

Task: Tell a story from two points of view (PAGES 32–33)

See *Teacher's tips: making tasks work* on pages 13–14.

Preparation: listening

1   a   In pairs, students describe the pictures on pages 32–33. Introduce the characters and explain that students need to know the vocabulary in the box to understand the story. Ask students to tick the words that they already know before they use them in their mini-dictionaries.

b   Get students in pairs to say which words are illustrated in the pictures. Check the answers with the class.

2   Ask students to discuss their ideas for the story. Get a few ideas from the class and point out the old lady at the window. Ask what students think she is doing/thinking. Do not give answers at this stage.

3   [cassette] [3.2] Put the students into two groups (A and B) to listen to Bill's account and the old lady's account. Choose one student in each group to control the recording, and send them to a quiet place to listen to it. Tell students to make notes and to listen as many times as necessary. If a group finishes quickly, put the students in pairs to practise telling the story.

Task: speaking

1   Put students into pairs from their own group. Introduce the phrases in *Useful language a* and give students a few minutes to think about how to use them. Give students time to practise re-telling their accounts. Walk round the room providing further vocabulary and helping with any misunderstandings.

2   Put the students into A-and-B pairs. Ask students to tell both complete stories before finding the differences and any information only mentioned by student A or B. While students speak, walk round the class and note common problems with the use of narrative tenses.

3   Go through the phrases in *Useful language b* on page 33. Give students time to think about how they can use them to compare the stories. Make a list of the differences and missing information. This can be done as a class with you writing ideas on the board.

ANSWERS
The differences
1   Bill said it was midnight; the old lady said it was one o'clock in the morning.
2   Bill said it was snowing heavily; the old lady said it was a clear night.
3   Bill said he and Frank were falling over because the ground was slippery and that they weren't drunk; the old lady said they were drunk.
4   Bill said they were laughing and calling for help; the old lady said they were shouting, swearing and behaving aggressively.
5   Bill said they were holding onto the cars so that they didn't fall over; the old lady said they were trying to break into the cars.
Information one person mentioned, but the other didn't
According to Bill, there was ice everywhere; the police shouted at them; they tried to talk to the police
According to the old lady, there was a full moon; she called the police; the events happened in a nice neighbourhood.

4   Put students into small groups to discuss the questions. Check ideas and opinions as a whole class.

Language focus 1 (PAGES 34–35)

Verb forms in the narrative

See *Teacher's tips: using a discovery approach in the teaching of grammar* on page 8.

Remind students of the story of Bill and the old lady. Put students into pairs and set the activity. Check answers with the class and then refer them to the *Analysis* for explanations. Draw attention to the form of the Past perfect continuous and the similarities with the Past continuous form.

ANSWERS
See tapescripts on page 163 of the *Students' Book*.

Analysis

Students should be quite familiar with the Past simple, Past continuous and Past perfect simple. This will help them understand the Past perfect continuous.

1 Put students into pairs to read the information and answer the questions. Refer them to sentences 1–8 in the previous exercise for help and examples. Check answers and go through the language notes below.

ANSWERS AND LANGUAGE NOTES
Past simple: *A police car drew up; two police officers got out; it was very, very cold; There was thick ice; I had to get up; I heard this dreadful noise; they were drunk; I realised; I called the police*
Past perfect simple: *I had gone to bed*
Past continuous: *I was coming home; We were laughing; I was getting back into bed; what was going on*
Past perfect continuous: *it had been snowing; They had obviously been drinking*

a the Past simple
b the Past continuous (*was/were + -ing*)
c the Past perfect simple (*had + past participle*) and Past perfect continuous (*had + been + -ing*)

2 Get students to do this in pairs, then check the answers with the class.

ANSWERS AND LANGUAGE NOTES
a 1 b 2

It is important that the action has duration in sentence a, because it tells us there must have been a lot of snow, and in sentence b, because it emphasises the action that was in progress (and was interrupted) at the beginning of the main events of the story. In both sentences, the duration gives the background to the main events.
To check students' understanding, use the following questions.
• Is it a single action, or is it repeated?
• Is it an instant action, or is it long?
• Did it start before the main events (and continue after them)?

PRACTICE

1 [3.4] In pairs, students describe the pictures on page 34. Check ideas and, if necessary, teach *give a sharp poke*; *grateful*; *panic*. Refer students to the *Analysis* on page 34 and *Language summary A* on page 146 for help with the answers. When students have finished, play the recording, pausing after each story to check answers. If students find story a difficult to complete, play the recording after this story and check answers – this will give them an example for stories b and c.

ANSWERS
See tapescript on page 164 of the *Students' Book*.

Pronunciation

1 a [3.5] Play the sentence and ask students to follow in their book. If they have problems hearing the stress, hum the pattern without the words, e.g. 'm mMmm Mm' (*An Australian woman*). Tell students that the most important words are stressed and the other words are often weak, e.g. *an, from*. Point out that the pauses come when one piece of information ends and the next begins.

b [3.5] Play the recording and ask students to compare their answers. Check answers with the class.

ANSWERS
Although a little surprised at this // as she had not noticed a tunnel on that route before // she carried on.

c [3.5] Put students into pairs to underline the words. Play the recording to check answers.

ANSWERS
But after half an hour of twisting and turning // she ran out of petrol.

2 Ask students to read the three sentences a few times while you walk round the class and correct. Then give them time to underline words in the rest of the story before practising the whole story. Make sure all students get a chance to speak. Walk round the room noting common errors with stress patterns. When they've finished, briefly go through a few of the errors but do not correct too much. If students find this difficult, regularly get them to read short texts out loud.

2 a If your class is confident, get students to do the second option. If not, let them choose which option they do. Refer them to the ideas and allow them time to make notes. Walk round the class providing any vocabulary they need.

b Put students into small groups and give a time check so that all students get a chance to speak and ask questions. Note errors with narrative tenses and correct at the end of the activity.

ADDITIONAL PRACTICE

RB **Resource bank:** 3A Sidney and the circus (narrative tenses; verb–adverb combinations for travel and movement), pages 121–122

Workbook: Past simple, Past continuous and Past perfect in narrative, page 23; Past perfect simple or continuous, page 23; Past simple/continuous and Past perfect simple/continuous, page 24

Writing (PAGE 36)

A narrative

1 Focus attention on the picture, and ask if any students have been to the Grand Canyon or what they know about it. Give students a minute to read the text and answer the question. Check the answer and ask students if they agree with Mrs Brown. If necessary, pre-teach *mules*; *park ranger*; *hikers*; *shade*; *legs like jelly*; *vanished* and *tossed* (*the plane around*).

2 Put students into pairs and tell them they are going to write a story later but must first think about narrative structure. Do the first example as a class and ask students where they found the information in Paragraph A. Walk round the room to help students with the other answers. Check answers and go through the language notes below.

> **ANSWERS AND LANGUAGE NOTES**
> * **Paragraph A:** *the main characters; the setting* (this gives the reader a picture to start from)
> * **Paragraph B:** *the narrator* (this means the reader can identify with the narrator – very important)
> * **Paragraph C:** *an unexpected problem* (the unexpected adds drama and keeps the reader interested)
> * **Paragraph D:** *an interesting new character* (this helps keep the reader interested)
> * **Paragraph E:** *the climax; dialogue* (a good story shouldn't reach the climax too early – dialogue can make the events more dramatic)
> * **Paragraph F:** *an amusing conclusion; the beginning* (this helps 'complete' the story – the reader understands why they have read the story)

3 a Give students time to think of a topic. You could give an example of your own to remind them of a similar incident.
b Emphasise they must only structure the story at this stage and make notes to refer to later. Ask them to check they have used a structure similar to the one in exercise 2, if possible.

4 Give students time to write their first draft, and tell them not to worry about mistakes because they will be able to write it again later. When they check the narrative tenses, refer them to *Language summary A* on page 146.

5 If time is short, students write the final draft for homework.

Language focus 2

Continuous aspect in other tenses

See Teacher's tips: using a discovery approach in the teaching of grammar on page 8.

Analysis 1 & 2

Put students into pairs and set the cartoon activity. Check answers as a whole class.

> **ANSWERS**
> 1 've been waiting 2 's been bringing 3 've cut
> 4 'll break 5 'll be waiting

1–2 Students complete the table in the *Analysis* box. Check they have completed it correctly, and then ask them to discuss the question. Go through the language notes. Refer students to *Language summaries B* and *C* on page 147.

> **ANSWERS AND LANGUAGE NOTES**
> 1 **Present perfect simple:** *I've cut*
> Form: *has/have* + past participle
> **Present perfect continuous:** *They've been waiting /*
> *He's been bringing*
> Form: *has/have* + *been* + *-ing*
> **Future simple:** *You'll break / I'll be*
> Form: *will* + infinitive (without *to*)
> **Future continuous:** *Your mother and I'll be waiting*
> Form: *will* + *be* + *-ing*
>
> Highlight the contractions in the examples above. Also, point out the word order in questions, and the contractions in negative forms. For example:
>
> *Have you hurt yourself? / No, I haven't.*
> *How long have they been waiting? / They haven't been waiting long.*
> *When will you be home? / I won't be late. Will you be waiting?*
>
> 2 The continuous shows duration or repetition.

PRACTICE

1 Put students into pairs and do the first example as a class. To check understanding, ask students: *Is it an instant action or does it continue for a long time? Does it happen once or many times?* Give students time to do the other items, and make sure they discuss why they have chosen a particular ending. Check answers and go through the language notes.

> **ANSWERS AND LANGUAGE NOTES**
> a *it's been raining* (continues for a long time)
> b *or you'll miss the train* (happens once)
> c *I've been running up and downstairs all morning* (happens many times)
> d *I'll be working* (continues for a long time)
> e *I've dropped a glass on the floor* (happens once; an instant action)
> f Both endings are possible, but they change the meaning: *so I'll go to work on the bus next week* emphasises that the decision is made at the time of speaking; *so I'll be going to work on the bus next week* emphasises that the action happens many times.
> g *I'll be having my dinner at that time* (continues for a long time)

2 a 📼 [3.6] Play the recording, pausing after each part to let students note their ideas. Put students into pairs to compare. If students have problems, play the recording again, pause after each part and give more time for students to decide.

b 📼 [3.7] Play the recording without stopping. Ask how many they guessed correctly. Play the recording again, pausing after each part to let students write the questions. Ask students to compare their answers, then check as a whole class.

> **ANSWERS**
> See tapescripts on page 164 of the *Students' Book*.

c Explain that students are going to ask each other the questions, and go through the example. Give students time to change the questions. Put them into pairs and ask them to note the answers. Finally, ask a few students to tell the class something interesting they learnt about their partner.

ADDITIONAL PRACTICE

RB **Resource bank:** 3B Continuous snakes and ladders (simple and continuous verb forms of various tenses), pages 123–125

Workbook: Present perfect simple or continuous, page 26; Future simple or continuous, page 27

Real life (PAGE 38)

Dealing with unexpected problems

1 📼 [3.8] Focus students on the picture and elicit what problems might happen in a restaurant. Explain that students are going to hear about unexpected problem in four places. Then play the recording, pausing after each part to let students note their answers. Check as a class.

> **ANSWERS**
> 1 a in a restaurant
>   b a waiter and a customer called Mr Reid
>   c Mr Reid has booked a table for two, but the waiter has given it to someone else.
> 2 a on the phone
>   b Jacqui, a hairdresser/receptionist, and Jane Parry, a customer
>   c Jane has an appointment that morning with a hairdresser called Fiona, but Fiona won't be coming in that day.
> 3 a at a museum
>   b a ticket seller and two students
>   c The students would like to buy tickets for the museum, but the museum is closing in ten minutes.
> 4 a in a bank
>   b a bank clerk and a customer
>   c The customer wants to change euros into Czech crowns straightaway, but the bank doesn't have any Czech crowns.

2 Students work in pairs. Tell them not to worry about individual words because the whole phrase has the meaning. Check answers and go through the language notes.

> **ANSWERS AND LANGUAGE NOTES**
> **Acceptance:** *That's fine. / Right, I see. / I don't see why not.*
> **Annoyance:** *Oh, what a nuisance. / This is ridiculous! / Oh, no! You're joking! / I don't believe it! / Oh, for goodness' sake!*
> **Regret:** *Oh, dear! / Oh, that's a pity. / Oh, what a shame!*
>
> Explain that intonation can change the meaning of a phrase, e.g. *Right, I see* can express annoyance if said with 'annoyed' intonation, and *Oh, no! You're joking!* can sound more or less annoyed depending on the intonation. Generally, *Oh, what a nuisance* and *Oh, no! You're joking!* are not as strong as the other phrases to express annoyance.

Pronunciation

📼 [3.9] Play the recording, pausing after each sentence for students to repeat. Correct if necessary.

3 a Put students into pairs and ask them to note down at least one unexpected problem for each situation. If time is short, give only one or two situations to each pair. For feedback, get one or two ideas for each situation. Elicit ideas from the class and write them on the board.

> **POSSIBLE ANSWERS**
> 1 They don't take credit cards; the credit card machine is broken; they don't accept your particular card; your card is refused (there's no credit).
> 2 The concert is full; you have to pay by credit card and you don't have one; the two tickets are for separate seats.
> 3 They're too busy; your computer is too old to fix; it's very expensive.
> 4 They only have yesterday's copy; they don't have any at all; they don't have the one you want.
> 5 You don't know the name of the ward; they'll only give information to close relatives; they have no record of your friend.
> 6 They don't have black; they're very expensive; they don't have your size.
> 7 They've only reserved a room for one night; they've reserved the wrong type of room; they have no record of your reservation.
> 8 It's full; it's very expensive; your car is too big to go in.

b Give students time to choose the two problems and to prepare their conversations. Circulate, providing vocabulary and language they need. Ask the pairs to practise their conversations for five minutes. Correct pronunciation and language use. Finally, ask for volunteers to act out their conversations.

ADDITIONAL PRACTICE

RB **Resource bank:** 3C Problems, problems! (language for responding to unexpected problems), page 126

Workbook: Real life: Dealing with unexpected problems, page 27

Study ... (PAGE 38)

Noticing and remembering useful collocations

Emphasise the importance of collocations, as some students will believe that single words are more important. For more practice of collocations, refer to *Learner-training worksheet 4*.

1–2 Get students to read through the information and then find the collocations on page 36 of the *Students' Book*. If you are doing this in class, ask students to compare their answers in pairs before you check as a class. If students are doing it for homework, check answers in the next lesson or provide a copy from the *Teacher's Resource Book*.

ANSWERS
- lovely, narrow; heavy; next, previous
- have
- set out; take off
- couldn't wait; no problem

3 Ask students to discuss the question in pairs. Elicit their ideas and go through the suggested answers.

ANSWERS
a The definition is clear and the example sentence is a good idea (probably the most useful information).
b The different collocations are useful, but the meaning isn't given.
c No meaning is given and the collocations are very basic (probably the least useful information).

4 Check that the collocations students choose are true collocations and that they have recorded them usefully.

Practise... (PAGE 39)

This section can be done independently by students or you can use it for further practice of the language areas covered in Module 3, or as a test.

1–6 If students find exercises 1–6 difficult, refer them to the appropriate pages in the *Students' Book* for help. Provide the answers either by checking as a class or giving students a copy from the *Teacher's Resource Book*.

ANSWERS
1 Narrative tenses
a a background event
b an event which happened before the other events
c a background event
d a main event in the story
e an event which happened before the other events
f a main event in the story

2 Narrative phrases
a 6 b 2 c 5 d 1 e 3 f 4

3 Past perfect simple and continuous
a had been playing b had met
c had been waiting d had never seen

4 Continuous aspect
a I've hurt b I've been coming

c Both alternatives are correct.
d Neither alternative is correct.
e We've finished f We'll be watching
g I've been trying h has won

5 Collocations with mishaps
a your elbow, your head b your bag, your ID card
c your keys, your ticket d a bus e some ice f a drink

6 Unexpected problems
a Oh b For c it d This e You're f What
g see h shame

Pronunciation
Voiced and unvoiced sounds (1):
/tʃ/, /dʒ/, /θ/ **and** /ð/

a [3.10] Ask if students can pronounce the sounds listed. If students can produce the sounds, play the recording for them to compare. If not, play the recording and elicit the sounds. Encourage students to touch their throats to 'feel' the vibration. Point out the only difference between the pairs of sounds is that one vibrates and the other doesn't.

b [3.11] Put students into pairs and ask them to say the sounds and listen to each other. Write the phonemic symbols on the board and elicit answers from students, writing the words under each symbol as you go. It is not important if some of the words are under the wrong symbol at this stage. Play the recording, pausing after each word to ask students if it is written under the correct symbol. Erase and write again if necessary.

ANSWERS
See tapescript on page 164 of the *Students' Book*.

c In pairs, students listen carefully, and correct each other if necessary. Walk round the class correcting the sounds.

Remember! (PAGE 39)

Give students a few minutes to tick the boxes, or ask them to do this at home if it is a personal record of achievement.

Mini-check (PAGE 158)

This can be done in class, or set for homework. You can refer students to the *Language focus* sections in Module 3 or the relevant *Language summaries* on pages 146–147 for help.

ANSWERS
1 run out 2 up 3 broke 4 slipped 5 left 6 arrived
7 had been waiting 8 was travelling 9 had promised
10 had broken 11 have been running 12 At 13 for
14 in 15 What 16 All 17 whispering 18 You're joking!
19 that he's telling 20 snowing

module 4

The mind

Reading and speaking (PAGES 40–41)

1 Introduce the topic by asking students to read the title and describe the pictures on pages 40–41. Elicit the meaning of *gender gaps* and ask if students think men or women are better at different things. Keep the atmosphere light to avoid students becoming too emotional or upset.

   Either put students into male–female or same-sex pairs to answer the questions. Check *tends to be* or ask students to use their mini-dictionaries. Give students a few minutes to do the activity. If the pairs are male–female, check answers as a whole class. If they are same-sex pairs, form new male–female pairs and ask students to compare their answers, then check answers as a whole class.

2 Put students into pairs, introduce the text and give them a few minutes to discuss the statements. Give them about two minutes to read the text, and tell them not to worry about problem vocabulary at this stage. Check answers as a whole class.

ANSWER
Statement c is true according to the text.

3 Working individually, students read the text again and underline the sections that give the information. Tell them to guess the meaning of unknown words from the context. Put students into pairs to compare answers, and encourage them to use their own words and not just to read from the text. Check answers as a whole class and ask students which lines in the text gave them the information.

ANSWERS
a The male brain weighs about 1.3kg; the female brain weighs 10 percent less (lines 2–4).
b 'Grey matter' helps us think; 'white matter' helps us transfer information (lines 12–15).
c Women are better than men at doing a lot of things at the same time (lines 21–28).
d Men have better spatial abilities than women (lines 30–32).
e Male toddlers tried to climb the barrier or push it down; female toddlers showed distress and tried to attract help (lines 43–46).
f Women needed verbal and emotional skills to control and educate their babies; men needed spatial skills to hunt (lines 52–54).

4 Put students into pairs and explain that guessing meaning from context is an important skill, because using dictionaries interrupts your reading and makes you read slowly. Emphasise that it is not always necessary to be 100 percent correct when guessing, but it is important to understand the general idea. Ask students to describe the meanings in their own words and to make notes to help them remember. Check answers as a whole class. Write some of their suggestions on the board and ask students to choose the best definition for each word/phrase. If the definitions are unclear, elicit or give example sentences.

   Only refer students to the answers below if they have found this activity very difficult.

ANSWERS
a *come up with*: to think of (an idea, plan, or reply)
b *the latter*: the second of two people or things just mentioned
c *sources*: things, places, or people that you get things from
d *more adept at*: better at (something that needs care or skill)
e *multi-tasking*: doing a lot of activities at the same time
f *come out on top*: be the best/better than other people
g *tackling*: dealing with (a difficult job or problem)
h *ancestors*: people, or members of your family, who lived a long time ago

5 Give students a few minutes to think about the questions, and check *typical* and *exception* if necessary. Put them into small groups to exchange ideas. Make sure they explain their opinions and ask each other questions. For feedback, ask a few students to tell you about someone else in their group.

ADDITIONAL PRACTICE

Workbook: Listen and read: Driving each other crazy, page 28

Vocabulary (PAGE 41)

Qualities of mind

See *Teacher's tips: working with lexis* on pages 9–10.

1 Make sure students only use their mini-dictionaries for the words they can't guess. Check answers as a whole class and go through the language notes below. Elicit or give example sentences if necessary, e.g. *I never ask my sister for help because she's so bossy and won't let me decide how to do things*.

ANSWERS AND LANGUAGE NOTES
a *bossy* (used with a negative meaning)
b *emotional* (used with a negative or positive meaning)
c *articulate* (used with a positive meaning)
d *sympathetic* (used with a positive meaning)
e *stubborn* (normally used with a negative meaning)
f *practical* (used with a positive meaning)
g *co-operative* (used with a positive meaning)
h *self-confident* (used with a positive meaning)
i *intuitive* (normally used with a positive meaning)
j *aggressive* (normally used with a negative meaning)

2 Give the students a few minutes to do this individually. Walk round the class helping with any language they need to change the sentences. Put students into pairs to explain, and ask each other questions about, their answers.

3 Give students five to ten minutes to write their sentences. Walk round the class helping with language and correcting if necessary. Put students into pairs or small groups to explain, and ask each other questions about, their sentences. Ask a few students to tell the class the most interesting or the funniest/strangest information they heard.

ADDITIONAL PRACTICE

Workbook: Vocabulary: Qualities of mind, page 28
Vocabulary booster: More qualities of mind, page 30

Task: Analyse the results of a quiz
(PAGES 42–43)

See *Teacher's tips: making tasks work* on pages 13–14.

Preparation: listening

1 Introduce the short text and give students thirty seconds to read it and tick the points they find surprising. Put them into pairs to compare answers before eliciting ideas from a few students.

2 a Put students into pairs and make sure they know who is student A and who is student B. Direct them to the correct page in the *Students' Book*. Tell them they are going to use their quiz to interview the other student. They must not answer the questions for themselves.

b Give students a few minutes to check unknown words. Walk round the class helping with meaning and pronunciation, or ask students to use their mini-dictionaries. Words you could check are (Quiz A, page 42) *judging, task, non-fiction, fantasy, science fiction, background music*; (Quiz B, page 138) *straightaway, manual, measure, option, intuition, visualise, jump around* (in a magazine), *ticking things off*.

Task: speaking

1 Put students into their A-and-B pairs. Tell them not to look at each other's quizzes. Get student A to ask their questions first, and suggest they circle 'a' or 'b' depending on their partner's answers. Set a time limit of three to four minutes. Tell them to ask their partner to repeat a question if they do not understand it. When the time limit is reached, get student B to ask their questions and circle the answers. Ask them to count the 'a' and 'b' answers and to write the numbers at the bottom of the quiz. They must not tell their partner the result.

2 a [4.1] Explain that the recording will help students analyse the results of the quiz. Most of the language in the box is explained in the listening or can be guessed from context. However, if your class is worried about unknown vocabulary, pre-teach *linear thinking, logical thinking, verbal skills* and *the big picture*, or give students a few minutes to check in their mini-dictionaries. If they use their mini-dictionaries, say each word/phrase for them so that they can hear the sound. Play the recording without pausing. Ask students to compare answers, and then check as a whole class.

ANSWERS
Left-brained people: linear thinking; logical thinking; verbal skills; learning by explanation
Right-brained people: intuition; interest in the 'big picture'; artistic creativity; the ability to visualise; learning by doing

b [4.1] Put students into pairs and set the questions. Tell students that *in this respect* (question 2) refers to the *typical score* (question 1), i.e. is there any difference between the typical score of men and women? Give them a few minutes to answer the questions, then play the recording again if necessary. Check answers as a whole class.

ANSWERS
1 a balance of 'a' and 'b' answers
2 Yes, men tend to get more 'a' answers than 'b'.
3 Yes, you can learn to improve the less dominant side of your brain.

3 Students work individually for about five minutes to prepare their explanations. Ask them to make notes if necessary but not to write sentences. Refer them to *Useful language a* and walk round the class providing any other vocabulary or phrases they need. Do not refer them to the tapescript for recording 1 because this will encourage them simply to read it to their partner. When they have finished preparing, put students into the same A-and-B pairs as in exercise 1 and set a time limit for the activity. Give a time check halfway through so that all students get a chance to speak. Encourage them to ask questions if their partner's explanation is unclear.

4 Students work individually for one or two minutes to think about the questions. If necessary, check *revealing, upbringing* and *encourage*, and refer them to *Useful language b* for ideas. Then, put the A-and-B pairs from exercise 1 into larger groups (ideally two or three pairs forming one group). Give them plenty of time for the discussion, and tell them to give full explanations and to ask one another questions. While they are talking, walk round the class noting common errors and correct these briefly at the end of the activity.

Language focus 1 (PAGES 44–45)
The passive

See *Teacher's tips: using a discovery approach in the teaching of grammar* on page 8.

1 Ask students if they have heard of the abbreviation *IQ* and if they know what it stands for – 'intelligence quotient' – a number representing someone's ability to reason, compared to the statistical average for their age, which is taken to be 100. For example, someone might say *He's very intelligent – he's got an IQ of 130*. It is measured by using problem-solving tests. Tell students that the questions in this exercise are the kind used in IQ tests. Give students a maximum of five minutes to answer the questions. Explain that for question b, they have to choose from shapes 1–4 the best one to fit in the blank square. If they find a question too difficult, tell them to go to the next one. Emphasise that it doesn't matter if they can't answer a question. Refer them to page 142 to check answers. Put them into pairs to discuss which question they found easiest or most difficult.

2 Introduce the text by writing *Mensa* on the board and asking students what this organisation is. (The word *mensa* means 'table' in Latin. The name stands for a round-table society, where race, colour, creed, national origin, age, politics and educational/social background are irrelevant.) Give them a minute to read the text, and then put them into pairs to answer the question and explain their reasons. As feedback, ask students to put their hands up if they would like to join Mensa, and elicit a few reasons for and against.

Analysis 1

1 Explain that students are going to revise or learn about the passive, and put them into pairs to answer the questions. Teach *founded* by giving/eliciting *started* or *begun*. Copy the passive sentence onto the board, elicit the form and go through the language notes below. Then ask students to find more examples in the text, and write a few on the board to highlight form using different tenses.

ANSWERS AND LANGUAGE NOTES
Passive sentence: *The society* **was founded** *in 1946 by Roland Berrill and Lancelot Ware.*
Form: *be* (in the appropriate tense) + past participle

In the examples from the text, show students that the basic form remains the same, but you can change the tense of *be* to express different grammatical meanings:

to be accepted (infinitive of *be* + past participle)
was ... known (Past simple of *be* + past participle)
should be used (modal verb + *be* + past participle)
are drawn (Present simple of *be* + past participle)
are organised (Present simple of *be* + past participle)
is ... known (Present simple of *be* + past participle)
have been made (Present perfect of *be* + past participle)

2 Put students into pairs to discuss the statements. Check answers as a whole class and go through the language notes.

ANSWERS AND LANGUAGE NOTES
a True. (If necessary, write the active sentence from exercise 1 (*Roland Berrill and Lancelot Ware founded the society in 1946*) on the board. Underline the agent in this sentence, and in the passive version which you wrote on the board earlier.)
b True. (Point out this is often true but not always, e.g. in the passive sentence in exercise 1, the agent is important and known but the writer has chosen the passive because it is appropriate to this type of writing.)
c False. (It is used more in formal contexts, and can sound unfriendly and too impersonal in informal contexts.)
d True.

3 Read through the information and refer students to *Language summaries A* and *B* on page 147.

Practice

1 🔲 [4.2] Introduce the text by asking students to read the title and elicit another word for *smartest*, e.g. *most intelligent, brainiest, cleverest.* Put students into pairs and set the activity. If necessary, help students with vocabulary or refer them to their mini-dictionaries for the following: *establish, genius, claim, drop out, goals, defeat, give up, remark*. If students find the activity difficult, refer them to the statements in *Analysis 1*, exercise 2, and *Language summaries A* and *B*. Play the recording and ask students to compare their answers. Check answers as a whole class.

ANSWERS
See tapescript for recording 2 on page 165 of the *Students' Book.*

Analysis 2
Alternatives to the passive

1–2 Read through the information and ask students to find the sentences in the two texts, then put them into pairs to compare. Check answers with the class and go through the language notes below. Refer students to *Language summary C* on page 147.

ANSWERS AND LANGUAGE NOTES
a *It is not known how many marriages have been made at Mensa meetings!*
b *intelligence 'should be used for the benefit of humanity.'*
c *it is said that the average score is around 100.*
d *books, which have been translated into many different languages.*

Point out that the active sentences in exercise 2 are more conversational and less formal than in the texts on pages 44–45. In informal conversation, we use an alternative to the passive if there is one. *You* means *anyone; they* means *people* or the *authorities / the people who are responsible for this; people* means *the people who know this* or sometimes *people in general. We* can be used to substitute the passive in a similar way. As English becomes less formal, these forms are increasingly used in written texts.

2 Put students into pairs and do the first example as a whole class, highlighting how the form changes. Tell students to help each other with vocabulary or use their mini-dictionaries, if necessary. Check answers as a whole class. If students have found this difficult, write some of the active sentences and their passive equivalents on the board. Then highlight the changes by eliciting the form from the students.

ANSWERS
b You can only see brain cells with a microscope.
c We still don't know exactly how many aspects of the human brain work.
d People think that the right side of the brain is the 'artistic' side.
e In fact, we use both sides of the brain when we listen to music.

f You can't feel pain in the brain, because it has no nerves.

g Someone has calculated that messages in the brain travel at over 250 kilometres per hour!

h In ancient times, people believed that the purpose of the brain was to cool the blood.

i Someone has suggested that our brains haven't changed much since prehistoric times.

j They are doing research into how the brain works.

ADDITIONAL PRACTICE

[RB] **Resource bank:** 4A Passive scrabble (passive tenses and passive forms), pages 127–128

Workbook: Passives, page 31; Choosing active or passive, page 33; Formed and conversational use, page 35

Writing (PAGE 46)

A formal letter

1 [4.3] Explain that students are going to write a formal letter of complaint. To introduce the topic, focus them on the advertisement on page 46 and teach *boost* and *unique* by eliciting/giving a similar word or phrase (e.g. *increase/extend*, *the only one*). Ask if students have seen similar advertisements before and if they have tried these methods. Set the questions and play the recording. Put students into pairs to compare, and then check answers as a whole class. Play the recording again if necessary.

ANSWERS
The course promises to boost your brainpower. The 'special package' includes twelve booklets on methods; CD-ROMs of exercises; eight CDs of classical music; three months' supply of vitamin supplements. It costs €150 plus €5.95 postage and packing.

2 Put students into pairs, introduce the characters and set the question. Stress that these are sentences that Phillip says not writes. Briefly check answers as a whole class.

ANSWERS
The course arrived later than advertised
The exercises take longer than claimed.
The exercises are not enjoyable as promised.

3 **a, b** Give students one minute to read the text, and ask if there are any additional complaints Phillip has. (Answer: he can buy the vitamins and CDs at his local supermarket for half the price.) Put students into pairs to underline the words/ phrases he uses and discuss the question in b. Check answers and go through the language notes below.

ANSWERS AND LANGUAGE NOTES
The grammar and vocabulary of the letter are more formal, as indicated below:
You told me / I was told that (active becomes passive)
I'd / I would (no contraction)
get/receive (a Latin-based word is used)

it in forty-eight hours, but actually / the course within forty-eight hours whereas in fact (no colloquial phrasing)
it took nearly three weeks. / it took almost three weeks to arrive. (more detail)
Your ad / Your advertisement (no abbreviation)
said/promised (vocabulary with more specific meaning)
that the exercises / that the necessary exercises (more detail)
only take / would be enjoyable and take only (more detail; changed word order)
ten minutes a day, but / ten minutes a day to complete. However, (longer, more complex sentences, here broken up by a new sentence)
I've worked out / I have calculated (no contraction; a Latin-based word is used)
that they take / that in order to complete the exercises suggested, it would take (more detail)
more like two hours a day. / closer to two hours a day. (no colloquial phrasing)
And another thing – / Furthermore, (no colloquial phrasing)
I just cannot / I totally fail to (exaggeration of meaning)
understand/comprehend (a Latin-based word is used)
how you can say / how you can describe (vocabulary with more specific meaning)
these boring exercises / these tedious exercises (exaggeration of meaning, through use of a less common word)
are enjoyable! / as enjoyable, or suggest that they will 'open up your imagination'. (more detail)

c Put students into pairs and ask them to underline the words/ phrases in the text. Check answers, and refer to the language notes above if necessary.

ANSWERS
1 Following   2 purchased   3 dissatisfied
4 whereas in fact   5 to complete
6 I have calculated   7 I totally fail to comprehend
8 I am of the opinion that
9 I … demand a complete refund of everything that I have paid

4 Give students a few minutes to find the phrases. Elicit some examples and write them on the board. Check that students understand the phrases.

ANSWERS
Other useful phrases: Following our telephone conversation; I am writing to complain about; the product and service that I have received; for a number of reasons; Firstly; Finally; a total waste of both my time and money

5 Ask students if they have seen advertisements like the one on page 139 before and if they have tried a course like this. Get them to choose one of the languages, and check *P&P* (postage and packing). Put them into pairs to think of four things that went wrong, and then elicit examples and write them on the board. Tell students they can use any of the ideas on the board or their own. Students write the letter in class, or for homework if time is short.

Writing, exercise 5: alternative suggestion

Writing, exercise 5: alternative suggestion

If your students need to improve their writing skills, follow the above procedure until the letter-writing begins. Then ask students to order their ideas and write a first draft. Walk round the class helping with language and correcting mistakes. Ask students to give their draft to another student to check and then to use the other students' suggestions to write the final draft. Students write the final letter in class, or for homework if time is short.

ADDITIONAL PRACTICE

Workbook: Improve your writing: A formal letter of apology, page 34

Language focus 2 (PAGE 47)

have/get something done

Introduce the text, give students a very short time to read it and ask them which they think is the best piece of advice. Put them into pairs to think of other ideas for keeping your brain healthy. Finally, elicit a few ideas and ask students if these are better than the ideas in the text.

Analysis

1–2 Put students into pairs to answer the questions. Go through the answers, the language notes and the additional information in exercise 2 as a whole class. Refer students to *Language summary D* on page 147 for more information.

ANSWERS AND LANGUAGE NOTES

The verb form is active, and in the imperative: (subject) + verb.
In the second sentence, someone else does the testing (and is often paid to do it).
The verb form is passive, and in the imperative: *have* + subject + past participle. (This is a very common usage in English and can be used in any tense. We often use *done* instead of a more specific verb, e.g. *I'm getting my car done*, when the meaning is understood from the context, i.e. it is most likely that *done* here means *repaired/serviced* because this is a very common situation.)
Another example in the text is *get your blood pressure checked*.

PRACTICE

1 Put students into pairs and, if necessary, do the first example (picture b) with them. Check answers and go through the language notes below.

ANSWERS AND LANGUAGE NOTES

b *He's having his hair cut.* (Show that we keep the tense, the present continuous, exactly the same. Point out

the contraction (*he's = he is*) and show the form: *have* (in this case *having*) + subject (*his hair*) + past participle (*cut*).)
c *They're painting their house.*
d *They're having their house painted.*

2 Put students into pairs to write their sentences. Walk round the class helping with form and any unknown vocabulary, e.g. *contact lens; highlighting; manicure; pedicure; alterations; ironing*. Check answers with the class and write a few examples on the board. Elicit the form of the examples you write and go through the language notes below.

ANSWERS AND LANGUAGE NOTES

At Harringtons Optician's, you can:
have/get your eyes tested.
have/get contact lenses fitted.
have/get your glasses cleaned and repaired.

At Finola's Beauty Salon, you can:
have/get your face massaged. (But it would be more natural to say *have a face massage.*)
have/get your hair cut/styled/conditioned. (It is very common to say *I'm having/getting my hair done.* This follows the *have* + subject + past participle form, but uses *done* as a non-specific reference to the action. *Done* is also used to refer to the action for a second time, e.g. *I'm getting my hair cut on Friday. I'm getting it done for the party.*)
have/get your hair highlighted.
have/get your nails manicured/cut. (*I'm having a pedicure* would be more natural than *I'm having my nails pedicured.*)

At Flair Dry Cleaning & Ironing Service, you can:
have/get your clothes ironed.
have/get your clothes dry-cleaned.
have/get your clothes altered.
have/get your clothes collected and delivered free.

3 [4.4] Set the questions and play the recording. Put students into pairs to compare, and then check answers as a class. Give students plenty of time to make notes and prepare their dialogues. Walk round the class helping with vocabulary and correcting language use. Give them about five minutes to practise the dialogues, and give more correction if necessary. Finally, ask a few pairs to perform a dialogue for the rest of the class. If time is short, reduce the number of dialogues you ask students to prepare.

ANSWERS

Flair Dry Cleaning; alterations

ADDITIONAL PRACTICE

Workbook: *Have/get something done*, page 34

Wordspot (PAGE 48)

mind

See *Teacher's tips: working with lexis* on pages 9–10.

1 Focus students on the diagram and explain that *mind* can be used as a verb, as a noun and in compound adjectives. Give an example of these from the diagram. If you think your class will find this exercise difficult, check that students understand the language in the explanations and the phrases in the diagram, or ask them to use their mini-dictionaries. You may need to check the meaning of: *it doesn't concern you*; *unprejudiced*; *to come third*; *blocking*; *ceiling*; *scheme*. Do a few examples as a class and tell students they might need to change the form of the phrase. Then give students a few minutes to complete the exercise. Check answers as a whole class.

> **ANSWERS**
> b Mind your own business!
> c open-minded; make up your mind
> d my mind went blank
> e speak their mind
> f something on your mind
> g I don't mind
> h Never mind.
> i changed my mind
> j Bearing in mind
> k Would you mind moving
> l absent-minded
> m Mind your head!
> n To my mind

2 [4.5] Put students into pairs to discuss their answers. Tell them to guess unknown vocabulary from the context or use their mini-dictionaries. Play the recording to check answers.

> **ANSWERS**
> See tapescript for recording 5 on page 165 of the *Students' Book*.

3 Show students how the dialogues in exercise 2 clearly contextualise the phrases with *mind*. Emphasise that they should make the situation and the characters' moods clear. While they are writing, walk round the class helping with vocabulary, checking that their conversations clearly illustrate the *mind* phrases, and correcting if necessary. If some students finish early, ask them to write more conversations. For feedback, ask a few pairs to read one of their conversations to the class.

ADDITIONAL PRACTICE

Workbook: Wordspot: *mind*, page 35

Listening (PAGE 49)

Song: *You were always on my mind*

1 a Introduce the song by showing students a picture of Elvis Presley or asking if they have heard of him. Get students to tell you a few things about him. If students have not heard of him, give them some of the facts below:
- American
- popularly called the 'King'
- one of the most popular rock-and-roll singers in the West
- died in 1977 at the age of 42
- made a lot of films.

The song *Always on my mind* was a hit for Elvis in 1972. It has been covered by a number of singers/groups, most famously the Pet Shop Boys in 1987.

Put students into pairs to complete the activity.

b [4.6] Play the recording for students to check their answers. Check answers as a whole class, and play the recording again if necessary.

> **ANSWERS**
> See tapescript for recording 6 on page 165 of the *Students' Book*.

2 Ask the class to make sure their answers are mostly correct. Emphasise that some of the answers are very similar and students should decide which one fits best with the mood/meaning of the song. Go through the answers as a class and check students understand *guess*, *suppose* and *blind* (metaphorical sense).

> **ANSWERS**
> a I was always thinking about you.
> b needed to
> c a last opportunity
> d I suppose
> e unimportant
> f I didn't know what was happening.

3 Students do the activity individually and then compare with their partner. Elicit a few answers from students and, finally, ask them if they think the relationship has finished. (Answer: the use of the Past simple suggests that the relationship has probably finished. However, the words *Tell me that your sweet love hasn't died* and *Give me one more chance* show that the singer hopes it hasn't finished completely.)

> **ANSWERS**
> **Things he's sorry he did:** he didn't treat her well; he didn't love her enough; he didn't say and do little things; he didn't hold her when she was lonely; he never told her how happy he was with her; if he made her feel second best.
> **Things he'd like her to do:** tell him that she still loves him; give him another chance.

ADDITIONAL PRACTICE

RB **Resource bank:** 4B It's all in the mind (expressions with *mind*), page 129

Consolidation modules 1–4 (PAGES 50–51)

It is primarily intended that you do this in class time, allowing students to work in pairs or small groups. However, we have noted below which of the activities could be set for homework with the follow-up activities done in class. Emphasise to students that the *Consolidation* activities are for revision purposes and are not tests.

A Vocabulary: Word hunt

This section could be done as a competition by giving students a time limit and asking them to find as many words as possible in that time. The pair with the most words wins. Make sure the students read the instructions and the page references carefully. Either check answers after each section or at the end of section 8. Alternatively, students can use their mini-dictionaries to check their answers. This section could be set for homework.

ANSWERS
1 a spectacular b world-wide c blend
   d siblings
2 a inept b shy c grotesque d dull
3 a low-fat b self-esteem c bad-tempered
   d co-ordination
4 a wealthy b optimistic c penniless
   d valuable
5 a life jacket b lifeguard c social life
   d private life
6 a set out b under-dressed c took off
   d I was so terrified I could barely … / nervous wreck
7 a aggressive/bossy/stubborn
   b articulate/co-operative/sympathetic/practical/self-confident/intuitive
8 a make up your mind b Mind your own business!
   c Never mind. d you've got something on your mind

B Active and passive verb forms

Students do this individually while you walk round the class and help. Put them into pairs to compare answers. This section could be set for homework.

ANSWERS
1 was arrested
2 tricked
3 was telling / told
4 persuaded
5 had been placed
6 to be removed
7 returned
8 found
9 had disappeared
10 had been taken
11 arrested
12 was boarding
13 had been paid for
14 am not usually deceived
15 said
16 was returned

C Speaking: Forming nouns and adjectives

1 Students can work alone or in pairs for this activity. Check answers as a whole class or ask students to use their mini-dictionaries.

ANSWERS
b creative c determined d enthusiastic e fit
f good-looking g honest h optimistic i persistent
j self-confident k talented l wealthy

2 Students work individually before forming groups to discuss their opinions. Tell them the group needs to agree on a final list for each job. Encourage them to explain and ask each other questions about their ideas. Finally, elicit answers from each group and ask the other groups if they agree. If time

is short, cut the number of jobs or qualities. Alternatively, give a different job to each group rather than ask them to do all three.

D Listening: Passive forms with *have* and *get*

1 a [C.1] Ask students to read the table, and then play the recording, pausing after each section to give students time to write notes. Put students into pairs to compare, and then check answers as a whole class. Play the recording again if necessary and check students understand *lasered*, *short-sighted*, *tattoo*, *dyed*, *cool*, *extensions*, *plaits*.

ANSWERS

Name	What they had done	Where/ When	How they felt at the time	How they feel about it now
Karen	Had her eyes lasered	At a private clinic in London; about five years ago, at the end of an afternoon	Really nervous	Really glad
Nigel	Had a tattoo done	In Manchester city centre; about five years ago, on his eighteenth birthday	A bit scared	Loves it
Penny	Had her hair dyed royal blue and had blue extensions put in	Doesn't say where; when she was at university	Fabulous; really cool	Embarrassed

b Give students a few minutes to think about their answers, and then put them into groups to discuss them. Encourage students to explain and ask each other questions about their ideas.

E Speaking: Real life

1 Make sure students try and think of a phrase before looking at the relevant page.

POSSIBLE ANSWERS
a Well, I'd better be off. / Right, I'd better get back to work
b Excuse me, could you help me?
c Just ignore him/her/it/them. / There's no point in getting upset about it. / Don't take any notice of him/her.
d Just ignore them. / Don't take any notice of them. / Try not to worry about it.
e Oh, what a nuisance. / Oh, no! You're joking! / This is ridiculous!
f Oh, no! You're joking! / Oh, what a shame! / Oh, dear! / Oh, that's a pity.

2 Give students plenty of time to prepare their dialogue. Walk round the class providing vocabulary, and correcting if necessary. If time is short, ask only a few pairs to act out their dialogues. If students write their dialogues, take them in to correct.

module 5

Unusual achievements

Reading and vocabulary
(PAGES 52–53)

Remarkable achievements

1 Focus attention on the pictures and headings, explaining that these people have all achieved something unusual. Check students understand *achievements*, *prestigious*, *prodigies*, *juggler*, *supergran* (a journalistic term for an older lady who has done something outstanding). Put students into pairs or small groups briefly to discuss what the achievements might be, and then elicit a few ideas.

2 Set the activity and give students a few minutes to read the articles and check their predictions. Put them into pairs to compare their answers and to summarise the information in the articles orally. Walk round the class helping with vocabulary or ask students to use their mini-dictionaries. In open class, get a different pair to summarise each article, and ask the other students to add anything if necessary. Do not correct how students express their ideas but do focus on students' understanding of the articles.

> **ANSWERS**
> 1 won the award for Europe's Most Influential Businesswoman
> 2 graduated with Maths degrees from Warwick University
> 3 broke the world record for juggling a football non-stop
> 4 first woman to circle the globe solo by helicopter
> 5 first African American to win an Oscar for Best Actress

3 a Put students into pairs and check that they understand the words in bold, or ask them to help each other and guess from the context. Tell them to use their mini-dictionaries only for words they cannot guess. To give an example of the activity, focus students on Fabiola Arredondo and ask them which of the items (1–9) could refer to her. Elicit ideas and get students to explain why, pointing out that they may disagree with each other. Individually, students complete the activity.

b Put students into pairs or small groups and refer them to the speech bubbles on page 52 for language they can use. Encourage them to explain their answers fully and to ask questions to clarify their partner's answers. Walk round the class and listen for errors in the Present perfect, which you can refer to later in *Language focus 1*. Finally, check ideas as a whole class and encourage students to explain their answers and persuade others.

> *Reading and vocabulary*, exercise 3: **language note**
>
>
>
> Although the aim of this activity is not grammatical, it is useful background for the *Language focus* and *Task* sections later in this module. Briefly, show students that many of these sentences contain the present perfect, and

ask/explain why (i.e. because they describe recent achievements, still relevant now, with the focus on the action rather than on when it happened). Do not make this a big focus or spend too long on it because it will interrupt the flow of the lesson.

4 a Tell students that there is no 'right' answer; they should put the achievements in order according to their own opinion. Give them a few minutes to decide on the order and think about their reasons. Then put them into pairs or small groups to compare. If possible, each group should agree on an order for the achievements. Encourage students to explain their answers and ask each other questions about their opinions. For feedback, ask each group for their list and their reasons. If you have a small- to medium-sized class, ask other groups to agree/disagree, then write a final list on the board. If you have a large class, choose only a few groups to read their list to the others.

b Either ask the students to discuss the questions in groups or as a whole class.

ADDITIONAL PRACTICE

Workbook: Vocabulary: Remarkable achievements, page 36

Language focus 1 (PAGES 54–55)

Perfect tenses in the past, present and future

See *Teacher's tips: using a discovery approach in the teaching of grammar* on page 8.

1 [5.1] To introduce the topics, ask students to look at the pictures, briefly say what each person is doing and guess what their achievements are. Then set the activity and give students a short time to read through the prompts. Play the recording, pausing after each section to give students time to write notes. Ask students to compare in pairs, and then check answers as a whole class. Play the recording again if necessary.

> **ANSWERS**
> **Elsie Gamble**
> Date she began at Coteswood School: 1927
> School fees then: £3 a term
> School fees now: £700 a term
> **Git Kaur Rhandawa**
> Number of driving tests taken before she passed: forty-seven
> Amount of money spent on driving lessons: more than £10,000
> **James Hughes**
> Saw first film: at the age of six
> Number of films seen up to now: nearly 10,000
> Number of films sees a year: about 800

2 Put students into pairs and give them a few minutes to complete the sentences and find the examples. Check answers as a whole class and elicit the basic form of each

41

tense. You can go through the answers while you discuss the questions in the *Analysis* below.

ANSWERS AND LANGUAGE NOTES

1 *has been a teacher for more than seventy-five years.* (Tense: Present perfect. Form: *has/have* + past participle.)
2 *she had finally passed her driving test.* (Tense: Past perfect. Form: *had* + past participle.)
3 *will have seen 20,000 films.* (Tense: Future perfect. Form: *will* + have + past participle.)

Analysis

The idea in this *Analysis* is for students to understand the general concepts that are common to all verbs in the perfect aspect, rather than worrying about details that are different. The Future perfect is focused on again later in the course, and *Language focus 2* on pages 58–59 looks in more detail at the differences between the Present perfect simple and continuous.

1–3 You can go through the questions as you check the answers to *Language focus 1*, exercise 2. Put students into pairs to answer the questions, and refer them to the timelines to illustrate the three forms. If students have problems interpreting the first timeline, draw it on the board and explain how it illustrates the Present perfect. Walk round the class while students do the activities to help with any misunderstandings. Go through the answers and language notes as a whole class. Clarify problems with meaning by referring to the timelines and the examples in *Language focus 1*, exercise 2. Clarify problems with form by writing example sentences on the board and eliciting the form. Refer students to *Language summary A* on page 148 for more information.

ANSWERS AND LANGUAGE NOTES

1 **Present perfect**
  She is a teacher now. She became a teacher more than seventy-five years ago.
a The Present perfect links the present and the time **before** now. (Elicit/highlight the form: subject + *have* (*'ve*) / *has* (*'s*) / *haven't* / *hasn't* + past participle. Question: *have/has* + subject + past participle?)
2 **Past perfect**
  The action *she had passed* happened first.
b The Past perfect links a time in the past with the time **before** that. (Elicit/highlight the form: subject + *had* (*'d*) / *hadn't* + past participle. Question: *had* + subject + past participle?)
3 **Future perfect**
  He'll see his 20,000th **before** he's forty.
c The Future perfect links a time in the future with the time **before** that. (Elicit/highlight the form: subject + *will* (*'ll*) / *won't* + have + past participle. Question: *will* + subject + have + past participle. Example: *Will he have seen 20,000 films?*)

PRACTICE

1 Introduce the topics by asking students if they recognise any of the people in the photos on page 55. Get them to say what they are doing, and what they think their achievements were. Put students into pairs and do the first example as a whole class. Emphasise that there is one extra time word. Ask students to guess unknown vocabulary from the context or to use their mini-dictionaries. If necessary, help with some of the following words/phrases yourself as you walk round the class: *ranked*; *retire*; *victim of injury*; *intensity*; *professional tennis circuit*; *TV commentator*; *coach*; *rowing team*; *take up*; *take part*; *surviving*; *well into their sixties*; *at the current rate*; *albums*. If students find the activity difficult, refer them back to the *Analysis*, and to *Language summary A* on page 148. Check answers as a class and go through the language notes, referring to the timelines in the *Analysis* if necessary.

ANSWERS AND LANGUAGE NOTES

1 *has sold* (from the past to now)
a *since* (refers to the time at which the action began)
b *the time* (the action happened before she was eighteen)
2 *had won* (before she was eighteen)
3 *had already retired* (the adverb goes after the auxiliary)
c *then* (refers to the time at which the action began)
4 *has become* (she is still a successful TV commentator and coach now)
5 *have won* (from 100 years ago to now)
6 *has discovered* (no one discovered it in the past and no one knows it now)
7 *had only taken up* (the adverb goes after the auxiliary)
d *before* (before two years ago)
e *by* (between now and his ninety-fifth birthday)
8 *will have taken part* (between now and his ninety-fifth birthday)
9 *have been* (they were and still are)
f *over the last* (for thirty-five years and now)
10 *will have sold* (between now and 2010)
g *by* (between now and 2010)
The unused time word is *ago*. This refers to the period between the beginning of the action and now, e.g. *five years ago.*

---

2 Students work individually to complete the sentences. Emphasise that they do not have to do them all. Walk round the class, checking sentences and providing any vocabulary students need.

3 Ask students to take it in turns to read a sentence to their partner. Encourage students to ask each other for more information as they go through the sentences. Emphasise that they need to choose one of their partner's sentences to read to the class. If you have a large class, ask only a few students to read the most interesting sentence out loud.

ADDITIONAL PRACTICE

RB **Resource bank:** 5A A wonderful life (Present perfect: various uses), page 130

Workbook: Future perfect or simple, page 36; Perfect tenses in the past, present and future, page 37

Vocabulary (PAGE 56)

Verb–noun combinations

See *Teacher's tips: working with lexis* on pages 9–10.

The aim of this exercise is to show students the importance of collocations generally, as well as learning these particular phrases. For extra information and practice, do *Learner-training worksheet 4* on pages 108–109.

1 Tell students you are going to look at some common verb–noun combinations. Give an example (e.g. *have a shower*) and elicit a few more from students (e.g. *do your homework*; *take a photo*; *have breakfast*). Students do the activity individually or in pairs. When they have checked in their mini-dictionaries, briefly elicit answers from the class and check that they understand the phrases.

> **ANSWERS**
> 1 win   2 beat   3 raise   4 set   5 show
> 6 cope with   7 make

2 The aim of this activity is to check that students understand the phrases in exercise 1. While they work, walk round the class to make sure their answers are good examples of the phrases. Encourage them to explain to their partner why they have chosen a particular answer, e.g. i *My uncle has always shown an interest in me because he ...*

Vocabulary, exercise 2: alternative suggestion

If you are short of time, elicit the examples in exercise 2 while you are checking the answers to exercise 1. This will tell you if students have understood the phrases.

Vocabulary: additional suggestion

Explain that noticing and remembering word combinations is very important in English. Put the following suggestions for remembering these combinations on the board and ask students to decide which are the most useful:
- underlining them in things that you read
- writing them in your vocabulary book
- repeating them to yourself   .
- making sentences of your own with them
- making posters for the wall to remind you of them.
Ask students to read the text *Prodigies graduate* to find any useful verb–noun combinations. Students can then use the method(s) they chose from the board to record and remember these combinations. If time is short, ask students to record the combinations for homework and then compare with another student in the next lesson.
Possible combinations
graduate with a Maths/English/Business degree
achieve a first-class degree
have regrets
accepted at university
take her exams (A levels)

ADDITIONAL PRACTICE

RB **Resource bank:** 5B Word combinations (verb–noun word combinations), page 131
Workbook: Vocabulary: Verb-noun combinations, page 38

Task: Talk about an achievement you find amazing (PAGES 56–57)

See *Teacher's tips: making tasks work* on pages 13–14.

Preparation: listening

1 Explain that students are going to talk about a great achievement, and check that they understand *amazing*. Focus them on the pictures and ask them to describe who/what they can see. Set the activity and do the first example as a whole class, eliciting why the aeroplane is an important piece of technology. Put them into groups for the rest of the activity, and ask them to help one another with vocabulary or to use their mini-dictionaries. Alternatively, pre-teach some or all of the following: *basic*; *scientific advance*; *cure*; *outstanding leadership*; *period of crisis*; *step*; *human rights*; *incredible*.

2 Go through the list and elicit examples from each group. Alternatively, ask students to move round the room comparing answers with other students and changing their example if they hear a better one. When you/they have gone through the list, set the question in exercise 2. Check the meaning of *collective*, and put students back into their groups to discuss the question.

3 [5.2] Introduce the recording and ask students to read the questions. Check that they understand *category*; *fall into*; *admire*. Play the recording and tell students to write notes, not sentences. Pause after each speaker to allow students time to write. Put them into pairs to compare their answers, then play the recording again. Check answers as a whole class. If students have found this activity very difficult, play the recording again, pausing after each section to elicit the answers.

> **ANSWERS**
> See tapescript for recording 2 on page 166 of the *Students' Book*.

Preparation: listening: alternative suggestions

If you think your students are not interested in / do not have a wide enough general knowledge for the topics in the *Students' Book*, you could choose from the following:
- the greatest achievements in their own country in the last 150 years
- the achievements that they personally have benefited from (e.g. women might say they have benefited from laws ensuring equality of pay)
- the greatest inventions of the last 150 years
- the inventions of the last forty or fifty years that have made the most difference to their lives
- the worst inventions of the last 150 years.
Provide a list to which students can add their own ideas. When they have done this, do exercise 2 as in the

Students' Book. Do not do exercise 3. Then follow the procedure for *Task: speaking* on page 57.

Task: speaking

1 Students can work alone or in pairs. Set a time limit for students to choose their topic. Let students choose for themselves but try to ensure that a range of topics is covered.

2 If students worked in pairs in the previous stage, keep them with their partner. As an example for this stage, refer to one of the recordings in exercise 3 on page 56 and show students how the three points are included. Ask students to make notes but not to write a full version of the talk. While they are preparing, walk round the class providing any language they need. After about six minutes, stop the activity and go through the *Useful language* box, explaining any problem vocabulary. Give students more time to continue preparing and to think about how they could use the phrases in the *Useful language* box.

3 If students have previously worked in pairs, divide them into different groups. Give each student equal time to speak, and ask the other students to note any questions or comments while they listen. Give a short time at the end of each talk for students to ask these questions. While the students are speaking, make a note of language errors for correction and analysis after the activity.

4 Keep students in their groups and set the questions. Give them a few minutes for the discussion and then elicit a few ideas from the class.

Task: speaking: alternative suggestions

- If students are very nervous about speaking alone, put them into pairs to prepare and give their talks, taking it in turns to speak.
- If you have a very large class, students can work in pairs to reduce the number of talks given in stage 3.
- If you are short of time, or you think students will need a lot of time to prepare this task, give students time in class to choose the topic, and go through the *Useful language* with them. Then ask students to prepare their talk for homework, but emphasise that they should make notes rather than write a full version. In the next lesson, before students give their talks, allow a few minutes for them to practise silently what they are going to say and to ask you for help with language if necessary.
- If you do not think students will have enough to say about one achievement, suggest that they talk about two or three achievements. When they give their talks, the students listening could decide which of the achievements is the greatest.
- If your students need a greater challenge, ask some or all of them to give their talks to the whole class or to record their talks on cassette for later analysis and correction.
- If you have a large class and will not be able to listen to all the students give their talks, ask them to record

their talks on cassette for you to listen to later. Write some notes on each student's talk and give this to them in the next lesson.

Language focus 2 (PAGES 58–59)

More about the Present perfect simple and continuous

See *Teachers' tips: using a discovery approach in the teaching of grammar* on page 8.

Put students into pairs to discuss their answers. Encourage them to explain their answers if they can, and to guess if they are not sure. Briefly check answers but do not give/elicit explanations at this stage.

> **ANSWERS**
> 1 b   2 b   3 b   4 b   5 a   6 b

Analysis

1–2 Keep students in pairs and ask them to read through the information and complete the activities. Tell them to focus only on the correct forms (a or b) from the cartoons. Walk round the room to help with language points if necessary. Check answers as a whole class and go through the language notes. Refer students to *Language summary B* on page 148 for further information and examples.

ANSWERS AND LANGUAGE NOTES
Remind students that they looked at the general differences between simple and continuous forms in Module 3, and that these are true for all simple and continuous forms, including the Present perfect simple and continuous. Then explain that both forms link the past and present, and ask students to look again at the correct sentences under the cartoons and think about how they are linked to the present (e.g. in 1b the goal is scored in the past, the match is now finished and the team has won). Then go through the answers and language notes below. Refer students to the cartoons to show them that the action is repeated, momentary, finished, etc.

1 a 6b; Present perfect simple. (*Own* is a state, and state verbs are not normally used in the continuous form.)
  b 1b; Present perfect simple
  c 1b, 3b, 5a; Present perfect simple. (The result of the action is emphasised.)
  d 2b, 4b; Present perfect continuous
  e 4b, 5a; Present perfect continuous and Present perfect simple. (The difference between 4b and 5a is that in 4b the action is repeated and unfinished, while in 5a it is repeated and finished. The 'finished' aspect means we use the Present perfect simple. Also, if a number is given, e.g. *five reports* in 5a, we always use the simple form because we are emphasising the completion.)
  f 2b, 4b; Present perfect continuous

2 a 2b emphasises the duration and 4b emphasises the repetition and the duration.

b **Sentence 1:** because the winning goal is only scored once, not repeated.
Sentence 5: because he has finished the five reports. If we use the continuous form, it means he writes the five reports at the same time and he isn't finished yet.
Sentence 6: because *own* is a state, and state verbs are not normally used in the continuous.

PRACTICE

1 a Put students into pairs and set the activity. Walk round the class helping students if necessary. Refer them back to the *Analysis*, and to *Language summary B* on page 148, for further help. Check answers as a class and elicit/give reasons for each answer.

ANSWERS AND LANGUAGE NOTES
1 *has lost* (action lasted for a moment and is finished)
2 *has changed* (action is finished) or *has been changing* (action is repeated, i.e. *a lot* of different hairstyles, but this is not as probable)
3 *has been going* (action is repeated; *a lot* tells us it has happened more than once)
4 *has felt* (action is repeated and probably finished) or *has been feeling* (action lasts for a period of time and is unfinished)
5 *has broken* (action lasted only for a moment)
6 *has passed* (action is finished, and the result is emphasised)
7 *has been studying* (action is repeated and lasts for a period of time)
8 *has already done* (action is finished)
9 *has spent* (action is finished) or *has been spending* (action is not finished, i.e. they might continue spending money)
10 *has been* (action is finished and only happened once) or *has been going* (action is repeated)
11 *has been forgetting* (action is repeated)
12 *has left* (action is finished)

b Students work individually and choose at least five of the sentences. Give them a few minutes to think about how to form the question. Write the first question (*Have you lost some/any money recently?*) and the short answers (*Yes, I have / No, I haven't*) on the board, and highlight the forms. Set a time limit for students to ask as many other students as possible, and encourage them to ask additional questions for more information. Tell them to note the students who answered yes to their questions. Finally, put students into groups to talk about what they discovered. Remind them they will need to use the third person (e.g. *Johann has been abroad a lot this year*).

2 a Put students into pairs and give them a few minutes to discuss possible answers.

b Ask students to read the introduction (*Jane knew that her flatmate …*) to check their predictions. Show them that the first one has already been done, and ask them to write 2–9 in the other boxes.

c [5.3] Play the recording for students to compare, and then check answers as a whole class, eliciting why the Present perfect is used. Play the recording again if necessary.

ANSWERS
1 Hi, Marina … what's the matter? You've been crying again, haven't you?
2 No, I'm fine. I've just been watching a sad film, that's all.
3 Oh, I see. Tell me, have you heard anything from Andrew today?
4 Who? Oh, him. No. I haven't thought about him all day, actually.
5 Oh, really? So you've forgotten about him already, have you?
6 No, it's not true. I've been trying to get through to him all day.
7 Haven't you managed to speak to him, then?
8 No. I've left about ten messages on his voice mail. Oh, why doesn't he phone?
9 Marina. Your phone … it's ringing. Aren't you going to answer it?

3 a Give students about ten minutes to write and practise their dialogues. Walk round the class checking the use of the Present perfect and contractions. Provide vocabulary if necessary.

b If you have a large class, put students into groups to act out their dialogues. Ask them to take notes on any differences between the dialogues. When they have finished, elicit answers to the two questions.

Pronunciation

1 a [5.4] Introduce question tags by writing the two sentences on the board and highlighting the form. (If the main part of the sentence is positive, the question tag is negative and vice versa. The auxiliary is used in question tags, not the main verb.) Play the recording, check answers and draw an 'up' or 'down' arrow on the question tags on the board.

ANSWERS
down; up

b Students discuss the questions in pairs. Check answers and go through the language note.

ANSWERS AND LANGUAGE NOTE
She already knows the answer to the question. (It is common to use a question tag to show sympathy or understanding, or to ask for confirmation.)
She is really asking the question.

2 a [5.5] Play the recording, pausing after each sentence for students to write. Emphasise that they can use their knowledge of perfect tense grammar to help them form the sentences. Put students into pairs to compare. Check answers as a whole class and write the sentences on the board, highlighting the form if necessary. Then play the recording again and ask students to draw the arrows. If students have

problems hearing the intonation, pause after each sentence and repeat it yourself with exaggerated intonation. Check answers as a whole class by drawing the arrows on the board.

b Either put students into pairs to practise the sentences, or play each sentence again and ask the class to repeat. Correct the intonation as necessary.

ANSWERS
See tapescript for recording 5 on page 166 of the *Students' Book*.

ADDITIONAL PRACTICE

RB **Resource bank:** 5C Who's worked for the CIA? (Present perfect simple and continuous), pages 132–133

Workbook: Present perfect simple or continuous, page 40

Wordspot (PAGE 60)

first

See *Teacher's tips: working with lexis* on pages 9–10.

1 Put students into pairs and ask them to help each other complete the activity before checking in their mini-dictionaries. Go through the answers and language notes with the class. If necessary, check the meaning of the phrases by eliciting/giving more example sentences, or ask students to summarise the meaning in their own words.

ANSWERS AND LANGUAGE NOTES
a *first impressions*
b *At first* (means there is a contrast/change between the first and second parts of the sentence; compare with *first of all*, which means the first thing to do/say)
c *on first name terms*
d *first-class* (make sure students do not confuse this with *first-class travel/ticket*)
e *first aid*
f *at first sight*
g *first of all*
h *first thing*
i *in first place*
j *first-choice*
k *in first gear*
l *first language*

2 Do one or two examples with the class and then put them into pairs to complete the activity. Tell them to look at the words around the phrase to decide if it is a noun or an adjective. Check answers as a whole class.

ANSWERS
a first-class, first-choice
b first impressions, first language, first aid, in first place, in first gear

c love at first sight, (be) on first name terms, first thing (in the morning).
d at first, first of all

3 Introduce the activity by asking students to look at exercise 1 and memorise the meanings. Ask them not to look at page 60 when they are trying to answer the questions on page 142. Students can work alone or in pairs. Check answers with the class, and ask students how many they answered correctly.

> ### *Wordspot*, exercise 3: alternative suggestion
>
> To make this more competitive, put students into pairs and get them to ask each other alternate questions. The student with the most correct answers wins.

ANSWERS
a first language
b (be) on first name terms
c at first
d first thing (in the morning)
e first-choice
f first-class
g love at first sight
h in first place
i first impressions
j first aid
k first gear
l first of all

ADDITIONAL PRACTICE

Workbook: Wordspot: *first*, page 41

Study ... (PAGE 60)

Improving your accuracy when speaking

You can use the *Study* ... section at the end of the module or earlier, depending on your students' needs. Students can do it for homework, or in class time if they need teacher guidance or if you want them to discuss the information in pairs/groups.

1–2 Introduce the activity by eliciting the meaning of *accuracy*, and why it can be a good thing. It is useful to contrast *accuracy* with *fluency*, and to show why both are necessary. Check students understand *identify*; *as well as you can*; *feedback*. Ask students to read the list and answer the questions. Emphasise that there are no 'right' or 'wrong' answers. Put them into pairs to compare answers and explain why they have chosen particular ideas. Finally, elicit some extra ideas from the class and write these on the board for others to copy.

Note: when you do speaking-accuracy activities during the course, elicit the techniques students chose and ask them to use these. In feedback, ask students if the techniques were successful or not.

Practise ... (PAGE 61)

This section can be done independently by students or you can use it for further practice of the language areas covered in Module 5 or as a test.

1–5 For each exercise, make sure students read the instructions carefully. Demonstrate *cross out* in exercise 5. If students find exercises 1–5 very difficult, refer them to the appropriate pages in the *Students' Book* for extra help. Provide the answers either by checking as a whole class or giving students a copy from the *Teacher's Resource Book*.

ANSWERS
1 **Perfect tenses**
a F, T, T   b T, NS, T   c T, F, T   d T, T, F
2 **Present perfect simple and continuous**
a 4   b 8   c 3   d 2   e 2, 5   f 1, 3, 6   g 7   h 6
3 **Time words**
a over the last   b before   c By   d By the time
4 **Verb–noun combinations**
a an award / the final / a competition
b an important issue / money / standards
c a good example / someone a challenge /
  a world record
d a fortune / progress / something possible
e a difficult boss / financial problems / university life
5 **Phrases with *first***
assistance, ceiling, choose, expressions, speed, tongue, type

Pronunciation spot

Dipthongs (1): /eɪ/, /əʊ/, /aɪ/ **and** /aʊ/
a 🔊 [5.6] Explain that diphthongs are made by combining two vowel sounds. Demonstrate this by pronouncing the vowels /e/ and /i/ separately, and then 'gliding' them together to make /eɪ/. Check that students understand the four words. Then play the recording, pausing after each word for students to repeat. If students cannot hear the sounds, model the words yourself and exaggerate the diphthongs.

b Put students into pairs and ask them to say the words to each other. Walk round the class, saying the words for students if necessary.

c 🔊 [5.7] Play the recording, pausing after each set of words for students to change their answers if necessary. Check answers as a whole class, eliciting the words, modelling them yourself or playing the recording again. While pairs practise the words, walk round the room correcting pronunciation.

ANSWERS
1 danger / face / made   2 cope / host
3 life / rivals / while   4 however / now

Mini-check (PAGE 159)

This can be done in class or set for homework. You can refer students to the *Language focus* sections in Module 5 or the *Language summaries* on page 148 for help.

ANSWERS
1 made   2 take   3 won   4 raise   5 set
6 had been raining   7 had been sitting; sat
8 has been working   9 had learnt/learned
10 will have lived   11 had made   12 I've left
13 Have you finished   14 He's been trying
15 I've written   16 I've never seen   17 at   18 with
19 of   20 in

Remember! (PAGE 61)

Give students a few minutes to tick the boxes, or ask them to do this at home if it is a personal record of achievement.

module 6

Getting it right

Reading and vocabulary
(PAGES 62–63)

1 Put students into pairs and ask them to describe the pictures. Then ask them to read the titles and check that they understand *treat*, *survive*, *deal with*, *avoid*. Set the questions, and ask students to help each other with unknown vocabulary and to use their mini-dictionaries. Tell them not to read the text yet.

2 Get students to write a list for each situation. Allow five minutes and ask them to write at least two ideas in each list. Emphasise that they must not read the text yet.

3 Give them time to read the text, and tell them not to worry about new words. Then put them back in their groups to discuss the questions. Elicit answers and ideas from the class but do not deal with unknown vocabulary. If students had language problems when writing their lists in exercise 2, briefly elicit the forms used in the text to express advice (imperatives, and *if/when* + a present tense + imperative) and tell students they will focus on these in more detail later.

4 Put students into pairs. Tell them they should try and guess the meaning by reading the text around each word. Emphasise that it is not important to be 100 percent correct. Go through the answers as a whole class or ask them to check in their mini-dictionaries.

5 Ask students to answer as many of the questions as possible without reading the text again. Tell them to guess the meaning of unknown vocabulary rather than use their mini-dictionaries. However, if your students have a lot of problems with vocabulary, you could pre-teach *the flow of blood*; *cut off circulation*; *hallway*; *kneel*. Then ask them to read the text again to answer the questions they are unsure of. Encourage them to answer in their own words rather than using the sentences in the text. Check answers as a class.

POSSIBLE ANSWERS
a Because it might reduce / stop / cut off circulation / the flow of blood.
b Because there are machines using electricity and gas, and there is a danger of fire.
c Hallways are enclosed and provide protection from falling bricks; also, they have little furniture to fall over and hurt you. Inside walls have no glass to break and cut you.
d Because it tells you how near the storm is.
e If you lie flat, your body surface increases and gives a bigger area for the lightening to strike/hit.

6 If you have a large class, put students into groups for the discussion. Give students a few minutes to think about their answers first. Finally, elicit some answers from the class.

> **_Reading and vocabulary_: alternative suggestion**
>
> If you do not think students will be interested in the topics, do the reading/listening in the *Workbook* (page 42) for discussion in class and set this one for homework.

ADDITIONAL PRACTICE

Workbook: Vocabulary booster: Worst case scenarios

Task: Make a list of tips on *How to …* (PAGES 64–65)

See *Teacher's tips: making tasks work* on pages 13–14.

Preparation: reading and listening

Elicit some of the advice students read about on pages 62–63, and check students understand *tips* and *dos and don'ts*. Explain that later they are going to make lists of dos and don'ts on one of the topics. Ask them to match each topic to a picture (*How to give up smoking* does not match to a picture) and explain any unknown vocabulary.

a These activities give students examples they can use in *Task: speaking*. Put students into pairs and emphasise that they should guess the answers. Elicit which text matches which topic.

ANSWERS
1 How to learn a foreign language
2 How to dress well
3 How to stay fit
4 How to find the perfect partner
5 How to learn to play a musical instrument

b [6.1] Play the recording for students to check their answers. Play the recording again if necessary. Ask students to underline useful phrases they could use when presenting their lists and go through the language notes below. Set the question, and give students a few minutes to discuss and explain their opinions. Finally, elicit a few ideas from the class.

ANSWERS AND LANGUAGE NOTES
See tapescript for recording 1 on page 166 of the *Students' Book*.
a *Take every opportunity* + *to* infinitive
b *resist the temptation* + *to* infinitive
c *You should* (*never*) + infinitive
d *Always remember.* (The speaker should pause after this phrase before beginning the next.)
e *Be careful not* + *to* infinitive. (This phrase is not normally used in a positive sense, e.g. ~~Be careful to look when you cross the road~~ . We use *make sure* instead.)

f *You might (easily) + infinitive.* (Note the position of the adverb.)
g *if you're (not) used to + -ing.* (*Be used to doing* means you are accustomed to it, or it isn't strange for you.)
h *make an effort + to* infinitive.
i *make sure + subject + Present verb form.* (This can be used in a positive sense, e.g. *Make sure you do your homework,* or a negataive sense.)
j *Start by + -ing*
k *allow plenty of time for + noun/-ing*

Task: speaking

1 a Give students time to choose a topic. Make sure that they know they can change the title or choose another topic.

b While students are working, walk round the class providing any vocabulary they need. About halfway through the activity, refer students to the phrases they underlined in *Preparation: reading and listening*, exercise b, and go through the *Useful language* box giving brief examples if necessary. Then ask them to finish their lists and think about whether they can use any of this language.

2 Put students into new groups, with people who have worked on different topics. Ask them to take turns to introduce their topic and to go through their lists. At the end of each list, encourage the other students to make comments.

3 Give students a few minutes to discuss the question, and then elicit ideas from each group.

Language focus 1 (PAGES 66–67)

Use and non-use of articles

See *Teacher's tips: using a discovery approach in the teaching of grammar* on page 8.

1 Introduce the topic by asking students to look at the picture and tell you what the boy is doing. Elicit *chew gum* and *blow a bubble with gum.* Put students into pairs, check that students understand *object to* and give them a few minutes to discuss the questions. Elicit a few ideas from the class.

2 Ask students to read the titles, and check that they understand *concentrate* and *aid.* Give them a short time to read the text. Tell them not to worry about unknown words, or the alternatives in Part B, a–p. Put them into pairs to compare answers before checking as a class. If necessary, get students to check a few items of unknown vocabulary in their mini-dictionaries, or explain them yourself.

ANSWERS
Title 2 is the best.

3 Do some examples with the class. Make sure they understand that *a* and *an* are indefinite articles, and *the* is a definite article. Elicit 'zero article'. Put them into pairs to complete the activity. Check answers as a class but do not give explanations at this stage.

ANSWERS
Indefinite articles: a new study, a link
Definite articles: the author, the study, The link, the production, the brain
Zero articles: Teachers, people, gum, chewing, memory, oxygen

Analysis 1

Explain that there are many rules and exceptions when using articles in English, and it is necessary to memorise these. Encourage students to think about the use of articles in their own language and to note where English is the same or different.

1–2 Before they start, check that students understand *mentioned, unique, ordinals* and *superlatives* by eliciting meaning or giving examples. Put them into pairs to read through the information, find the examples in the text (exercise 1), and think of more examples (exercise 2). Check answers as a class, go through the language notes and ask students to read through *Language summaries A1* and *A2* on page 149. If students cannot find or think of examples, refer them to the *Language summaries* before you check answers.

ANSWERS AND LANGUAGE NOTES
1 a *a new study.* (There are many new studies and we do not know which one yet.)
   b *the study, The link.* (Show students in the text where these have been mentioned before.)
   c *the author.* (There is only one author.)
   d *Teachers, people.* (The text does not specify which teachers or people. This is a very common use of the zero article in English and is different in many other languages. Get students to translate the relevant parts of the text into their own language to demonstrate the difference.)

If students ask about *the production of oxygen*, explain that this is an example of the common pattern *the + noun + of + noun.* Elicit/give more examples: *the top of the mountain, the north of France, the back of the house.*

2 a *a kilo of, a large amount of, a couple of, a number of.* (But *a several, a twenty,* and *a ten* are incorrect.)
   b *the third, the twenty-fifth, the 100th*
   c *the best, the most beautiful, the most interesting*
   d *the next, the previous, the final.* (Point out that *last* and *next* can be used without an article, but this changes the meaning. *Last* = 'the one before this one', e.g. *last night. The last* = 'the final one', e.g. *the last day of our holiday.*

PRACTICE

1 Students complete the activity in pairs while you walk round the class helping with any problems. If students find this difficult, refer them back to *Analysis 1* and *Language summaries A1* and *A2.* Check answers with the class and elicit explanations if necessary.

ANSWERS

a *the* b *the* c – d a e – f *The* g –
h *the* i *the* j *the* k *the* l *the* m *the*
n *a* o *the* p *the*

2 If necessary, pre-teach *siesta*. Tell students that it is a short sleep, but do not say what time it is. Get students to work individually to complete the gaps, and then to compare their answers with a partner. Check answers with the class, then ask students to discuss the answers to the quiz.

ANSWERS

1 –	a	*the, –*	b	–	c	*the, –*
2 *a*	a	*the*	b	*the*	c	–
3 *a, the*	a	*the, –*	b	–	c	*the, –*
4 *the, the*	a	*the*	b	*the*	c	*the*
5 *the, –*	a	*the*	b	*the, the*	c	*the, –*
6 *the, the, –*	a	*the*	b	–	c	–
7 *the*	a	–	b	*the*	c	–
8 –	a	*the, –*	b	*the, –*	c	*the, the*
9 *(no gap)*	a	*a*	b	*the, –, –*	c	*the, a*
10 *the, –, –*	a	*the*	b	*the*	c	–

3 🔲 [6.2] Play the recording, pausing after each section. Ask students how many questions they got right.

ANSWERS

1 a 2 b 3 a 4 b 5 a 6 a 7 a 8 b
9 b 10 c

Analysis 2

Use of definite article with places and times

Explain that there are general rules for the use of the definite article with places and times, but there are also exceptions. It is necessary for students to learn the rules and the exceptions. Suggest that students notice the rule/exception each time they learn a new place name or time phrase.

Set the activity and do an example with the class to demonstrate that the information is in the quiz. For feedback, draw the table below on the board. Elicit answers from the students, writing the categories of place and time in the first or second column, and any exceptions in the third column. For example:

Definite article	No article	Exceptions
	countries	*the Czech Republic*

When the table is complete, ask students to read *Language summary A3* on page 149.

4 **a** This will work well with a class of up to twenty students. Divide the class into teams and refer them to the appropriate page in the *Students' Book*. Ask students to use their mini-dictionaries if necessary. Do not correct mistakes with articles at this stage, but do provide any vocabulary students need to write their own questions.

b Draw a table on the board with Team A in one column and Team B in the other. Ask one student in Team A to ask the first question, and give them two marks if the articles are correct. If the articles are wrong, elicit/give the correction. Ask Team B to answer the question, and give them two marks for a correct answer. Then ask one student from Team B to ask the first question from their quiz. Repeat this procedure until all the questions are finished.

ADDITIONAL PRACTICE

RB **Resource bank:** 6A The genuine article (use and non-use of articles, pages 134–135

Workbook: *a/an* and *the* – first and second mention, page 43; Articles: Making generalisations, page 43; Articles: *the* with places, page 44; Articles *a/an* and *the* with institutions e.g. school, page 44

Language focus 2 (PAGE 68)

Different ways of giving emphasis

1 Put students into pairs to discuss the first three questions. Introduce the characters, explaining that Hannah and Dan are friends or a couple. Give students a short time to read the text and to answer the last question. Tell them to ignore the handwritten symbols. Check that students understand *to be hopeless* (a relatively friendly way of saying 'to be disorganised or incompetent'); *you've got a nerve*; *to be grateful*.

2 🔲 [6.3] Explain that the handwritten symbols indicate missing words. Play the recording, pausing after each line with a symbol to enable students to do the activity. Do the first line with the class, showing students on the board how they can write in the missing words. Ask students to compare their answers in pairs, and then to discuss the questions.

ANSWERS

See tapescript for recording 3 on pages 166–167 of the *Students' Book*.

The conversation makes sense without these words, but the additions mean the speakers make their points more emphatically. Point out that they are not angry, just speaking with greater emphasis in the recording.

Analysis

Give students about five to ten minutes to do the activity. Check answers with the class and go through the language notes. Refer students to *Language summary B* on pages 149–150 for more information.

ANSWERS AND LANGUAGE NOTES

a *so* annoying; **absolutely** ridiculous; **extremely** grateful. Other examples: *really, completely, totally*. (These are called intensifiers.)

b *So* is used before an adjective, in *so annoying*. *Such* is used before a noun, in *You've got **such** a nerve!* (Both are used to emphasise the point. *Such* can also be used before an adjective + noun, e.g. *It's **such** a lovely day*.)
c *you **do** need to get yourself organised with keys.* The stress moves from the main verb to the auxiliary or, at least, the two words have equal stress.
d ***What you need** is some kind of system; **it was me who** found them.* (These are called cleft sentences, and are used to emphasise the particular thing or person rather than the verb.)
e *Where **on earth** ...?*

PRACTICE

1–2 [6.4] Match the first sentence with the class and elicit the meaning of *exhausted*. Put students into pairs to match the other sentences. When they have finished, use the first sentence and show how it can be made more emphatic. Tell students there may be more than one possibility in some cases. Use the recording to check answers, and refer students to the tapescript for recording 4 on page 167 if necessary.

Pronunciation

1–2 [6.4] Go through the information, and either ask a student to read the two examples with the appropriate stress or read them yourself. Ask students to look at the tapescript for recording 4. Play the recording, pausing briefly after each pair of sentences to give students time to mark the stress. Emphasise they need only mark the words that are specially stressed. Check answers as a whole class, playing the sentences again if students find this activity difficult.

> **ANSWERS**
> b really, so; really   c such; welcome
> d suppose; you   e earth; you
> f so; do   g earth; me
> h really, do; really   i Come; do
> j really; earth, me

ADDITIONAL PRACTICE

RB **Resource bank:** 6B Where on earth are we? (ways of adding emphasis; cleft sentences), page 136

Workbook: Different ways of giving emphasis, page 46; Cleft sentences, page 47; Pronunciation: Cleft sentences, page 47; So and such, page 48

Listening and writing (PAGE 69)

Taking notes

1 Introduce the topic by asking students if taking notes is important and if they are good at it. Explain that they are going to think about, and then practise different techniques for taking notes. Put students into pairs or small groups to answer the questions, and then elicit a few ideas from the class.

2 Explain that later they are going to hear a short lecture about Maria Montessori. Ask students to read the caption and elicit any additional information they know.

3 a Put students into pairs and do the first example (bullet point) as a class, checking that students mark the appropriate place in the notes. Do not pre-teach any of the items in the list, and encourage students to guess if necessary. Check answers as a whole class and elicit the meanings of the symbols and abbreviations. Demonstrate *underlining* and *highlighting* (if possible) on the board.

> **ANSWERS**
>
> | | |
> |---|---|
> | MH | **MARIA MONTESSORI:** |
> | U | **Biographical Notes** |
> | Q, Ab | 'Among greatest educators of C20th' |
> | Q | |
> | B, S | • pioneer of education for <12s |
> | B, H | • founder of Montessori schools |
> | X, Q, | * 'Follow the child' |
> | Q | |
> | | |
> | SH | **Early life** |
> | Ab, Br | b. Ancona (Italy) 1870. Middle-class family. |
> | S, Ab | Studied medicine @ Rome Uni. |
> | Br | First woman graduate of medicine (1896). |
> | Ab | contact w/ children of poor families when working as physician |
> | | |
> | SH | **Development of Montessori schools** |
> | BR, Ab | Founded first school (at request of govt.) 1907. From 1910, worked only in children's education |
> | Ab | First Montessori schools opened in USA 1911 |
> | S, Ab, S | Wrote >20 books on educ. theory & practice. |
> | | Developed Montessori method. |

b Give students a few minutes to discuss the questions, and then elicit other techniques and write them on the board. Ask students to explain/demonstrate their techniques if necessary.

> **ANSWERS**
> Most of the techniques are used to save time while writing or to highlight the most important points. Quotation marks are used to show someone's words or opinion.

4 a [6.5] This activity will probably be challenging, and it is important that students do not panic. Emphasise that the main aim is to practise the different techniques in exercise 3. Tell them it is not necessary to understand

everything, and that you will play the recording more than once. Do not play the recording more than three times.

b Give students time to read their notes, and to alter them if necessary. Then ask them to read their partner's notes to see if they included more or less information. Finally, ask them to decide where the notes are good, where they could be improved and which techniques they found useful.

5 Put the students into small groups. Ask them to use their notes to answer the first question. Students then discuss the second question. Elicit a few ideas from the class.

ADDITIONAL PRACTICE

Workbook: Improve your writing: Taking notes: abbreviations, page 48; Writing notes, page 49

Real life (PAGE 70)

Giving advice and making suggestions

1 Introduce the topic by asking students if they have ever wanted to study or work in an English-speaking country. If your class is in an English-speaking country, ask students why they chose to study there. Then write 'englishadventure.com' on the board, ask students what they think this is, and elicit or pre-teach *discussion forum*; *log on*; *ESL* (English as a second language). Set the questions and give students a few minutes to read and take notes. Put students into pairs to compare, and then check answers with the class.

> **ANSWERS**
> a the best country to study English in
> b Australia, New Zealand, Malta, England, the USA, Ireland
> c **Australia:** Sydney is an international city; plenty of foreign students
> **New Zealand:** beautiful countryside
> **Malta:** quiet; good weather; friendly people; everyone speaks English
> **England:** friendly people; good food
> **The USA:** the best ESL programme (*you can't beat it*)
> **Ireland:** the friendliest people in the world

Pronunciation

🔲 [6.6] First, ask students to underline the phrases for giving advice in the texts. Check answers and briefly go through the language notes below:

> **ANSWERS AND LANGUAGE NOTES**
> See tapescript for recording 6 on page 167 of the *Students' Book.*
> *Take my advice* + imperative
> *You could always try* + noun
> *Have you thought of* + -ing
> *The most important thing is* + to infinitive
> *I'd* (*I would*) + infinitive + *if I were you.* (We can also use *was*, but *were* is generally considered more correct.)
> *If you ask me, you can't beat* + noun. (We can also say: *If you ask me,* + noun + *is the best place/thing to do.*)

> *Try + -ing*
> *How about + -ing*
>
> Ask students to close their books so that they can concentrate on listening to the phrases. Play the recording and pause after each phrase for students to repeat. Correct their pronunciation if necessary, focusing on all or some of the following areas:
> • linking, e.g. *You could ‿ always, Have you thought ‿ of*
> • sentence stress, e.g. ask students to mark the stressed words in each phrase
> • pitch, i.e. the pitch is quite high in all the phrases to show friendliness and politeness.

2 Give students a few minutes to write their advice, and walk round the room providing any vocabulary they need. Then put students into pairs to read their sentences to each other. Tell them to pay attention to the pronunciation. Finally, ask a few students to tell you the best piece of advice they heard.

ADDITIONAL PRACTICE

Workbook: Real life: Giving advice and making suggestions, page 49

Study ... (PAGE 70)

Guessing from context

1 Explain that guessing meaning from context is an important skill and that students should not worry about understanding every word in a text. If they stop at every new word, they will not be able to read efficiently. Go through the information in the bullet points and set the activity. Tell students not to use their mini-dictionaries at this stage. Check answers as a whole class and elicit the information they used to decided if the word was a noun, verb, etc.

> **ANSWERS**
> a verb b noun c verb d adverb e noun
> f adjective

2 Set the activity and emphasise that students should guess the words before checking in their mini-dictionaries. Put students into pairs to compare how many words they guessed correctly. Encourage students to guess meaning from context as much as possible during the rest of the course.

Practise ... (PAGE 71)

This section can be done independently by students or you can use it for further practice of the language areas covered in Module 6, or as a test.

1–5 For each exercise, make sure that students read the instructions carefully. If students find exercises 1–5 very difficult, refer them to the appropriate pages in the *Students' Book* for extra help. Provide the answers either by checking as a whole class or giving students a copy from the *Teachers' Book.*

ANSWERS

1 Articles
a My brother works as <u>a</u> travel representative in Canada.
b <u>The</u> President of <u>the</u> USA has resigned!
c <u>The</u> Sahara is <u>the</u> largest desert in Africa.
d He was <u>the</u> last person to see <u>the</u> victim alive.
e I'll see you next week. (no additional articles)
f <u>The</u> weather is better in <u>the</u> south of <u>the</u> country.
g I live near <u>the</u> hospital.
h He'll be here in <u>the</u> morning.

2 Ways of giving emphasis
a so b did c What d It e on f such

3 Verb forms
a to translate b wear c not to overdo
d finding e don't appear f injure; to taking

4 Phrases for *How to* …
a 3 b 5 c 4 d 2 e 6 f 1

5 Giving advice and making suggestions
a advice b could c doing d most
e were/was f If g contacting h coming

Mini-check (PAGE 159)

This can be done in class, or set for homework. You can refer students to the *Language focus* sections in Module 6, or the relevant *Language summaries* on pages 149–150 for help).

ANSWERS

1	the	2	the
3	an	4	–
5	a	6	did
7	of booking	8	to practise
9	to doing	10	were
11	a	12	not
13	on	14	in
15	such	16	about
17	What	18	If
19	It	20	the

Pronunciation spot

a **[cassette]** [6.7] Ask if students can pronounce the sounds. If students can produce the sounds, play the recording for them to compare. If not, play the recording and elicit the sounds after each word. Encourage students to touch their throats to 'feel' the vibration.

b **[cassette]** [6.8] Put students into pairs and ask them to say the words and listen to each other, then decide which of the three sounds each one is. Play the recording for students to check.

ANSWERS
See tapescript for recording 8 on page 167 of the *Students' Book*.

c Get students to practise saying the words in pairs.

d Put students into pairs to decide how to pronounce each sound. Check answers, then get them to practise reading the text aloud in pairs.

ANSWERS
Children /tʃ/ should /ʃ/ through /θ/ purposeful /s/ just /dʒ/ activities /z/ with /ð/ purpose /s/ choice /tʃ/ children /tʃ/ choose /tʃ/, /z/ rather /ð/ Toys /z/ which /tʃ/ serve /s/ specific /s/, /s/ purpose /s/ therefore /ð/ discouraged /s/

Remember! (PAGE 71)

Give students a few minutes to tick the boxes, or ask them to do this at home if it is a personal record of achievement.

module 7

Big events

Vocabulary and speaking (PAGE 72)

Events and celebrations

1 **a** Put students into pairs to look at the pictures and elicit *celebrations*. Give them a few minutes to answer the questions and explain why they would/wouldn't like to attend. Elicit a few ideas from the class and ask if students have been to any events like these.

b Get students to find as many items as possible without pre-teaching any words, then check the rest during feedback or ask them to use their mini-dictionaries. To prepare for exercise 2, elicit *signing autographs* (picture 4) and *football match* (picture 1).

2 Explain that you are going to find out how much students can remember about the pictures. Give them a few minutes to look again, and then ask them to turn to page 139 and answer the questions in pairs. When they have finished, ask them to look at the pictures again to see how much they remembered. Check answers as a whole class and go through the language notes below.

ANSWERS AND LANGUAGE NOTES
1 Possibly Japan or Korea, because the people are in traditional dress as worn in these countries.
2 Picture 3. (At football matches (picture 1) and public events (pictures 4 and 5), the people are normally called *spectators*. We can also use *supporters* for picture 1.)
3 Five (pictures 1–5). (We do not use *crowd* to refer to a group of people at a 'personal' or family event. A *crowd* normally means the people do not know each other.)
4 Picture 2.
5 Signing autographs.
6 Possibly Italy because they are supporting the Italian football team, or another country because this is an international match.
7 *Fight the fees.* (Teach *fees* and point out that this is probably a student demonstration against college/university fees.)
8 Picture 5.

3 Give students a few minutes to think about their answers before putting them into small groups to discuss the questions. Encourage them to explain their answers, and to ask each other questions for more information.

ADDITIONAL PRACTICE

Workbook: Vocabulary: Events and celebrations, page 50

Vocabulary 2 (PAGE 72)

Extreme adjectives

1 To introduce the activity, remind students of the collocation a *huge crowd*, elicit the meaning of *huge* and

match it to *very large* in column B. Put students into pairs to complete the activity. Check answers as a whole class and, if necessary, elicit examples of the words in column A to check meaning. Write each word in column A on the board and elicit/mark the stress.

ANSWERS AND LANGUAGE NOTES
a 2 *huge*
b 11 *tiny*
c 12 *terrifying*
d 3 *deafening* (normally pronounced as two syllables – /defnɪŋ/)
e 8 *freezing*
f 7 *gorgeous* (pronounced as two syllables)
g 1 *furious* (pronounced as three syllables)
h 4 *soaked*
i 9 *terrible*
j 6 *hilarious* (pronounced as four syllables)
k 5 *starving*
l 10 *exhausted* (pronounced /ɪgˈzɔːstɪd/ or /egˈzɔːstɪd/)

2 Write *very, quite, really, absolutely, completely* and *totally* on the board, and ask students to match them to the adjectives in column A. Elicit answers from the class and write each adjective next to the appropriate intensifier.

ANSWERS AND LANGUAGE NOTES
We have to use an 'extreme' intensifier with an extreme adjective. *Very* is not an extreme intensifier, and so cannot be used with the extreme adjectives.

Highlight the following points.
• *Really* and *quite* can be used as either extreme or non-extreme intensifiers, and can go with both extreme and non-extreme adjectives, e.g. *exhausted* and *tired*. When *really* is used with a non-extreme adjective, i.e. *really tired*, it means 'very'. When *quite* is used with a non-extreme adjective, i.e. *quite tired*, it means 'not very'. When *really* and *quite* are used with extreme adjectives, they have the same meaning as 'absolutely'. When *quite* means 'not very', it is not stressed; when it means 'absolutely', it is stressed.
• *Absolutely* and *really* can be used with all extreme adjectives.
• *Quite, completely* and *totally* can only be used with certain extreme adjectives.
  – *Quite* can be used with *terrifying, deafening, soaked, terrible* and *exhausted*.
  – *Completely* can be used with *soaked* and *exhausted*.
  – *Totally* can be used with *deafening, soaked* and *exhausted*.

3 Students do this activity individually or in pairs. Pre-teach *referee sent off the home team's captain*; *front row*; *projected*; *got off to a great start*; and *fans*, or ask students to use their mini-dictionaries.

ANSWERS AND LANGUAGE NOTES
a freezing   b tiny   c terrifying   d soaked
e furious   f deafening   g terrible   h huge
i exhausted   j hilarious   k starving   l gorgeous

ADDITIONAL PRACTICE

Workbook: Vocabulary: Extreme adjectives, page 50; Pronunciation: Stress in extreme adjectives, page 51

Task: Describe a memorable event
(PAGES 74–75)

See Teacher's tips: making tasks work on pages 13–14.

Preparation: listening

1 Many of the phrases in the box were introduced in *Vocabulary and speaking* on page 72. If necessary, check students understand *memorable event*; *peace march*; *religious*; *performance*; *royalty*. Set the activity. Ask students not to describe the events in detail because they will be doing this later.

2 [7.1] Ask students to read the questions. Check that they understand *take place*; *mentioned*; *atmosphere*. Emphasise that they may not be able to answer every question for all the speakers. Play the recording, pausing after each speaker to give students time to write notes. Put students into pairs to compare while you walk round the room to see how many answers they have. Play the recording again if necessary. If students have answered most of the questions, go to exercise 3 without checking answers with the class. If students have found this listening difficult, check as a whole class and focus on any problem vocabulary in the answers below. Do not refer students to the tapescript at this stage.

ANSWERS
1 a an anti-war demonstration
   b not stated where; March or April this year
   c other demonstrators
   d positive; very moving
2 a the 800th or 850th anniversary of the founding of Moscow
   b outside St Basil's in Red Square, Moscow; a few years ago
   c an orchestra, a choir and Muscovites (people from Moscow)
   d absolutely amazing/incredible, because so lively, noisy and emotional
3 a a Nirvana concert
   b London; 1991 or 1993
   c their boyfriend, the audience and the band
   d just amazing (no explicit answer)
4 a a New Year's Eve Festival
   b Brazil; the 31st December
   c the people they were staying with and the people on the beach
   d really magical

3 Put students into pairs, and encourage them to guess any unknown vocabulary or use their mini-dictionaries. When they have checked their answers, focus them on *utterly spectacular* (sentence 8) and *just completely came alive* (sentence 14), and go through the language notes below.

ANSWERS AND LANGUAGE NOTES
See tapescript for recording 1 on pages 167–168 of the *Students' Book*.

Explain that:
• *utterly* is an intensifier we can use with some but not all extreme adjectives (see page 73 for other examples), and students need to check before using it
• *just* adds more emphasis to *completely*, and can also be used alone with some but not all extreme adjectives, e.g. *it was just incredible* (speaker 1); *It was just amazing* (speaker 3).

Task: speaking

1 Introduce the task and give students a couple of minutes to decide which celebration(s) they are going to talk about. If students feel they do not have much to say, encourage them to choose more than one celebration. Walk round the class prompting ideas and providing vocabulary. After a few minutes, go through *Useful language a*, giving brief examples if necessary. Then give them a few more minutes to think about how they could use this language and the phrases from *Preparation: listening*, exercise 3.

2 Give students a few minutes to think about their questions, and go through *Useful language b* with the class. Then put them into pairs for the interviews and tell them to take notes. Give a time check halfway through the activity so that all students have a chance to speak and ask questions. Make a note of errors for later input and listen particularly for errors with relative clauses or quantifiers, which can be corrected after *Language focus 1* and 2.

3–4 If you have a large class, put students into groups for these exercises. Give students a few minutes to go through their notes first, and set a time limit for the summaries. Ask students to think about the questions in exercise 4 while they listen. When all the summaries are finished, put the students into groups to discuss exercise 4, or elicit answers from the class.

Language focus 1 (PAGES 76–77)
Relative clauses

1 Introduce the topic by asking students to talk about the pictures on page 76. Set the questions and give students thirty seconds to read the texts. Put them into pairs to discuss their answers, and then elicit a few ideas from the class.

2 [7.2] Students work individually or in pairs. If necessary, pre-teach *servants*; *treat*; *florists*; *parades*; *excursions*; *according to legend*; *gravesides*; *skull*. When students have finished, play the recording, pausing after each gap to allow them to change their answers if necessary. Refer students to the tapescript to check answers.

Analysis

Revision

If this is not revision for your students, make sure you go
through the information carefully. Refer students to *Language
summary A* on page 150 and give further examples.

1 Underline the first relative pronoun with the class. Put
students into pairs to underline the other pronouns and
answer the question.

ANSWERS AND LANGUAGE NOTES
People: *who* (*that* can also be used to refer to people)
Places: *where* (*which/that* + preposition can also be used
to refer to places, e.g. *This is the house which/that I used
to live in*)
Things: *which/that* (*whose* is used to refer to people's
possessions, but there is no example in the phrases)
Times and dates: *when* (*that* is used after *One day* in
the example, because it does not refer to a specific time
or date)

2 When you check students' answers, demonstrate the
subject/object by re-writing the example sentences as below.

ANSWERS AND LANGUAGE NOTES
This is the outfit (*that*) *I'm going to wear.* = *I'm* (subject)
going to wear this outfit (object). The relative pronoun
can be omitted from this sentence because it refers to
the object.
That's the man who took the photographs. = *That man*
(subject) *took the photographs* (object). The relative
pronoun cannot be omitted from this sentence because
it refers to the subject.

Defining and non-defining relative clauses

Put students into pairs to answer the questions. In feedback,
write the example sentences on the board and highlight the
points made below. Finally, ask students to read through
Language summary B on pages 150–151.

ANSWERS AND LANGUAGE NOTES
a *Tanya Robson is the actress **who** won the Oscar for best
actress.* (If you cross out the relative clause, the
remaining sentence is *Tanya Robson is the actress.*
This does not have meaning.)
b *Tanya Robson, **who** won an Oscar for best actress, is
coming to the premiere.* (If you cross out the relative
clause, the remaining sentence is *Tanya Robson is
coming to the premiere.* This has meaning.)
c The second sentence needs commas: *Tanya Robson,
who won an Oscar for best actress, is coming to the
premiere.* (Non-defining relative clauses need
commas, dashes or other punctuation to act as
parentheses, as they contain extra, non-essential
information.)

PRACTICE

1 a Put students into pairs to complete the sentences, and
walk round the class prompting if necessary. If students
find this difficult, refer them back to the *Analysis* or *Language
summary* A. Check answers as a class and elicit the reason for
each. Then give students a few minutes individually to answer
the questions on a separate piece of paper. Emphasise that
students should only write single words or short phrases. As an
example, do the first few questions for yourself and write the
answers on the board.

ANSWERS AND LANGUAGE NOTES
1 not necessary (object)
2 not necessary (object)
3 *when* (time)
4 *who/that* (person and subject)
5 not necessary (object)
6 *whose* (possessive)
7 *whose* (possessive)
8 *where / in which* (place)
9 *when* (time)
10 not necessary (object)

b To demonstrate the activity, get students to look at the
speech bubbles on page 77 and ask you some questions about
the words you wrote on the board in exercise 1a. Put students
into pairs to do the same thing, and emphasise that they must
use a relative clause in their answers. For feedback, ask a few
students to tell the class something they have in common with
their partner or something interesting they heard.

2 Keep students in their pairs and go through the first
example on the board, deleting/adding words and
punctuation as necessary. Students should write their answers
in full. To check answers, write the original sentences on the
board and elicit the necessary changes.

ANSWERS
a Steve Redgrave, who has won medals at five
Olympic Games, is one of Britain's best-known
sportsmen.
b The Winter Olympics, which normally take place in
January or February, are held every four years.
c Madonna, who has been an international star for
over twenty years, had her first hit single in 1984.
d The annual bull-running festival takes place in
Pamplona, which is a city in northern Spain.
e Cuban singer Compay Segundo, who made his first
recording in the 1930s, found fame in the 1990s
with Latin group *The Buena Vista Social Club.*
f Eating and drinking are forbidden during the day
during the festival of Ramadan, which takes place
in the ninth month of the Muslim calendar.
g The Maracaña Stadium, which is in Rio de Janeiro,
has a capacity of 205,000 people.

Pronunciation

1 📼 [7.3] Read through the information with students. Play the example sentences and ask students to follow them in their books. If students cannot hear the intonation, say the sentences yourself and exaggerate the patterns. Play the recording again, pausing after each sentence for students to repeat, and correct if necessary.

2 📼 [7.4] Pause after each sentence for students to repeat. Then put them into pairs to practise all five sentences while you walk round the class correcting intonation and pauses. If necessary, play the recording again.

ADDITIONAL PRACTICE

RB **Resource bank:** 7A Relative clauses crossword (defining relative clauses), page 137; 7B What's buried at the bottom of the garden? (non-defining relative clauses), pages 138–139

Workbook: Defining relative clauses, page 51; Relative pronouns, page 52; Non-defining relative clauses, page 52; Prepositions in relative clauses, page 52

Reading and vocabulary

(PAGES 78–79)

1 **a** Introduce the topic and focus students on the pictures and titles. Put them into pairs to answer the questions, and check that they understand *centre around*. Tell them not to read the texts at this stage. Elicit answers and ideas from the class, and ask if anyone has heard of these festivals.

ANSWERS
1 radishes, Stilton cheese, hot (spicy) food, tomatoes

b Ask students to read the question first, then give them one minute to read the texts. Check answers as a whole class and ask students if their predictions were correct.

ANSWERS
Oaxaca in Mexico; December 23rd
Stilton in England; May Day
Albuquerque, New Mexico, in the USA; three days in March
Buñol in Spain; the last Wednesday in August

2 **a** Give students about five minutes to find the words in their mini-dictionaries, and then to discuss their ideas in pairs.

b Give them time to read the texts, then check their answers. Put them back into their pairs to discuss the question. Finally, elicit any additional facts about the festivals from the class.

ANSWERS
1 Stilton   2 La Tomatina   3 Stilton
4 Fiery Foods Festival   5 Oaxaca
6 Fiery Foods Festival   7 La Tomatina   8 Oaxaca

3 Explain that guessing meaning from context will help students increase their reading speed and that it is not

always necessary to be 100 percent correct. Check that students understand *banned*, *dizzy* and *start things off*, but do not use the phrases in bold to demonstrate meaning. Then give them five minutes to choose the definitions.

ANSWERS
a simple   b started   c strong-tasting or smelling
d strange and funny   e make you dizzy   f taste
g isn't suitable for you   h full of liquid
i start things off   j thrown

4 Give students five to ten minutes to discuss the questions. Walk round the class helping with vocabulary if necessary. For feedback, ask a few students to tell the class which food/ dish they would like to try.

ADDITIONAL PRACTICE

Workbook: Vocabulary booster: Describing, page 53

Language focus 2 (PAGE 80)

Quantifiers

📼 [7.5] Introduce the topic of food and check students understand *quantifiers* by eliciting 'expressions that describe quantities'. Do not pre-teach any of the quantifiers in the box. Put students into pairs to complete the gaps, then play the recording to check answers. Finally, ask students if they think the expert's advice is good.

ANSWERS
See tapescript on page 168 of the *Students' Book*.

Analysis

1 **a** Use *burgers* and *salt* from the previous exercise to explain what countable and uncountable nouns are, i.e. if a noun is uncountable, it does not have a plural form. Then put students into pairs to underline the words and answer the question. Check answers with the class before doing exercise b.

ANSWERS AND LANGUAGE NOTES
Countable: *burgers, apples, mushrooms.* (Use *human(s)*, and *tooth/teeth* as non-food examples.)
Uncountable: *salt, sugar.* (Use *evidence* as a non-food example.)

b Ask students to write the appropriate letter next to each quantifier.

ANSWERS AND LANGUAGE NOTES
Used with countable nouns: *a few, a number of, too many.* (These quantifiers are followed by a plural noun.)
Used with uncountable nouns: *very little, a great deal of, too much.* (*A great deal of* means 'a lot of'.)
Used with both: *any, a lot of, some, plenty of.* (When used with a countable noun, the noun will be plural.)

2 Give students a few minutes to discuss the sentences. If they find this activity difficult, refer them to *Language summary C* on page 151. Go through the answers with the class.

57

ANSWERS AND LANGUAGE NOTE

a   The first sentence has a neutral meaning, i.e. there are a large number of vegetables. The second sentence has a negative meaning, i.e. there are more vegetables than we need.

b   The first sentence means 'We have as much milk as we need.' The second means 'We have more milk than we need.'

c   The first sentence is negative/neutral, i.e. we may need to get some more soon. The second sentence emphasises the positive, i.e. there are still enough for you to have one.

d   The first sentence means 'I like certain pasta dishes, but not all of them.' The second sentence means 'I like all pasta dishes; I don't mind which one.' (Students might be surprised to see *any* used in a positive sentence. Point out that it is usually stressed in the sentence.)

PRACTICE

1   Go through the example with students and change it so that it is true for you. Then ask one or two students to change it so that it is true for them. Check students understand *fizzy drinks* and *shellfish* by asking for examples. Students decide on their sentences individually and then compare answers with a partner. Encourage students to ask their partners for more information.

2   Introduce the text by asking students what kind of person it is written for. Then ask them to read the text quickly, ignoring the alternatives a–j, and decide if it's good advice for a 'lazy cook'. Put students into pairs to complete the activity, and emphasise that they should explain their answers. Check answers as a whole class and elicit explanations.

ANSWERS

a   *some/any*. *Some* means 'a certain amount of'. *Any* means that it doesn't matter what type, but it's important to have some.

b   *a few/plenty of*. *A few* means 'a small number of'. *Plenty of* means 'more than you normally need'.

c   *plenty of*

d   *a few*

e   *Some/Any*. *Some* means 'certain, but not all'. *Any* means 'all'.

f   *too much*

g   *lots of/quite a few*. *Lots of* means 'a large number or amount of' (i.e. more than *quite a few*). *Quite a few* has a positive meaning.

h   *enough/plenty of*. *Enough* means 'sufficient for your needs'. *Plenty of* means 'more than you normally need'.

i   *something*

j   *Very few*

3   Students can do this individually or in pairs. Walk round the class providing any vocabulary they need. When they have finished, ask them to present their lists to the class. If you have a large class, put students into groups for the

presentation. Make a note of errors with quantifiers and provide corrections at the end of the activity.

ADDITIONAL PRACTICE

Workbook: Quantifiers, page 55

Real life (PAGE 81)

Awkward social situations

1   Introduce Bella and ask students where she is and why the situations are awkward. Elicit suggestions about what she could say.

2   [7.6] Play the recording and ask students if their suggestions in exercise 1 were the same or different. Ask students to read the tapescript. Explain phrases they do not understand, e.g. *a tiny portion*; *I couldn't possibly manage any more* (= I can't eat any more); *in the slightest*; *it doesn't agree with me* (= it makes me a little ill); *to bring someone out in a rash*; *not able to make it* (= can't come).

ANSWERS

See tapescript on page 168 of the *Students' Book*.

Pronunciation

[7.7] Tell students that polite intonation is very important because Bella is refusing invitations and offers. Play the recording and pause after each phrase for students to repeat. Correct if necessary.

3   a   Give students five to ten minutes to write their dialogues. If time is short, ask students to choose only one or two situations. Walk round the class providing vocabulary and modelling intonation for students to copy.

b   First, give students a few minutes in pairs to practise their dialogues and polite intonation. If time is short, select only a few pairs to act out their dialogues for the class.

ADDITIONAL PRACTICE

Workbook: Real life: Awkward situations, page 57

Wordspot (PAGE 82)

take

1   Put students into pairs and ask them to guess the meaning of any phrases they do not know. Tell students they will need to change the form of the verb *take* in most of the sentences. Check answers as a whole class and elicit/give more examples if necessary.

ANSWERS

a   take a photo of   b   takes place   c   take care of
d   taking a seat   e   take it seriously   f   taken notes
g   It takes   h   takes after   i   took part
j   take off   k   to take up   l   take your time

2 **a** 🔲 [7.8] Play the recording, pausing after each question to give students time to write their answers. Tell them they do not need to write full sentences.

b As an example, write the answer for question 3 on the board (*sit down*) and elicit the question from students. Then give them a few minutes to try and remember the other questions.

> **ANSWERS**
> See tapescript on page 168 of the *Students' Book*.

c Refer students to the speech bubbles as an example. For feedback, ask students to tell the class the most interesting/surprising thing they heard.

ADDITIONAL PRACTICE

Workbook: Wordspot: *take*, page 53

Study ... (PAGE 82)

Improving your reading speed

1 Introduce this section by asking students if they think reading quickly is important and if they are good at it or not. Elicit the things that prevent them reading quickly, and write a few ideas on the board, e.g. *unknown words*. Go through the introduction and the dos and don'ts with students, checking they understand *skip over*; *say the words to yourself*; *re-reading*; and *get distracted*, or ask them to use their mini-dictionaries. Then ask them to decide which tips might help with the problems you wrote on the board.

2 Give students a minute to decide which tips they are going to use. Make sure students do not read the text for more than sixty seconds. Put them into pairs to discuss whether the tips were useful, and then elicit a few opinions from the class. Encourage them to use these tips when they read other texts during the course.

Practise ... (PAGE 83)

This section can be done independently by students or you can use it for further practice of the language areas covered in Module 7, or as a test.

1–6 For each exercise, make sure students read the instructions carefully. If students find exercises 1–6 very difficult, refer them to the appropriate pages in the Students' Book for extra help. Provide the answers either by checking as a whole class or giving them a copy from the Teachers' Book.

> **ANSWERS**
> **1 Relative pronouns**
> a incorrect; *a shop **that**/**which** sells ...*
> b correct
> c correct
> d incorrect; *the couple **whose** house ...*
> e correct
> f incorrect; *the place **where** ...*
> g correct; but we can also say *the hotel **that** we're staying **at**/the hotel we're staying **at*** (with no relative pronoun)/*the hotel **where** we're staying* (without *at*).

> h incorrect; *the beach **where** he works* (without *at*)/*the beach he works **at*** (with no relative pronoun)
>
> **2 Relative clauses**
> a ... which the whole town depends **on**, has ...
> b This house, **in which** Dickens lived ...
> c ... computer system, **which** cost several ...
> d The receptionist, **who** was clearly ...
> e He is a man **to whom** the whole ...
>
> **3 Quantifiers**
> a more than a few   b more than we need
> c not much   d a lot of   e all of them
>
> **4 Awkward social situations**
> a possibly   b slightest   c to see   d afraid   e 'd
>
> **5 Extreme adjectives**
> a very big   b extremely hungry   c very bad
> d very funny   e very wet   f very beautiful
>
> **6 Phrases with *take***
> a take place   b take up   c take care of
> d take a seat   e take off   f take after
> g take your time   h take part

Pronunciation spot
Different pronunciations of the letter 'e'

🔲 [7.9] Put students into pairs and set the activity. Do the first category as a whole class. Tell students to say each given example, i.e. *Wednesday, revolutionary, celebration*, etc., so that their partner can hear the sound of 'e'. If students find this difficult, model the examples yourself as they do each category. Play the recording without pausing to check answers, and refer students to the tapescript if necessary. Then play the recording again, pausing after each category for students to repeat the words. Correct the sound of 'e' if necessary.

> **ANSWERS**
> See tapescript for recording 9 on pages 168–169 of the *Students' Book*.

Remember! (PAGE 83)

Give them a few minutes to tick the boxes, or ask them to do this at home if it is a personal record of achievement.

Mini-check (PAGE 159)

This can be done in class, or set for homework. You can refer students to the *Language focus* sections in Module 7 or the relevant *Language summaries* on pages 150–151 for help.

> **ANSWERS**
> 1 whose   2 which   3 where   4 which   5 when (*or no relative pronoun*)   6 which   7 made   8 place
> 9 waving   10 absolutely   11 terrifying   12 starving
> 13 exhausted   14 tiny   15 a bit of   16 very few
> 17 a bit of   18 much/plenty   19 no   20 any

module 8

Fame and fortune

Reading and vocabulary
(PAGES 84–85)

1 Introduce the topic by showing students pictures of famous people and asking what they are famous for. You could use the pictures in Module 1 (pages 8–9 and 12–13), Module 5 (page 53 – Halle Berry) or Module 7 (page 73 – Tom Cruise), or take in your own. Set the questions and check that students understand *in the news*. When students have finished, elicit answers. Write some of the ideas from students' lists on the board.

2 **a** Pre-teach *celebrity*, then give students a couple of minutes to read the titles and compare them with their own ideas. For feedback, refer to the list you wrote on the board in exercise 1, and ask students which of these ideas were mentioned. Then elicit additional ideas from the titles and check students understand *buy your way* and *formula*.

b Do not pre-teach any of the phrases in the box, but ask students to help each other with any unknown phrases or to guess the meaning. Put them into pairs, set the activity and make sure they do not read the text. Then elicit answers and use the pictures to check what the phrases mean, and elicit/teach *tightrope*, which will be required for exercise 3.

3 Give students two to three minutes to read the text. Tell them not to worry about unknown vocabulary at this stage. Put them into pairs to compare their answers. Then check as a whole class, but do not elicit/give too much detail (they will get more detail in exercises 4 and 5).

> **ANSWERS**
> See text on pages 84–85 of the *Students' Book*.

4 Set the activity. Check students understand *stars*, *risk*, *originality*, *talent*. Tell them to answer as many questions as possible without reading the text again. Then give them time to read and check before putting them into pairs to discuss the answers. When checking the answer to f, make sure students understand *obscurity* (section 5).

> **ANSWERS**
> b 5   c 1, 2   d 2   e 3   f 5   g 4   h 7   i 6   j 1

5 Put students into pairs and do the first example as a whole class. Ask students to underline the sentence or phrase in the text that gives each answer. Check answers with the class and point out that all except c are fairly common fixed expressions.

> **ANSWERS**
> b   a guaranteed crowd puller
> c   a lovable loser
> d   captured the imagination of

e   an overnight sensation
f   at the speed of light
g   takes on a momentum of its own
h   make it really big
i   follow in anyone else's footprints

6 Check students understand *appeal* and give them a couple of minutes to think about their answers. Put them into groups for the discussion. Encourage them to explain their answers, and to ask each other questions if necessary.

Vocabulary and speaking (PAGE 86)

The road to fame

1 To introduce the topic, remind students of the people they read about on pages 84–85. Give them about five minutes to discuss the questions, and then elicit a few ideas.

2 [T8.1] Students work in pairs or small groups. Check that they understand *rise and fall* (= to become famous or successful and then lose your fame or success). Set the activity and tell them to help each other with unknown phrases or guess the meaning before using their mini-dictionaries to check. Play the recording and ask students to change their answers if necessary. Check answers with the class and go through the language notes below.

> **ANSWERS AND LANGUAGE NOTES**
> Refer to the recording and the sentences in exercise 2. Point out that references in the sentences make it easier to put them in order, e.g. *child* in 1 is followed by *teenager* in 2; *a popular TV soap opera* in 4 is followed by *The soap* in 5; *a Hollywood movie* in 5 is followed by *The movie* in 6. Also, point out the use of *After several years* (4), *Soon* (7), *But* (8), *Slowly but surely* (9) and *Some years later* (10).

3 **a** Make sure students understand their roles. Refer them to the speech bubbles for examples of questions. Ask students to write notes rather than full sentences. While they are preparing, walk round the class providing vocabulary and any other help they need.

b Give them about five minutes to act out the interview in pairs, and tell them to add additional questions/information as they speak. Then select a few pairs to act out their interviews for the rest of the class.

ADDITIONAL PRACTICE

Workbook: Vocabulary: The road to fame, page 58

Listening and writing (PAGES 86–87)

Song: *Do you know the way to San José?*

1 **a** To introduce the topic, you could remind students that the character in *The road to fame* on page 86 got *a starring role in a Hollywood movie*. Put the students into pairs to discuss the questions and check that they understand *models* by asking what models do.

b Explain that they are going to listen to a song about a woman who goes to Hollywood. Check that students know Hollywood is in LA (Los Angeles). Students make their predictions individually and then compare with a partner. Tell them not to read the text of the song. Elicit a few predictions and write them on the board.

2 [T8.2] Give students a few minutes to read the text of the song and fill the gaps. If they cannot immediately guess an answer, tell them to move to the next one. Emphasise they should not worry about unknown phrases at this stage. Play the recording and then get students to compare answers. Play the recording again, if necessary, and check answers as a whole class.

> **ANSWERS AND LANGUAGE NOTES**
> See tapescript for recording 2 on page 169 of the *Students' Book*.

3 Read through the questions and check that students understand *work out*. To increase the challenge in this activity, ask students to cover the text while answering the questions. Either play the recording to check answers or refer to the text. When eliciting answers to question f, ask students which of the predictions you wrote on the board in exercise 1b were correct.

4 Put students into pairs and ask them to underline all the phrases in the text before guessing the meaning. Emphasise that it is not important to be 100 percent correct or to understand every word in a phrase, but they should try and understand the general idea. If necessary, do the first example with the class by asking if the woman felt happy/contented in LA. Then ask students if she believes she will feel the same when she goes back to San José. When students have answered these two questions, you can elicit the meaning of sentence a.

> **POSSIBLE ANSWERS**
> a I'm returning to San José to become happier / more contented.
> b You can become a star very quickly. / They promise to make you a star very quickly. / You believe you can become a star very quickly.
> c But you do not become a star quickly. / The promise is not true.
> d All the people who falsely believed they could be stars are now doing ordinary / badly paid jobs.
> e The thought of being rich and famous is attractive.
> f The things you hoped for don't happen. / Your dreams and desires disappear.

5 Students may already have thought about the first question when guessing the meaning of *find some peace*

of mind in exercise 4. Emphasise that this question is asking for the students' own opinions.

6 Set the activity and go through the ideas provided. Give students five to ten minutes to plan their account, make some notes and decide which vocabulary from page 86 they are going to use. While they are planning, walk round the class providing any additional vocabulary and prompting ideas if necessary. Then ask students to write their final draft. If time is short, this can be done for homework. Take the final drafts from students and mark them, paying particular attention to their use of the vocabulary from page 86. You could also note any errors students make when linking their ideas and use these to introduce the *Writing* activities on page 92 in the *Students' Book*.

Language focus 1 (PAGE 88)

Gerund or infinitive?

See *Teacher's tips: using a discovery approach in the teaching of grammar* on page 8.

1 Explain that all the quotations are from famous people, and ask students if they recognise any of the names. Check students understand *prevent*, *recognise*, *achieve* and *immortality* by eliciting a similar or opposite word. Give them a couple of minutes to read the quotations and answer the question. Then put them into pairs to discuss their answers.

2 To check students understand *infinitive* and *gerund*, write an example of each on the board. Give them a short time to find examples in the text and compare their answers with a partner. Check answers with the class.

Analysis

1–2 Students work individually or in pairs to complete these exercises. Walk round the class to check they are underlining the appropriate examples, and correct if necessary. Make sure students use their mini-dictionaries to find the meaning as well as the form in exercise 2. Ask them to compare with a partner, and then go through the answers and language notes below as a whole class. Refer students to *Language summaries A* and *B* on page 152 for more information and examples.

> **ANSWERS AND LANGUAGE NOTES**
> **1**
>   **Gerunds**
> a *prevent* people *recognising* him. (Some verbs are followed by gerunds, but there are no explicit rules for this. When students learn a new verb, they also need to learn if it is followed by a gerund.)
> b *Being* a star ... *dreaming* of being one. (Grammatically, a gerund as the subject of a sentence is used in the same way as a noun. A gerund can also be used as an object, e.g. *I like watching TV*.)
> c *through* not *dying*. (We can also use *by* instead of *through* after *achieve*. Highlight the negative form, i.e. *not* comes between the preposition and the gerund. This form can also be used in the positive, e.g. *You will pass your exams through/by working hard*. The gerund is used as a noun in this example.)

Infinitives

a   *want to achieve*. (There are no explicit rules for this. When students learn a new verb, they also need to learn if it is followed by an infinitive.)

b   *make you feel*. (Other verbs that follow this pattern are *let* and *help* (though *help* can also take the *to* infinitive.)

c   *necessary to be rich*. (There are many adjectives which are followed by the infinitive. Students need to learn them as they go along.)

d   *works hard all his life to become well-known*. (Explain that *to become well-known* is the reason for *working hard* in this sentence. This pattern is very common.)

2   The following verbs are followed by gerunds: *avoid, deny, don't mind, have trouble*.
The following verbs are followed by infinitives: *expect, pretend, refuse, threaten*. (Emphasise again that there no explicit rules here, but that students need to remember if a verb takes a gerund or an infinitive.)

Analysis: alternative suggestions

To help students learn and remember the patterns, try the following.

- Make two posters, one for gerunds and one for infinitives, and put them on the wall of your room. As new verbs come up in class, ask students to add them to the appropriate poster.
- Test students regularly by giving them a list of verbs and asking them to decide which take the gerund and which take the infinitive.
- Encourage students to use their dictionaries to check if a verb is followed by a gerund or an infinitive.

PRACTICE

1 **a** Check that students understand *Have you got what it takes to be a celebrity?* by giving/eliciting a similar phrase, e.g. *Are you the kind of person who can be a celebrity? / Do you have the character/abilities necessary to be a celebrity?* Explain that some of the sentences are typical of someone who could become a celebrity. If students find this activity difficult, refer them to *Language summaries A* and *B* on page 152 of the *Students' Book*. When they have completed the gaps, go through the answers and language notes as a whole class.

ANSWERS AND LANGUAGE NOTES
1   *to go*
2   *taking*
3   *to remember*
4   *getting*
5   *to be*
6   *wait*
7   *to see*
8   *to make*
9   *appreciate*
10 *knowing*
11 *going*

12 *being*
13 *to make*
14 *to find*. (*Try* can be followed by a gerund or an infinitive. When it means 'make an effort (to do something difficult)', it is followed by the infinitive, as in this example. When it means 'experiment with (something) to see if it will work', it is followed by a gerund, e.g. *If you don't feel well, try taking some medicine.*)
15 *notice*
16 *not to know*. (Highlight the word order here.)
17 *not having*. (Highlight the word order here.)
18 *arrive*
19 *to make*
20 *to like*

b Check that students understand *potential*, and give them a few minutes to tick the appropriate statements. Briefly check answers as a whole class and ask students to explain their choice if necessary.

2 Set the activity and refer students to the speech bubble for an example. Give them a few minutes to think about how to form the questions. If they find this difficult, go through the following points with them.
- All the questions use either *Would you ...?* or *Do you ...?*
- They need to ask *Do you like ...?* in order to get the answer *I can't stand ...*
- They need to change the pronouns from *I* to *you*, *me* to *you*, *myself* to *yourself*, etc.
Put students into pairs to ask and answer the questions. Give a time check halfway through the activity so that all students get the chance to ask their questions. If time is short, tell students to ask each other just five of the questions.

ADDITIONAL PRACTICE

RB **Resource bank:** 8C Design your own soap opera! (verbs that take the infinitive or the gerund), pages 142–143

Workbook: Infinitives, page 59; Gerunds, page 59; Gerund or infinitive?, page 60

Language focus 2 (PAGE 89)
Different infinitive and gerund forms

See *Teacher's tips: using a discovery approach in the teaching of grammar* on page 8.

Put students into pairs and emphasise that they should try to explain why they have chosen a particular form. Briefly check answers but do not elicit explanations at this stage.

ANSWERS
1 b   2 b   3 b   4 b

Analysis

Give students a few minutes to find the examples and think about the form. Then go through the answers and language notes eliciting/giving explanations.

ANSWERS AND LANGUAGE NOTES

Explain that gerunds and infinitives can be used in different forms. As you go through the answers, highlight the different forms and their meanings (see below). These should not be too difficult because students are already familiar with passives, perfect and continuous forms, and the same rules of form and meaning apply here. When you have finished going through the language notes, read through *Language summary C* as a class for more examples of these forms.

a **Continuous infinitive:** 3b. Form: *to be + -ing*. (Used to show that the action expressed by the infinitive is in progress at a particular time, in this case at the moment.)

b **Perfect infinitive:** 4b. Form: *to have* + past participle. (Used to refer to the past, i.e. it's not possible to meet Marilyn Monroe now.)

c **Passive infinitive:** 1b. Form: *to be* + past participle. (Used here because the people who see celebrities are not specified.)

d **Passive gerund:** 2b. Form: *being* + past participle. (Used here because the people taking the photographs are not specified.)

PRACTICE

1 Students work individually or in pairs. Ask them to use their mini-dictionaries for unknown vocabulary. If they find this activity difficult, refer them back to the *Analysis* or *Language summary C*. Ask students to explain their answers.

ANSWERS
1 to be asked   2 to worry   3 asking   4 to be
5 to have worked   6 to have seen
7 to be released   8 to be seen

2 Introduce the texts and ask students what they expect to find in each. Elicit a few ideas and then ask students to read the texts quickly to check their predictions. Students will have seen most of the vocabulary earlier in this module, but check that they understand *paparazzi*, *ex-lovers*, *kidnap*. Put students into pairs to complete the gaps and refer them to *Language summaries A, B* and *C* if necessary. Check answers as a whole class and ask if students would prefer to be rich and famous or not.

ANSWERS
Ten things to worry about if you're rich and famous
1 being seen
2 Being followed
3 Not getting; to take
4 to be criticised
5 to sell
6 to have
7 finding
8 being kidnapped
9 selling
10 Not knowing

Ten things to worry about if you're **not** rich and famous
1 to be
2 being/getting invited
3 Not having; to be
4 to spend
5 to see
6 to have
7 to drive; to eat
8. to buy
9 to sell
10 being given

3 Go through the topics and elicit one thing to worry about in each case. Then allocate each group a different topic and give students five minutes to think of ideas. Suggest that one student in each group takes notes. Walk round the class providing vocabulary and correcting form if necessary. When they have finished, ask one student from each group to read their list to the class. Ask the other groups to add more ideas if they can.

> ### *Practice*, exercise 3: alternative suggestions
>
> • If you have a large class, add more topics to the list or ask students to decide on additional topics before you begin the exercise.
> • If the topics are not suitable for your students, prepare different ones in advance or ask students to decide on their own topics.
> • If you want to extend the activity, ask students to think of five things **not** to worry about as well.

ADDITIONAL PRACTICE

Workbook: Different gerund and infinitive forms, page 60

Task: Summarise an article
(PAGES 90–91)

See *Teacher's tips: making tasks work* on pages 13–14.

Preparation: reading and listening

1 Focus attention on the photos and title, and check students understand *celeb* (a colloquial abbreviation of *celebrity*) and *worshipper* (in this context, a person who admires something or someone to an extreme degree). Set the activity, and if students do not know the people in the pictures, give them some of the facts below:
• **Brad Pitt:** American Hollywood actor – has made many films
• **Jennifer Lopez:** American singer and actor (nickname 'J-Lo') – comes from poor background; now very rich
• **David Beckham:** British footballer – married to Victoria (previously 'Posh Spice', one of the Spice Girls).

2 Give students thirty seconds to read the article without their mini-dictionaries and to check the predictions they made in exercise 1. Read through the questions and check that students understand *key words* and *issues*. Then ask students

to answer as many questions as possible without reading the article again. Put them into pairs to compare notes and then ask them to read the article again, use their mini-dictionaries and add more information to their notes.

3 [T8.3] Set the question, play the recording and ask students to read their notes while they listen. If students find this difficult, play the recording again or refer them to the tapescript for recording 3 on page 169 of the *Students' Book*.

Task: speaking

1 If you/your students decide to do the first option in exercise 1, elicit some predictions about the articles before asking students to choose. Try to make sure there is a variety of articles chosen.

If you/your students choose the second option, either make sure you bring some newspapers to the class, or tell students to find an article for homework and then do the task in the next lesson. The articles chosen should be a similar length to those on pages 140–141 in the *Students' Book*.

2 a Make sure students only write notes at this stage, using the notes they wrote in *Preparation: reading and listening*, exercise 2, as an example. Encourage them to use dictionaries or ask you about unknown vocabulary in the articles.

b Go through *Useful language a* and explain any problem phrases. Give students plenty of time to summarise their article. If necessary, refer them to the tapescript for recording 3 as an example. Walk round the class providing any language they need.

3 Make sure the students in each group have summarised different articles. Go through *Useful language b* and explain any problem phrases. Ask students to make notes about their opinions while they listen to each summary. To finish the activity, ask students which article was the most interesting. For homework, students could read the articles they did not read for the task.

Task: alternative suggestions

a If you are short of time or have short lessons: this is quite a long task, so you could do it over two lessons. Do *Preparation: reading and listening* in one lesson, then allocate the articles to read and set the summaries to prepare for homework. In the next lesson, students can compare summaries with others who read the same article before continuing with *Task: speaking*, exercise 3 as normal.

b If you prefer to choose current newspaper articles for your students, you can still follow the same stages. Select three to five interesting articles that are appropriate for personal and general discussion points. Write the headlines on the board, elicit some predictions and then follow the procedure in *Task: speaking*, exercises 2 and 3.

Writing (PAGE 92)

Linking ideas and arguments

1 a Introduce the topic and do the first example as a class. Put students into pairs to do the rest, then check answers with the class.

ANSWERS
2 Whereas
3 Although
4 what is more; For this reason
5 Despite

b Show students that *However* introduces an argument/idea that is 'against', or that contradicts, the argument/idea in the first sentence. Go through the other categories and check that students understand *consequences*. Then ask students to complete the table. Check answers as a whole class and go through the language notes below. Refer to the sentences you wrote on the board in exercise 1a, and use arrows to show the alternative positions of the linkers.

ANSWERS AND LANGUAGE NOTES
1 *However/Although/Despite*. (These have the same meaning, but are used in different ways grammatically. *However* is an adverb. It usually comes at the beginning of the second sentence, and introduces the idea that contradicts that of the first sentence. It can also appear in the middle or at the end of the second sentence. It is followed and, if necessary, preceded by commas.
Although and *despite* both join two contrasting ideas in the same sentence. They can come at the beginning or in the middle of the sentence. Note the difference in form: *despite* is a preposition followed by a noun, a gerund or a pronoun; *although* is a conjunction followed by a clause with a subject and verb.)
2 *What is more*. (This is an adverb. It usually comes at the beginning of the sentence, but can come in the middle or at the end. Commas are needed.)
3 *For this reason*. (This is an adverb. It usually comes at the beginning of the sentence, but can come in the middle or at the end. Commas are needed.)
4 *Whereas*. (This is a conjunction. It joins two clauses together. Like *although*, it can come at the beginning or in the middle of a sentence. *Whereas* is used to **contrast** two different situations; *although* links ideas that **contradict** each other.)

2 This can be done as a whole class, individually or in pairs. As you go through the answers, show how the linkers can be substituted for those in the sentences in exercise 1a.

ANSWERS AND LANGUAGE NOTES
besides: 2. (This is an adverb like *what is more*. It is often used informally.)
furthermore: 2. (This is an adverb like *what is more*. It is more formal.)
nevertheless: 1. (The use is similar to *however*. It is usually more emphatic.)

therefore: 3. (The use is the same as *for this reason*. It is usually more formal.)

even though: 1. (The use is the same as *although*. It is a little more emphatic.)

in spite of: 1. (The use is exactly the same as *despite*.)

on the other hand: 1. (The use is similar to *however*. It is usually more emphatic.)

while: 1 and 4. (This can be used in the same way as *although* or *whereas*.)

Ask students to read *Language summary D* on page 153 of the *Students' Book* for more examples.

3 To introduce the topic of the composition, ask students to say what is happening in the picture and how the two men reading newspapers might feel. Read the title, check that students understand *banned* and briefly ask students for their opinions on the topic. Then, give them a few minutes to read the composition and tell you the writer's opinion. Put students into pairs and set the activity in the *Students' Book*.

> **ANSWERS**
> a Whereas   b Although   c What is more
> d even though   e For this reason
> f On the other hand   g therefore   h while
> i despite   j in spite of   k Nevertheless
> l However

ADDITIONAL PRACTICE

Workbook: Improve your writing: Linking ideas and arguments

Wordspot (PAGE 93)

big and *great*

See *Teacher's tips: working with lexis* on pages 8–9.

1–2 Introduce the activity by eliciting a couple of phrases with *big* and *great*. Go through the diagrams with the class and show how the meanings overlap in *large*. Then put students into pairs to complete the gaps.

> **ANSWERS**
> a big   b big   c big/great   d great   e great
> f big   g big   h great (*impressive*) / big (*physically large*)
> i great

3 Students can do this individually or in pairs. If they use their mini-dictionaries, tell them to look either for *big/great* or for the verb, e.g. in sentence a, students should look for *have*.

> **ANSWERS**
> a great   b big   c great   d big-   e great
> f big   g big   h great

4 The aims of this activity are to check that students understand the different meanings of *big* and *great*, and to provide practice. Encourage students to discuss their answers and to ask each other for more information.

> **ANSWERS**
> a open answer   b fantastic   c a bad thing
> d open answer
> e **Possible answers:** Shakespeare, Dickens, Austen
> f open answer
> g **Possible answers:** medicine, banking, football

ADDITIONAL PRACTICE

Workbook: Wordspot: *big* and *great*, page 63

Consolidation modules 5–8 (PAGES 94–95)

It is primarily intended that you do this in class time, allowing students to work in pairs or small groups. However, we have noted below which of the activities could be set for homework. Emphasise to students that the *Consolidation* activities are for revision purposes and are not tests.

A Use of articles

Students can do this individually or in pairs. Before completing the gaps, ask them to read through each text quickly to find out what it is about. Check answers as a whole class. This section could be set for homework.

> **ANSWERS**
>
> | 1 | | 2 | |
> |---|-----|---|-----|
> | a | The | a | a |
> | b | – | b | – |
> | c | a | c | – |
> | d | the | d | the |
> | e | the | e | the |
> | f | – | f | a |
> | g | a | g | – |
> | h | the | h | – |
> | i | the | i | an |
> | j | the | j | the |
> | k | the | k | a |
> | l | the | l | a |
> | m | The | m | a |
> | n | *The* | n | – |
> | o | The | | |
> | p | – | | |
> | q | – | | |
> | r | – | | |

> **Consolidation: exercise A: alternative suggestion**
>
> Use the first text as revision and go through the answers eliciting explanations for the use or non-use of articles. Then set the second text and encourage students to refer to the first text for information on whether to use articles or not.

B Word combinations

1 Check that students understand the difference between *Big events* and *Unusual achievements* by eliciting or giving examples of each (see Modules 5 and 7). If students cannot remember the meaning of any items, tell them to search the relevant modules or use their mini-dictionaries. When students compare their answers, tell them not to give definitions of the words.

ANSWERS
BE: cheering, spectators, a huge crowd, a procession, waving flags, media attention
FF: a huge mansion, make a fortune, be in the public eye, media attention, get your big break
I: bandage, infection, painful, a wound, hurt yourself
UA: beat the record, win an award, raise money, be in the public eye, media attention

Consolidation: exercise B1: alternative suggestion

If you want to make the exercise more competitive, put students into pairs to categorise the items. The first pair to finish wins.

2 Give students a few minutes to think of definitions. Emphasise that they should only use their mini-dictionaries if they cannot remember the items. Then ask them to test their partners.

C Perfect tenses: Record breakers

Students can work individually or in pairs. Before answering the questions, ask them to read through each text quickly and to decide which they find the most surprising or most interesting. Check answers as a whole class. This section can be set for homework.

ANSWERS
1 a has held
   b had been
2 c had taken
   d had been walking
3 e had been married
   f had been living
4 g has been collecting
   h has collected
5 i have used
   j had ever tried
6 k had been waiting
   l had first proposed
7 m has been increasing
   n will have reached
8 o has been touched
   p had suffered

Consolidation: exercise C: alternative suggestion

Put students into pairs or small groups and divide texts 1–8 equally among the groups. When they have finished their text(s), put students into larger groups, making sure there is at least one student from each of the original groups. Ask them briefly to tell the other students what their text is about. Then ask them to explain why they chose particular forms. Finally, ask the whole class which text they thought was most surprising/interesting, etc.

D Relative clauses

1–2 [C1] Before students do the exercise, ask them to read through each text quickly to find out what it is about. If necessary, pre-teach *pushchair* and *dragged* in the first box. Do the first example as a whole class and elicit why the relative pronoun *who* is correct. Walk round the class, prompting students if necessary, and then play the recording to check answers.

ANSWERS
a 2 who was unaware of what was happening
   3 whose pushchair had been dragged along for nearly a kilometre
   4 who saw the whole thing happen
b 5 who has been suffering for years
   6 which (that) had been stuck in his spine for almost forty-eight years
   7 who will be having an operation to remove the tooth
   8 which happened off the Gold Coast
   9 where he had been swimming

E Speaking: Two-minute talk

1 Give students a couple of minutes to choose their topic, and make sure that there is a variety of topics in each group. Ask students to keep their topic secret at this stage. Students prepare their talks individually while you walk round the class, providing vocabulary if necessary. Tell them to make notes but not to write the complete talk.

2 Set the activity for students to do while they listen, and ask them to guess the topic at the end of each talk. Do not allow students to talk for more than two minutes.

module 9

Mysteries, problems, oddities

Vocabulary and speaking (PAGE 96)

Strange events

1 Put students into pairs and introduce the topic by asking them to describe the pictures on page 97. Elicit *bend spoons*; *the Northern Lights*; *a pack of cards*; *mysteries*. Do not ask students to talk about similar events, or strange things that have happened to them, because they will do this in exercise 3. Ask students to guess the meaning of unknown vocabulary as they match the phrases. When you go through the answers, check students understand all the phrases.

> **ANSWERS**
> a 8   b 2   c 10   d 9   e 1   f 6   g 4   h 5
> i 3   j 11   k 12   l 7

2 Give students a few minutes to check the words and decide their answers before putting them into pairs to compare. Encourage them to explain their answers and ask each other for more information.

3 Give students a couple of minutes to think about their answers before putting them into groups. Ask them to give details in their answers and to ask one another questions. When they have finished, get a few students to tell the class the strangest thing they heard in their groups.

ADDITIONAL PRACTICE

Workbook: Vocabulary: Strange events, page 64

Listening (PAGE 97)

Mysteries of everyday life

1 Introduce the topic by contrasting 'everyday life' with the strange events on page 96. Focus students on the pictures and elicit *sneeze*, *tickle*, *ticklish*, *yawn* (students should be able to guess the meaning of *sleepwalk*). Also teach *hiccup* by demonstrating it. When students have discussed the questions, get a couple of answers from each group.

2 Go through the questions and check students understand *bald*. Students answer the questions individually before comparing with their partner. Do not elicit answers at this stage.

3 **a** 📼 [T9.1] Give students a few minutes to find the words in their mini-dictionaries, then elicit the pronunciation of *diaphragm*. Set the question and ask students to see how many phrases they can match without listening to the recording. Then play the recording and ask students to compare answers with their partner. Briefly check answers as a whole class, but do not elicit answers to exercise 2 at this stage.

> **ANSWERS**
> a   testosterone
> b   a state of panic
> c   pre-adolescent boys, stress
> d   oxygen, the soul
> e   the diaphragm, swallowing rapidly
> f   the Middle Ages, the Bubonic Plague

b 📼 [T9.1] To help students, you could pre-teach the words *cause*, *result*, *origin*, *victim*. Then play the recording and ask students to list the phrases under these headings. Ask students to compare and explain their answers.

> **ANSWERS**
> Testosterone in the body causes baldness.
> A state of panic is a result of being tickled – this leads to laughter.
> Pre-adolescent boys are the most common victims of sleepwalking.
> Stress can be a cause of sleepwalking.
> The body's need for oxygen causes us to yawn.
> In ancient times, it was believed that your soul would leave your body as a result of opening the mouth.
> A sudden muscle movement in the diaphragm is the cause of hiccups.
> Swallowing rapidly causes hiccups to stop.
> The origin of 'Bless you' is the Bubonic Plague in the Middle Ages.

4 Put students into pairs to discuss the questions, and then elicit a few ideas from the class.

Language focus 1 (PAGES 98–99)

Modals and related verbs

Focus students on the picture and ask them what advice they could give to someone who sleepwalks. Ask students to cross out the incorrect modals. Do the first sentence as a class to demonstrate that not every sentence has an incorrect modal in it. When students have finished, check answers as a class. Then refer to sentence 1 again and elicit that *have to* is better than *ought to* in this context (though both are possible). Get students to look at the rest of the sentences and to choose which verb is best in the context. Do not check answers at this stage, because the *Analysis* box gives more information to help students with the answers.

> **ANSWERS**
> 1   both correct
> 2   both correct
> 3   *should* is incorrect
> 4   *mustn't* is incorrect
> 5   both correct
> 6   *can* is incorrect

Analysis

1–3 Put students into pairs, set the activities and go through the information in exercise 2. Allow plenty of time for students to answer the questions. Then go through the answers and language notes below, eliciting the form where necessary. It is important that students read *Language summary A* on pages 153–154 of the *Students' Book* before they do the *Practice* on pages 98–99.

ANSWERS AND LANGUAGE NOTES

1 a *have to* and *must. (Have to* is better in the context of sentence 1. Form: *have to* + infinitive without *to. Must* is better in sentence 2 if the culture strongly believes that covering your mouth is the right thing to do. Form: *must* + infinitive without *to.)*

   b *ought to should. (Ought to* is possible in sentence 1, but is probably not strong enough in this context. Form: *ought to* + infinitive without *to. Should* is better in sentence 2 if covering your mouth in a particular culture is polite and considerate, but it would not be too rude if you didn't. Form: *should* + infinitive without *to.)*

2 a *must* in sentence 3. (The belief that this is true is usually based on evidence or strong opinion informed by the speaker's own feelings, e.g. *The hot weather in Singapore must be very uncomfortable.* Form: *must* + infinitive without *to.)*

   b *can* and *may* in sentence 5, and *may, might* and *could* in sentence 6. (In sentence 5, *can* and *may* both express a present possibility. *Can* expresses slightly more certainty than *may*, and so is probably better in this context, i.e. a lot of research has been done and doctors are fairly sure. In sentence 6, the modals *may, might* and *could* have exactly the same meaning and express a degree of certainty about the future. Form: modal + infinitive without *to.)*

3 Because *can* is used to express general possibilities (sentence 5), i.e. sleepwalking is also a possible sign of other things, not only stress. *Can* cannot be used for specific possibilities (sentence 6).

PRACTICE

1 Introduce the topic by focusing students on the picture, elicit *earthquake* and ask what the connection between the dog and the earthquake might be. Then ask if they know anything about how animals can be used to predict natural disasters. On the strength of this discussion, pre-teach *behaviour; perceive changes; magnetic field; impending disaster*. Set the activity and do the first example with the class, eliciting why *must* is not appropriate. When you check answers, ask students to explain their choices.

ANSWERS
b has to   c can   d mustn't   e can   f mustn't
g have to   h shouldn't   i should

2 Students work in pairs. They should know most of these animals, but you should take pictures of a bat, camel and

tiger into class or ask students to find the translation in their bilingual dictionaries. Check students understand *high-pitched sounds; survive in the wild; tusks*. Explain that more than one animal may fit some of the sentences. When students have finished, go through the language notes below.

ANSWERS AND LANGUAGE NOTES
a   *camels; can* (= ability)
b   *elephants, tigers; could, may, might* (= possibility)
c   *bats; can't* (= negative ability)
d   *horses; must* (= necessary not to) or *should* (= a good idea not to); *may, might, could* (= possibility). Explain that if we use *never have to* here, it means there is no obligation to do it – this does not make sense in the context.
e   *snakes; can* (= general possibility)
f   *sharks; have to, must* (= necessary)
g   *cats; could* (= ability)
h   *elephants; must* (= obligation). Explain that if we use *don't have to* here, it means there is no obligation to do it – this does not make sense in the context.

3 **a** Introduce the topic of fact versus myth by eliciting examples of each. Check that students know *rib, tarantula, turkey, plughole, ostrich*. Then give students a couple of minutes to read the statements individually and to decide which three are true.

b Go through the language in the speech bubbles and highlight the difference in meaning between *This must/can't be true* (based on evidence and strong opinion) and *I know for a fact this is/isn't true* (definitely true or not). Give students about five to ten minutes to discuss the statements.

c [cassette icon] [T9.2] Play the recording to check answers, and ask students to note any additional information.

ANSWERS
See tapescript for recording 2 on page 170 in the *Students' Book.*

ADDITIONAL PRACTICE

Workbook: Vocabulary booster: Modal and related verbs, page 64

Wordspot (PAGE 99)

wrong

See *Teacher's tips: working with lexis* on pages 9–10.

1 Introduce the vocabulary by eliciting a few expressions with *wrong* from the students. Ask them to read expressions a–i and to tick the ones they know. Then put students into pairs to match the expressions to the definitions.

ANSWERS
a 7   b 9   c 2   d 5   e 1   f 3   g 4   h 6   i 8

2 The aim of this activity is to check understanding of the expressions and help students remember them. Give students a few minutes to read the expressions and definitions

again, and then re-write the sentences on page 139 without looking at the *Wordspot*. Tell them they may need to change the form. When they have finished, tell them to compare their answers with the expressions in the *Wordspot*.

ANSWERS
a the wrong way up
b went wrong
c was completely wrong
d the wrong way round
e There's something wrong with
f in the wrong place
g What's wrong?
h there's nothing wrong with him
i a wrong number / someone who had got the wrong number

ADDITIONAL PRACTICE

Workbook: Wordspot: *wrong*, page 65

Language focus 2 (PAGES 100–101)

Past modals

See *Teacher's tips: using a discovery approach in the teaching of grammar* on page 6.

1 Explain that students are going to hear the story of a mysterious disappearance. Ask them to tick the words or phrases in the box they already know and to use their mini-dictionaries for the others. Give them about five minutes to discuss the pictures, and then elicit some ideas.

2 [T9.3] Give students a couple of minutes to read the questions. Play the recording without stopping and ask students to write just one or two words for each answer. Put students into pairs to compare answers, and play the recording again if necessary. If students find this activity very difficult, tell them to read the tapescript.

ANSWERS
See tapescript for recording 3 on page 170 of the *Students' Book*.

3 [T9.4] Give students a few minutes to think about the question before comparing with their partner. Play the recording without stopping and ask students if their explanation was the same. Play the recording again if necessary.

ANSWERS
See tapescript for recording 4 on page 170 of the *Students' Book*.

4 [T9.5] Put students into pairs and ask them to guess the answers if they are not sure. Note that in sentence g both alternatives are possible. Play the recording, pausing after each sentence, and ask students to check their answers. Then briefly go through the answers with the class.

ANSWERS
See tapescript for recording 5 on page 170 of the *Students' Book*.

Analysis

1 Elicit an example of a modal verb (e.g. *could*) and a related verb (e.g. *managed to*) from exercise 4. Then put students into pairs to complete the activity.

2 Elicit or give the perfect form: modal + *have* + past participle, before students start the activity. Check answers and go through the language notes below, writing the form of the modals on the board. Then ask students to read *Language summary B* on page 154 in the *Students' Book*.

ANSWERS AND LANGUAGE NOTES
1 a *had to* in sentence b. (Form: *had to* + infinitive without *to*. Meaning: an obligation in the past. *Had to* is the past of *must* or *have to*. The negative form is *didn't have to,* which means 'it wasn't necessary' or 'we weren't obliged'.)
   b *could* in sentence c. (Form: *could* + infinitive without *to*. Meaning: an ability in the past. *Could* is the past of *can* for ability.)
   c *managed to* in sentences a and e. (Form: *managed to / didn't manage to* + infinitive without *to*. Meaning: see *could* below.)
   d *couldn't* in sentence d. (Form: *couldn't* + infinitive without *to*. Meaning: an inability in the past.)
   Could is wrong in sentences a and e, but correct in sentence c, because it means 'theoretically, this person was able to do this.' If we want to say the person actually did it, we use *managed to* or *was able to.*
2 The perfect form is modal (+ *not*) + *have* + past participle.
   a *must have* in sentence f. (Contrast this meaning with *can't have* below.)
   b *might/could have* in sentence g. (*Could have* is used when it was possible for something to happen, but it didn't. We cannot use *could not have* to express a negative possibility, e.g. ~~The hotel manager could not have conspired~~ – this sentence means 'The hotel manager did not have the ability to conspire'. We use *might not have* to express negative possibilities in the past.)
   c *can't have* in sentence i. (This has the opposite meaning of *must have*.)
   d *should (certainly) have* in sentence h. (*Certainly* is used to add emphasis.)

PRACTICE

1 Do the first example as a whole class and explain that *Perhaps … sent* becomes *might have sent*, because it expresses the same level of possibility and is in the past. Students should not find it difficult to understand the change from *had the ability* to *could*. Ask students to work individually or in pairs to complete the exercise, and walk round the room correcting any problems with modals. If students have found this exercise very difficult, write the sentences on the board and highlight the changes as you check the answers.

ANSWERS AND LANGUAGE NOTES

b *The doctor must have sent a letter with Eleanor when she went to his surgery.*

c *The British Embassy should have checked this.*

d *Eleanor might have had to wait for a long time at the doctor's surgery.*

e *Eleanor managed to get back to the hotel with the medicine successfully eventually.*

f *They can't have removed Mrs Redwood's signature from the hotel register.*

g *They might not have taken Eleanor back to room 342 when she returned to the hotel. It might/could have been a different room.* (We cannot use *could not have taken* in the first part of the sentence because we need to express a negative possibility. Compare this with the second part of the sentence where both *might* and *could* are correct – this is a positive possibility.)

h *It is a shame that Eleanor didn't manage to persuade embassy officials to believe her.* (We use *didn't manage to* and not *couldn't* because we are talking about a specific occasion.)

i *The authorities shouldn't have put a young girl like Eleanor in a Mental Asylum.*

j *Eleanor might/could have invented the whole story.*

2 Show students that the second part of each item is an explanation that provides the context. Do the first sentence together, eliciting/explaining that if the speaker saw the glasses in the kitchen a few minutes ago, then it is logically impossible that they were left at work (so *can't have left* is the correct answer). Then put students into pairs to complete the exercise.

ANSWERS

a   can't have left
b   might/could have left
c   could have studied
d   had to study
e   must/might/could have got lost
f   can't have got lost
g   can't have gone
h   must have gone
i   had to buy
j   must have bought

3 [T9.6] Explain that students will hear six people talking, and that the sentences summarise what the people say. They have to match the sentences to the six people. Give students a couple of minutes to read the sentences. Then play the first person on the recording and ask students which sentence it belongs to (c). Play the rest of the recording, pausing after each person to allow students to match them to a sentence. Check answers as a whole class, and play the recording again if necessary.

ANSWERS

1 c   2 f   3 d   4 e   5 a   6 b

Pronunciation

1 [T9.7] Explain that the bold words and syllables in the examples show the stress, and all the other syllables are weak. Play the recording, pausing after each sentence for students to repeat. If students cannot hear the weak forms, model them yourself, only saying the sounds written in phonemic script, then play the recording again.

2 [T9.8] Play the recording, pausing after each sentence to allow students to write. Ask them to compare with a partner and, if necessary, play the recording again. If students have found this very difficult, tell them to look at the tapescript for recording 8 to check their answers. Set the question and while students are working, write the sentences on the board. Check answers as a whole class, mark the stressed words and highlight the weak forms on the board.

3 [T9.8] Pause the recording after each sentence and ask students to repeat. Correct the stressed and weak forms if necessary.

4 If you have done the pronunciation activity above, remind students of the sentences in *Practice*, exercise 3. Give an example of your own for one of the sentences. Encourage students to pay attention to pronunciation while they discuss the sentences. Walk round the room correcting stressed/weak forms and making a note of any errors in the use of modals. When they have finished, elicit a few answers from the class. Finally, elicit/provide corrections of the errors you noted.

Language focus 2: alternative suggestion

Students should be familiar with some of these modals and will be able to work out the meaning of the others from the present forms which they looked at in *Language focus 1*. However, if you think your students will be confused by dealing with all the modals at one time, you could divide the *Analysis* as follows.

* Follow the procedure for *Language focus 2*, exercises 1 and 2, on page 100. Then do exercise 4 a–e only and *Analysis*, exercise 1 (*managed to, had to, could, couldn't*).

* Follow the procedure for *Language focus 2*, exercise 3, on page 100. Then do exercise 4 f–l only, and *Analysis*, exercise 2 (*must have, might have, could have, should have, can't have*). Use exercise 2 on page 101 for practice of past modals.

You could take a break between the two *Analysis* exercises or even do them on different days. If there is a significant gap between the two exercises, make sure you reintroduce the story of Eleanor and Clara Redwood before you begin the second exercise. Note that present and past modals are used in *Practice*, exercises 1 and 3.

ADDITIONAL PRACTICE

RB **Resource bank:** 9A The maze of terror! (modal verbs of deduction in the past and present), pages 144–146

Workbook: Past modals, page 66

Task: Solve the mysteries
(PAGES 102–103)

Preparation: reading and vocabulary

1 Do this activity as a whole class. Set the question and check students understand *unsolved*. If students cannot think of an example, provide one yourself to prompt ideas.

2–3 Focus attention on the photos and titles for each text and ask students if they have heard of any of these mysteries. Then give them five to eight minutes to read and refer to their mini-dictionaries. Emphasise that they should ignore the questions at this stage. Give the pairs a few minutes to summarise the stories. Tell them just to use two or three sentences to summarise the key point of each story.

Task: speaking and listening

1 Put students into groups and allocate a different story to each group. If you allow the students to choose their own story, make sure each group has a different one. Emphasise that students should work individually to think about the questions; walk round the class to provide help if needed. Then go through *Useful language a* and give students a couple of minutes to decide how they could use these phrases in their answers.

2 Give students five to ten minutes to discuss the story in their groups. Tell them to ask each other questions if they need clarification. Encourage them to reach an agreement.

3 **a** Keep students in the same groups and emphasise that they must agree on which story to read. Give them a few minutes individually to read the story and answer the questions. Before they begin the discussion, remind them of *Useful language a*. Walk round the class providing vocabulary if needed.

b Go through *Useful language b* and give the groups about five minutes to prepare their presentation. Walk round the class and provide any words or phrases they need. Ask the group either to nominate one person to present their solutions or to do it as a team. At the beginning of each presentation, ask students briefly to remind the class of the story.

4 [T9.9] Set the question and play the recording. Ask students to note where the explanation is different from theirs. You could ask students to make notes only on the story they presented in exercise 3b, or on all the stories that were presented. Give them a few minutes to discuss the recording in their groups, and then elicit answers. Finally, ask the class which they think is the strangest story and why.

> ### Task: speaking and listening, exercise 4: additional suggestion
>
> Ask students to find another mysterious story (on the Internet, in books, or one they already know). Tell them to summarise the story for homework and then present the solutions in the following lesson. Alternatively, ask students to present the story and ask other students in the class to suggest possible solutions.

> ### Task: alternative suggestions
>
> - If you know of any mysterious stories currently in the news, you could use these instead of one or all of the stories in the *Students' Book*.
> - If time is short, cut the number of stories. Students could read the stories you cut for homework and then discuss them in the following lesson.
> - If time is short, cut *Task: speaking and listening*, exercise 3a, and ask students to do exercise 3b with reference to the first story they read (in *Task: speaking and listening*, exercises 1 and 2).
> - If one or two groups are a lot faster than the others, tell them to do exercise 3a but allow the slower groups to skip this and do exercise 3b with reference to the story they read in exercises 1 and 2.
> - If students find *Task: speaking and listening*, exercise 4, very difficult, tell them to read the relevant parts of the tapescript for recording 9 on page 171 in the *Students' Book*.

ADDITIONAL PRACTICE

Workbook: Listen and read: Coincidences, page 68

Real life (PAGE 104)

Saying what's wrong with things

1 Ask students if they have ever taken anything back to a shop because it went wrong, and what happened. Put them into groups to discuss their experiences. Focus attention on the photos and elicit what the items are. Without referring to the box, ask what could go wrong with these things. Explain that students can treat the dress and jumper as a single item of clothing. Then set the activity, and ask students to use their mini-dictionaries if necessary. When you check answers with the class, it would be useful to teach/elicit the form, e.g. Present simple or Present continuous.

> **ANSWERS**
> **Mobile phone:** It doesn't work; It isn't charging; There's a part missing.
> **CD:** It doesn't work; It's scratched.
> **Item of clothing:** It's got a hole in it; It doesn't fit; It's shrunk in the wash; It's the wrong size; It's got a stain on it; It doesn't suit you; It's the wrong colour.
> **Meal (pizza):** It's burnt; It isn't what you ordered.
> **Glass:** It's chipped; It's scratched.

2 [T9.10] Set the activity and ask students to copy a bigger version of the table into their notebooks. Check they understand *receipt*; *proof of purchase*; *to change/exchange goods*; *a blank screen*. Play the recording without pausing and then ask students to compare their answers. Play the recording again, pausing after each section to check answers. Finally, ask students if they thought the staff were reasonable / behaved politely.

> **ANSWERS**
> See tapescript for recording 10 on page 171 of the *Students' Book*.

3 Put students into pairs and ask them to read the suggestions in the book. Add any other suggestions necessary to prompt ideas from the students. Give them about ten minutes to prepare their dialogues and practise. Walk round the class providing any additional vocabulary they need. Ask a few pairs to act out their dialogues for the class, and finish by providing any essential correction work.

Real life: additional suggestions

If this kind of dialogue is likely to be important to your students in their work, or because they live in an English-speaking country, adapt the suggestions in the *Students' Book* to situations you think your students will find particularly useful. You could record your students acting out their dialogues and replay them to analyse errors and discuss better ways of saying things.

ADDITIONAL PRACTICE

RB **Resource bank:** 9B What's wrong with it? (language for complaining), page 147

Workbook: Real life: Saying what's wrong with things, page 69; Improve your writing: An e-mail about a problem, page 71

Study ... (PAGE 104)

Improve your listening

Introduce this section by asking students if they have problems listening to spoken English. If the answer is yes, elicit a few problems and write them on the board. Then read through the introduction and tips, checking that students understand *panic*; *lose the sense of*; *pick it up*; *sub-titles*; *download sound files*; *accents*; *the vast majority*. Ask students if any of the tips could help with the problems you wrote on the board earlier. Encourage them to use these tips when they listen to recordings during the course.

Practise ... (PAGE 105)

This section can be done independently by students to encourage them to monitor their own learning and achievement. However, you can also use this section for further practice of the language areas covered in Module 9, or as a test. If you are testing students, make sure they do not look at the *Language summaries*, *Real life*, *Vocabulary* or *Wordspot* activities until they have finished each exercise or all five exercises. Students can do this for homework, or in class time if they need teacher guidance or you want them to work in pairs/groups.

1–5 For each exercise, make sure students read the instructions carefully. If students find exercises 1–5 very difficult, refer them to the appropriate pages in the *Students' Book* for extra help. Provide the answers either by checking as a whole class or giving students a copy from the *Teacher's Resource Book*.

ANSWERS
1 Modal verbs
a It's not a good idea to say anything.
b I say you're not allowed to say anything.
c I'm sure that this isn't the right way.
d It's not necessary to tell him.
e I'm sure that's Tim at the door.
f It's possible for it to snow in March, it sometimes happens.
g Perhaps the match will be postponed.

2 Past modal verbs
a the same
b different. (The first sentence means that it was a good idea, but we didn't do it. The second sentence means that it was necessary and we probably did it.)
c the same
d different. (The first sentence means that it was possible, but he didn't do it. The second sentence means that it was possible and he did it.)
e different. (The first sentence means that it's a good idea generally and now. The second sentence means that it was a good idea in the past, but you didn't do it.)
f different. (The first sentence expresses my opinion that they didn't understand. The second sentence expresses the fact that they weren't able to understand.)

3 Strange events
a coincidence b hoax c miracle
d supernatural e premonition f telepathy

4 Saying what's wrong
a 7, 9 b 2, 4 c 1 d 5, 8 e 3, 6

5 Phrases with *wrong*
a I'm sorry, you must have got the wrong number.
b Unfortunately, things went wrong from the start.
c They put it the wrong way up.
d There's absolutely nothing wrong with this.
e You're wearing your pullover the wrong way round.

Pronunciation spot
Dipthongs (2): /ɪə/ and /eə/

a 🔊 [T9.11] Explain that diphthongs are made by combining two vowel sounds and demonstrate by separating the vowels /i/ and /ə/, and then 'gliding' them together to make /ɪə/. Check that students understand *cheer*, then play the recording. If students cannot hear the sounds, model the words yourself and exaggerate the diphthongs. Elicit the diphthongs from the class and ask them to repeat the words.

b 🔊 [T9.12] Put students into pairs, ask them to say the words to each other and decide if they go with *here* or *there*. Walk round the class, saying the words for student if necessary. Play the recording, pausing after each set of words for students to change their answers if necessary. Check answers as a whole class, eliciting the words, modelling them yourself or playing the recording again.

c While pairs practise the words, walk round the room correcting pronunciation.

Remember! (PAGE 105)

Give students a few minutes to tick the boxes, or ask them to do this at home if it is a personal record of achievement.

Mini-check (PAGE 160)

This can be done in class, or set for homework. You can refer students to the *Language focus* sections in Module 9 or the relevant *Language summaries* on pages 153–154 for help.

ANSWERS

1	up	2	with
3	something	4	scratched
5	fit	6	You don't have
7	He can't be	8	Can I
9	You mustn't/can't	10	You shouldn't
11	could	12	need
13	must	14	could
15	should	16	have
17	disappearance	18	suspicious
19	mysterious	20	explanation

module 10

Getting together

Vocabulary (PAGE 106)

Getting together

1 Start by asking students how often they meet their friends, what day(s), what they do, etc. Use the discussion to elicit the meaning of the verb *get together* and the noun *get-together*. Set the activity. Ask students to copy list B and then write the appropriate people from list A in each category. *Note*: it is possible for ex-classmates to go on a date, for colleagues to go to a school reunion and so on. However, to help students understand the meaning of the events in list B, limit answers to the people in list A that clearly demonstrate the meaning.

> **ANSWERS**
> **an appointment**: business associates, clients
> **a blind date**: strangers looking for a partner
> **a business meeting**: business associates, clients, colleagues
> **a celebration meal**: boyfriend and girlfriend, colleagues, friends, guests, relatives
> **a conference**: business associates, clients, colleagues, delegates, political leaders, speakers
> **a date**: boyfriend and girlfriend, strangers looking for a partner
> **a dinner party**: friends, guests
> **a family get-together**: relatives
> **a housewarming party**: friends, guests, neighbours
> **a school reunion**: ex-classmates, friends
> **a summit meeting**: delegates, political leaders, speakers

2 Ask students to copy a bigger version of the table into their notebooks, then do the first one as a whole class. To check answers, list the verbs on the board, add the events and go through the language notes below.

> **ANSWERS AND LANGUAGE NOTES**
> *have*: *an appointment, a blind date, a business meeting, a celebration meal, a conference, a date, a dinner party, a family get-together, a housewarming party, a school reunion, a summit meeting*
> *make*: *an appointment, a celebration meal, a date.* (*Make a meal* means 'cook or prepare food'. *Make a date* means 'agree on a time to meet someone'.)
> *go on*: *a blind date, a date*
> *attend*: *a business meeting, a conference, a summit meeting*. (*Attend* has a similar meaning to *go on*, but is more formal in use. It is different from *have* because it does not necessarily mean you will contribute to the meeting, e.g. *I'm attending a conference on Friday* – but I'm only going to listen to the speakers.)

3 Check that students understand that a *get-together* is an informal event. Give them time to think about their

descriptions individually. Walk round the room providing any vocabulary they need. Then give the groups time to describe their events, and encourage students to ask each other questions for more information. Give regular time checks so that all students get a chance to speak. For feedback, ask each group which get-together sounded the most fun, interesting, etc.

ADDITIONAL PRACTICE

Workbook: Vocabulary: Getting together, page 72; Vocabulary booster: Communicating, page 76

Reading (PAGES 106–107)

1 Check students understand *get in touch* and ask them to think of ideas for each category. Put them into groups to compare answers. Elicit ideas and write them on the board.

2 Give students time to read the article. Tell them not to worry about unknown vocabulary at this stage. Put them into pairs or small groups to answer the questions. When you have checked answers, ask students how many of the ideas that you wrote on the board in exercise 1 were mentioned.

3 Students read the questions and check the meaning of the words in their dictionaries. Ask them to read the article again before answering the questions. *Note*: some answers are not stated explicitly in the text and have to be inferred.

> **POSSIBLE ANSWERS**
> a Because, like fast food, it is convenient, quick and unromantic.
> b It's less anonymous because you meet the people face-to-face. It's less risky because there are other people around you, you meet the person (briefly) before a date and you don't have to spend the whole evening with a person you discover you don't like.
> c Because they are a 'modern' couple, and arranged marriages are usually associated with 'traditional' families.
> d Because they had similar upbringings and share a cultural/social background. Their values are the same.
> e Because you still have to meet different women and you marry the one you like.
> f Because it is completely Internet-based.
> g Because they are curious to find out what their schoolmates are doing.
> h Because fewer people read than they used to.
> i Because they don't normally get the chance to talk about their reading with other people.

4 Check that students understand *appeals to you least* and give them time to discuss the questions. If the second question is too sensitive, tell students they do not have to answer it. When they have finished, ask students which way of meeting people appealed to their group least and why.

Language focus 1 (PAGES 108–109)

Review of future forms

See *Teacher's tips: using a discovery approach in the teaching of grammar* on page 8.

⌨ [T10.1] Introduce the context and write the following questions on the board: *What do James and Richard discuss? What do they decide?* Give students a minute to read the dialogue and then elicit answers to these questions. (They discuss the time, how to get there and the traffic. They decide to drive, and to meet at about four.) Set the activity and do the first example with the class. Put students into pairs to complete the activity, and then play the recording to check answers. Do not elicit explanations at this stage.

ANSWERS
See tapescript for recording 1 on page 172 of the *Students' Book*.

Analysis

1–4 For each exercise, read through the information with students and then put them into pairs to answer the questions. After each exercise, check answers and go through the language notes below. Then read through *Language summaries A, B* and *C* on pages 154–155 in the *Students' Book*.

ANSWERS AND LANGUAGE NOTES
1 Questions b and d are used.
   Question b uses the Present continuous. Form: *be + -ing*. This is used to express definite arrangements, i.e. the time, date, place, etc. have been arranged.
   Question d uses the *going to* future. Form: *be + going to + infinitive*. This is used to express definite arrangements and general intentions for the future. It has a wider use than the Present continuous. We can always use *going to* instead of the Present continuous when talking about the future, but the reverse is not true.
   Examples of definite arrangements: (a) *I'm going to take*; (b) *are playing*; (c) *we're having*; (k) *'s dropping*
   Examples of general intentions for the future: (i) *Are you going to take*; (j) *I'm going to drive*
2 Sentence b expresses a new idea. (We normally use the Future simple (*will / 'll / won't* + infinitive to express ideas/decisions made at the time of speaking. Another example in the dialogue is (l) *I'll pick you up*.)
   Sentence a expresses an old idea. (We normally use the *going to* future for ideas/decisions made some time before the moment of speaking. We can also use the Present continuous in this way, e.g. (c) *we're having lunch over at my mum's*.)
3 In sentence d, the Present simple is used because it expresses a timetabled action. (The Present simple is also used for dates that are absolutely set, e.g. *My birthday's on a Saturday this year*.)
   In sentences f, m and o, the Present simple is used because it comes after conjunctions that refer to the future, i.e. the conditional words *if* and *in case*, and

the time word *before*. (The Present simple is used after other conditional words, e.g. *unless*, and time words, e.g. *after* and *when*.)
4 Other examples of predictions: *I'm sure Mum* (e) *won't mind*; *it's* (n) *likely to be pretty busy*
   Further examples: *Look at those clouds, it's going to rain* (based on present evidence – the clouds); *The radio said it may well rain next week; could/might/may/ will probably*

PRACTICE

1 Put students into pairs and ask them to explain their answers. Check answers with the class.

ANSWERS AND LANGUAGE NOTES
a *'re going to paint* (a future intention; the decision was made before the time of speaking)
b *are you going; 're staying; 're buying* (definite arrangements; we do not normally use *going to* if the main verb is *go*, e.g. ~~Where are you going to go~~?)
c *'re going to call* (a future intention); *is, is* (both used after *if*)
d *leaves* (a timetable action); *'m going to have* (a future intention) / *'m having* (a definite arrangement; the choice of form depends on the speaker's intended meaning)
e *'ll finish* (a new idea; the decision is made at the time of speaking)
f *'s going to send* (a prediction based on present evidence)
g *'ll have* (a new idea; the decision is made at the time of speaking.)
h *'ll make* (a new idea; forms part of main clause); *forgets* (used after *in case*; forms part of subordinate clause)
i *'re going to stay / 're staying* (a definite arrangement; both forms are possible)
j *'ll be* (a prediction based on a belief or expectation)

2 Go through the topics and check that students understand *career* and *sporting fixtures*. Ask students to make notes on their topics individually, and walk round the room providing vocabulary. Put them into pairs to give their talks, making sure they take turns. While they are speaking, note any errors with future forms and correct these at the end of the activity.

ADDITIONAL PRACTICE

RB **Resource bank:** 10B The Supasaver debate (ways of expressing the future), pages 149–150

Workbook: *Will* and *going to*, page 73; *Going to* and Present continuous for intentions and arrangements, page 73; Present simple, page 73; Predictions, page 74

Task: Decide who's coming to dinner (PAGES 110–111)

Preparation: listening

1 Put students into pairs to discuss the questions and then elicit ideas from the class. It is not important at this stage if there are some people your students do not recognise from the cartoons. However, if your students do not recognise any of the people, prompt them by writing the names on the board and give a few of the facts below:

- **Elvis Presley**: the 'King' of rock-and-roll music (now dead)
- **David Beckham**: English footballer
- **Marge Simpson**: character in *The Simpsons* (a hugely popular American cartoon series)
- **Nelson Mandela**: former president of South Africa and human rights activist
- **Hillary Clinton**: US senator and wife of Bill Clinton (former US president)
- **Charles Darwin**: proponent of the theory of evolution.

> **ANSWERS**
> The picture is unusual because these people would not normally have dinner together. Allow students to guess freely why the people are all together at the dinner table.

2 [T10.2] Read through the information with students. Explain that they are going to hear six people speaking one after the other, not in conversation together. Tell them to write notes, and that you will play the recording twice if necessary. Play the recording, pausing after each speaker for students to write. After you have played all six speakers, ask students to compare their answers. Check answers as a class.

> **ANSWERS**
> See tapescript on page 172 of the *Students' Book*.

3 Give students a minute to think about the suggestions, then put them into groups to explain their answers. Ask students if they would invite the person they chose and the people other students chose to the same dinner party.

Task: speaking

1 Ask students to think of three or four possible guests. Emphasise that they can choose anyone at all as long as they are well known. If necessary, prompt students by giving different categories, e.g. pop stars, actors, politicians. Give students time to make notes about their guests. Walk round the room providing the vocabulary. After a few minutes, stop the class and go through *Useful language a*. Then give them the rest of the time to complete their notes and to think about how to incorporate the phrases you have just looked at.

2 Do not form groups larger than four because there will be too many guests to talk about. Read the instructions in the book with the students, and then briefly go through *Useful language b*. Give students plenty of time for their discussion but make sure there is a time limit, e.g. eight minutes.

3 Read through the instructions in the book with students and check that they understand *seating plan*. Briefly, go through *Useful language c*. Give students a time limit (a

maximum of ten minutes) to complete the activity, and tell them to include themselves in the final seating plan. Make sure each student has a copy of the guest list and seating plan.

4 Form new groups, making sure that each student in the group has a different seating plan. Set a time limit of about ten minutes and give regular time checks so that all students get a chance to talk about their plan.

Language focus 2 (PAGES 111–112)

Future continuous and Future perfect

See *Teacher's tips: using a discovery approach in the teaching of grammar* on page 8.

This should mostly be revision for students. They have already seen the Future continuous (Module 3) and the Future perfect (Module 5).

1 Give students a minute to think about the questions. Check that they understand *chat rooms* and *text messaging*. Then put them into pairs to compare their answers. For feedback, ask the class which was the most popular form of communication.

2 Introduce the activity and check that students understand *posting* and *attitude towards*. Give them thirty seconds to read the text and then to compare their answers with a partner. When you elicit ideas from the class, check that they understand *face-to-face*; *catch up with friends*; *hi-tech bubbles*; and *exaggerating*, or ask them to look in their mini-dictionaries.

3 To introduce this activity, ask students if they think the writer of the text in exercise 2 is realistic. Individually, students then make brief notes about at least three ideas of their own. Tell them not to worry about the grammar at this stage. When students have finished comparing their ideas, go through the *Analysis* and then ask them to re-write or correct their notes using the appropriate forms of the future.

> ### Language focus 2, exercise 3: alternative suggestion
>
> If your students need additional practice of these forms, follow the procedure for exercises 1 and 2, go through the *Analysis* on page 111 and read *Language summary D* on page 155. Then do exercise 3 and ask students to focus particularly on the use of the verb forms. Walk round the class, providing help with the grammar if necessary.

Analysis

1–3 Put students into pairs to answer the questions. For exercise 3, check that students understand *in the normal course of events*. You can either check answers after each exercise or wait until students have completed all three exercises. Write the example sentences on the board and copy the timelines from page 155 of the *Students' Book*. As you check answers, elicit the form and demonstrate meaning using the timelines. Finally, go through *Language summary D* on page 155.

ANSWERS AND LANGUAGE NOTES

1   b   (The use of the Future continuous here is the same as in all continuous tenses, i.e. the action is in progress at a particular time – it began before this time and continues after.)

2   a   (The Future perfect is used here to emphasise the action will start and finish before 3000, i.e. we will not be able to speak in 3000 because we will lose our voices before then. *By* is commonly used with the Future perfect to express this idea.)

3   c   (The future continuous is used here to emphasise that the action is inevitable from the writer's point of view. The action will happen as a result of other actions and situations, but there is no specific/organised plan.)

PRACTICE

1 a Put students into pairs to look at the picture on page 112 and briefly discuss the questions. Then ask them to read the short text and use their mini-dictionaries to check their ideas.

b Do the example with the class and show students that they can find the information in the schedule on page 112. Emphasise that they will need to add words such as articles. If necessary, write the example on the board and highlight the form. If students find this difficult, do the second question with them and highlight the Future perfect form.

ANSWERS
2   He'll have arrived at São Paulo airport. He'll have driven from the airport to the hotel. He'll have checked in at the hotel.
3   He'll be resting.
4   Yes, he will.
5   He'll be arriving at the British Consulate. He'll be having lunch with the Consul.
6   He'll have had lunch with the Consul.

c If you think your students will find this difficult, do questions 1 and 2 with them and highlight the form on the board. Alternatively, refer them to *Language summary D* on page 155 for examples of the form.

POSSIBLE ANSWERS AND LANGUAGE NOTE
1   *What will Jay be doing between 12.00 and 12.45? / at 12.30?*
2   *What will he have done by 1.00?*
3   *What will he have done by 3.00?*
4   *Will he have met his fans by 4.00?*
5   *What will he be doing between 5.00 and 6.00? / at 5.15?*
6   *What will he be doing between 6.00 and 7.00? / at 6.45?*

Times may be expressed using either a full point (*12.00*) or a colon (*12:00*). The former style is normally used in British English. The latter style is normally used in American English, but is becoming more common in British English.

Pronunciation

1 🔊 [T10.3] Play the first sentence and ask students to count the words. They might count fewer words than are actually in the sentence, but you can use this later to highlight that the contractions are two words. Play the other sentences, pausing after each one to give students time to count. Then play the sentences again, pausing after each one so that students can write them. When they have finished, ask them to compare their sentences in pairs and to decide if they counted the correct number of words. Check answers by writing the sentences on the board, and highlight the contractions. If students cannot hear the pronunciation, model the sentences yourself and exaggerate the contractions. Show students that in the first sentence, we write *He'll have* but it is pronounced *He'll 've*. Make sure you do not give the contracted forms too much stress.

ANSWERS
See tapescript on page 172 of the *Students' Book*.

2 Put students into pairs and walk round the room correcting their pronunciation of the contractions.

2 Students can work individually or in pairs. Ask students not to answer the questions at this stage. Walk round the class prompting students by asking questions such as *When will the action start*? *When will it finish*? If necessary, refer students back to the *Analysis* on page 111 and *Language summary D* on page 155. Check answers as a whole class.

ANSWERS
a   Will you be driving anywhere this weekend? Where do you think you'll be going?
b   Will you be sitting on a bus or train at any time today? What will you be doing while you're travelling?
c   By the end of the year, will you have travelled abroad anywhere?
d   Will you be eating at home tonight? Who'll be doing the cooking?
e   Do you think you'll have got married five years from now?
f   Do you think you'll be studying English this time next year?
g   When do you think we'll have finished this book?
h   Do you think people will be speaking English as an international language in 100 years' time?
i   Do you think you'll have retired by the time you're sixty?

3 If you have a very large class, choose the first option. Give students a few minutes to think about their answers to the questions before speaking to other students. Encourage them to ask more questions to find out further information. When they have finished, ask a few students to tell the class the most interesting/surprising answer they heard.

ADDITIONAL PRACTICE

RB **Resource bank:** 10C How about ten thirty? (Future continuous and Future perfect), page 151

Workbook: Future simple, perfect or continuous, page 76; Future perfect or continuous, page 77

Writing (PAGE 113)

Types of message

1 a Introduce the topic by asking students if they ever write messages and why. Go through the options and give students a few minutes to complete the activity. When you check answers, ask students to tell you how they know in each case.

> **ANSWERS**
> 4, 2, 1, 3, 5

b Check any language students may not understand, e.g. *delighted*; *considerate*; *set the video*; *ASAP*. For *C U*, show that this sounds like *see you*, and explain that it is common in text messages to use combinations of letters instead of words.

> **ANSWERS**
> a   We're all delighted for you!!
> b   Much love
> c   Can you let me know if these flights suit ASAP?
> d   I'll be out of the office tomorrow (Fri)
> e   Best wishes
> f   Please be more considerate in future
> g   C U all then
> h   Hope you had a good day at work
> i   By the way, can you set the video for me

2 Put students into pairs to find examples and answer the questions. Check answers as a class and highlight any conventions that are very different from the students' own language. In particular, spend time eliciting what words are represented by the letters and numbers in message 4. Remind students that these are used because they sound like the word.

> **ANSWERS AND LANGUAGE NOTES**
> 1   Message 1: *[I've] Just heard ...*
>   Message 2: *[The flight] Depart[s from]: LONDON LHR [at] 06.10*; the arrival and return details are also examples of missing words.
>   Message 5: *[I] Hope you had ... / [I've] Gone to [the] supermarket ... / [Is] Pasta OK? / [I'll be] Back [at] about eight. / Ring me if [there is] any problem.*
>   (Use the examples to show that it is common to miss out subject pronouns, auxiliary verbs, prepositions, articles, and words we can guess from the context.)
> 2   Message 4: *evry1 = everyone, get 2together = get-together, 4 = for, 2 = to, @ = at, u = you, b = be, 1 = one, ne1 = anyone, l8 = late*
>   Message 5: *XX = kisses*
>   (In message 4, students might read *l8* as *18 = eighteen*, so tell them the first letter is an *L*.)
> 3   Message 1: *great news! / CONGRATULATIONS!! / it is about time!*
>   Message 2: *LONDON LHR / MILAN MALPENSA*

Message 4: *turn up!*
Message 5: *Thanx!*

> 4   Message 4: *arrangin = arranging, skool = school, plz = please, bck = back, cos = because, dnt = don't, wana = want to*
>   Message 5: *sthg = something, Thanx = Thanks, 'n' = and*
>   (Use the examples to show that letters are missed out when the reader can guess the word without them, e.g. *bck*. We also substitute incorrect letters when they sound the same as the original word, e.g. *skool*.)
> 5   Message 2: *ASAP = as soon as possible, LHR = London Heathrow, Fri = Friday, Mon = Monday*
>   Message 3: *a.m. = ante meridiem (Latin for 'before noon'), No. = Number*
>   Message 4: *fri = Friday*
>   Message 5: *L = the first letter of someone's name*
> 6   Message 4: *im = I'm, dnt = don't*
>   (Use the examples to show that the reader can understand the words without the punctuation.)
>
> **Formal messages:** 2 and 3. (Message 3 is particularly formal, so it doesn't use most of the features above. Emphasise that it is the situation and the relationship between the people that determine the level of formality, e.g. a note pushed under someone's door can be formal if it is addressed to a stranger and the situation is 'serious'.)
> **Informal messages:** 1, 4 and 5

3 Select the situations that are most relevant to your students. Ask students to use phrases and features from exercises 1 and 2. Get students to exchange messages and read each other's.

ADDITIONAL PRACTICE

Workbook: Improve your writing: Inviting a speaker, page 78

Real life (PAGE 114)

Dealing with problems on the telephone

1 Set the activity and mention any annoying telephone situations that students can relate to. Encourage them to describe fully any situations they have been in themselves, particularly if these are similar to those in the recording.

2 🔲 [T10.4] Play the recording and give students time between listenings to compare answers in pairs or small groups. When you check answers, make sure students understand *lose someone* ('be unable to hear someone on the telephone because of a bad signal'); *you're breaking up*; *put you through*.

> **ANSWERS**
> **Conversation 1**
> a   A customer is talking to a furniture shop / furniture delivery service.
> b   The customer is using a mobile phone on a train and keeps losing the other speaker.
> c   The customer says he'll call back.

Conversation 2
a   A customer is listening to a recorded message for a gas company, then talking to a member of the sales team, then a customer service representative.
b   The customer is transferred from one department to another.
c   The customer service representative wants to check the customer's information again.

Conversation 3
a   A travel agent is talking to a customer.
b   The customer is interrupted by delivery men and her son.
c   The travel agent says she'll ring back.

3 **a** [T10.5] Explain that students are going to listen to some of the phrases used in the three conversations. Pause the recording after each sentence to give students time to write.

b Give students a few minutes to discuss the questions. Then refer them to the tapescript for recording 5 on page 173 to check their answers, and the tapescript for recording 4 on pages 173–174 to underline other useful phrases.

c Play the recording again, pausing after each sentence for students to repeat. Correct their pronunciation if necessary.

4 Go through the options with students and check any problem vocabulary, e.g. *to hang up*; *to get cut off*; *problems on the line*. Encourage students to use phrases from exercise 3 and other useful phrases they underlined in the tapescript for recording 4. Walk round the class prompting with ideas and helping with language. If you have a large class, select only a few pairs to act out their conversations.

ADDITIONAL PRACTICE

Workbook: Real life: Dealing with problems on the telephone, page 79

Study ... (PAGE 114)

Using the Internet (1): Key pals

Start by asking students if they write e-mails and who to. Introduce the phrase *key pal* and go through the introductory paragraph. Ask students how having a key pal could be good for their English. Read through the information and encourage them to use the Cutting Edge website after the class. In future lessons, ask if students have used the site/found a key pal, and if it is useful for practising their English.

Practise ... (PAGE 115)

This section can be done independently by students or you can use it for further practice of the language areas covered in Module 10, or as a test.

1–6 For each exercise, make sure students read the instructions carefully. If students find exercises 1–6 difficult, refer them to the appropriate pages in the *Students' Book* for help. Provide the answers by checking as a class or giving students a copy from the *Teacher's Resource Book*.

ANSWERS
1 Future forms
a 2   b 1   c 4   d 3

2 Making predictions
a certainly   b well   c likely   d chance   e gets
f certain

3 Future continuous or Future perfect
a will be travelling   b will have run out
c will have finished   d will be having
e will have been

4 Getting together
a at the dentist's   b conference   c party
d reunion   e date   f associates

5 Words that go together
a 3   b 4   c 5   d 1   e 2

6 Phrases for problems on the phone
a Am I calling at a <u>bad</u> time?
b Could you speak <u>up</u> a bit, please?
c I'll have to <u>put</u> you through to another department.
d I'm calling <u>about</u> your flight to Prague next month.
e When <u>would</u> be a good time to ring back?

Pronunciation spot

'Hard' and 'soft' letters
Go through the information with students and elicit the sounds of the letters 'c' and 'g', or model them yourself.
a Do the first example (*activities*) as a whole class and then put students into pairs to do the rest.
b [T10.6] Play the recording to check answers. Put students into pairs to practise, and encourage them to correct each other's pronunciation of the sounds.

ANSWERS
/k/: *candlelit, candidates, curious*
/s/: *embrace, social, celebrate, once*
/dʒ/: *arrange, marriage, registered*
Exceptions: *angered* /g/, *eager* /g/, *gives* /g/ (not before 'a', 'o'. 'u', 'l' or 'r')
Other pronunciations: *signed* (the 'g' is silent), *activities* (before 't')

Remember! (PAGE 115)

Give them a few minutes to tick the boxes, or ask them to do this at home if it is a personal record of achievement.

Mini-check (PAGE 160)

This can be done in class or set for homework. You can refer students to the *Language focus* sections in Module 10 or the relevant *Language summaries* on pages 154–155 for help.

ANSWERS
1 tries   2 will have finished   3 will be flying   4 gets
5 'm taking   6 to get   7 working   8 to talk   9 fallen
10 stops   11 meeting   12 alive   13 date   14 faint
15 certain   16 guests   17 through   18 on   19 on
20 up

module 11

Interfering with nature

Reading and vocabulary
(PAGES 116–117)

See *Teacher's tips: working with lexis* on pages 9–10.

1 Introduce the topic by asking students what they can see in the picture on page 116 and, if possible, elicit some of the vocabulary in bold. Individually, students then find the words and phrases in their mini-dictionaries and complete the activity.

2 Give students a couple of minutes to read the text, and then check ideas as a whole class. *Note:* as the text uses words such as *theoretically* and *potential*, emphasise that some of the students' answers may be right – nobody knows for sure at this time. Ask students not to use their dictionaries at this stage because they will be working on vocabulary later.

3 a 🔲 [T11.1] Put students into pairs to discuss the numbers. Explain that they are going to hear sentences containing the numbers, related to the text. Play the recording without pausing, and get students to change their answers if necessary.

b Tell students that the sentences from the recording do not appear in the same way in the text. If necessary, do the first example with the class. Then give students about five minutes to fill the gaps before checking answers as a whole class.

> **ANSWERS**
> 1 75   2 20th   3 1980s   4 1 million   5 2,000
> 6 1997   7 6   8 35   9 2010   10 24-hour

4 Before students begin the activity, check that they understand *without an end in sight* and *considered superior*, but do not use the phrases in the text to explain them. Ask students to underline the answers as they find them. When you check answers, provide further examples if necessary.

> **ANSWERS**
> a doubtful whether   b indefinitely   c all but
> d identical   e justification   f get rid of
> g deteriorate   h elite

5 Give students time to think about their answers before putting them into their groups. Encourage them to explain their opinions, and ask each other questions. *Note:* It is suggested that you stick to the ideas in the text at this stage, rather then discuss recent interesting cases in the newspapers, as this may pre-empt the task later in this module.

ADDITIONAL PRACTICE

Workbook: Vocabulary: Modern medical science, page 80; Vocabulary booster: Illness and injury, page 84

Language focus 1 (PAGES 118–119)
Hypothetical situations in the present

See *Teacher's tips: using a discovery approach in the teaching of grammar* on page 8.

1 a Focus students on the pictures. Before they discuss the similarities and differences, you could pre-teach some vocabulary around the theme of changing things physically, e.g. *alter, improve, reshape, enlarge, enhance, make something bigger/smaller*.

b Give students a maximum of thirty seconds to read the text. Elicit the connection between the pictures and check that students understand *face-lift, nose job, chin reduction, implants, liposuction*.

2 a Put students into pairs or small groups and encourage them to explain their opinion. However, do not allow the discussion to go on too long.

b Read through the statements and check students understand *to spare; what really matters; end up; Barbie dolls; plastic surgery*. Give them a couple of minutes to think about the question individually. Then put them back into pairs or small groups to discuss the statements briefly.

Analysis

1 Check that students understand *imaginary* and *hypothetical*. Read through the sentences before putting them into pairs to discuss their answers. Check answers and go through the language notes below.

> **ANSWERS AND LANGUAGE NOTES**
> a   imaginary/hypothetical
> b   past
> c   imaginary/hypothetical
> d   past
> e   imaginary/hypothetical
> f   imaginary/hypothetical
>
> Emphasise that the past form is used to express imaginary/hypothetical situations. All the examples are used to talk about present or general time. To check meaning of the imaginary/hypothetical situations, ask students questions such as *Do I have $100,000?* (No), *Will I have it in the future?* (Probably not), *Will everyone go out and do the same thing / have plastic surgery?* (No / Probably not). It would be useful to summarise the different forms used to introduce hypothetical ideas, and add a few extra on the board:
>
> *If / If only* + Past simple
> *I wish* + Past simple. (*Wish* here expresses something that you want, but do not expect to happen. It does not express a simple desire.)
> *What if* + Past simple
> *It's time* + Past simple. (This often expresses disapproval of the current situation, e.g. *It's time you went out and found a job because I can't afford to pay for everything myself.*)

Imagine + Past simple (e.g. *Imagine you had $100,000 to spare …*)

Suppose + Past simple (e.g. *Suppose everyone went out and did the same thing …*)

2–3 Give students a few minutes to discuss their answers and then go through the language notes below. It is important that students read *Language summary* A on page 155 before they do the *Practice* activities on page 119.

ANSWERS AND LANGUAGE NOTES

2   Statement 1: *If I had $100,000 to spare, I'd probably do …* (We cannot contract I had in the first clause. *I'd* in the second clause = *I would*. Form: *would (not/n't)* + infinitive without *to*. We cannot make the double contraction ~~I'dn't~~.)
Statement 2: *I wish people would think less …*
Statement 3: *We'd all end up looking like …* (Show students the full conditional form by extending the second sentence of the statement, i.e. *If everyone went out and did the same thing, we'd all end up looking like Barbie dolls!* We do not need to write the first clause here, because it is expressed in the first sentence of the statement.

3   To help students with the difference in meaning, extend the sentences as below:
*I wish **you spoke** English – but you don't.*
*I wish **you'd speak** English – I know you can, but you don't want to.*
The first sentence expresses a wish about the present that is opposite to the real situation. The second sentence expresses a wish about the present/future that you do not expect to happen; this form is often used to express disapproval of people's behaviour. The meaning here is 'You could change this situation if you wanted but I don't expect you will.' If students have problems understanding this form, write a few more examples with a clearer context on the board: *I wish **you wouldn't smoke** in the kitchen – it's disgusting. / I wish **you wouldn't talk** while I'm trying to watch TV – it's very irritating.*

PRACTICE

1   **a** Students can do this individually or in pairs, while you walk round the room, helping with form and meaning if necessary. If students find this activity difficult, refer them to *Language summary* A on page 155. Check answers as a class and go through the language notes before students do exercise 1b.

ANSWERS AND LANGUAGE NOTES

1   *were/was.* (We use *were* with *he/she/it* but some people consider this too formal; *was* is acceptable. However, *were* is much more common in the phrase *If I were you*, e.g. *If I were you, I'd take a break now.*)
2   *went*
3   *lost, 'd look*
4   *would invent.* (This expresses a wish about the present/future that you do not expect to happen.)

b Focus attention on the pictures. For picture 2, check students realise they need to decide what the man in bed is

thinking (not the people at the party). Elicit a couple of examples from the students and then put them into pairs to write their sentences. While they are working, walk round the room providing any additional vocabulary they need. Compare answers as a whole class.

POSSIBLE ANSWERS

2   I wish they'd be quiet / shut up / turn the music down. I wish I were/was at the party.
3   I wish / If only we could afford / had enough money to buy that house. If I had £1,000,000, I'd buy that house.
4   I wish you'd tidy your room. It's time you tidied your room.

2   **a** Students can work individually or in pairs to complete the questions. Check answers as a whole class before students do exercise 2b.

ANSWERS

1   had; would you change; would you prefer
2   could
3   could; would
4   had; would you choose
5   could; would you be
6   could

b Give students a few minutes to answer the questions individually before comparing with their partner. Encourage them to explain their answers, and to ask each other for more information if necessary.

3   **a** Students work individually. Explain the activity and give a few true examples of your own. Walk round the room helping students with the verb forms and providing any vocabulary they need.

b Encourage students to explain their answers, and to ask each other for more information if necessary. For feedback, ask students to tell the class the most interesting/surprising/unusual thing they heard.

> ### *Language focus 1*: additional suggestion
>
> To create interest in the topic, bring in some advertisements for cosmetic surgery clinics either in English or in the students' own language. Ask students what they advertise and if they have ever seen advertisements like these. Avoid asking students if they, or anyone they know, has had cosmetic surgery.

ADDITIONAL PRACTICE

Workbook: Talking about hypothetical situations in the present, page 81; *I wish* and *If only*, page 82; It's time, page 82

Language focus 2 (PAGES 120–121)

Hypothetical situations in the past

See *Teacher's tips: using a discovery approach in the teaching of grammar* on page 8.

1 Focus students on the picture and elicit *tattoo*. Put students into pairs or small groups to discuss the questions, and then elicit a few ideas from the class.

2 📟 [T11.2] Introduce Stuart and set the questions. Give students a couple of minutes to think about the questions, and elicit a few possible answers. Play the recording without pausing and then ask students to compare their answers before checking as a whole class.

> **ANSWERS**
> He'd wanted a tattoo for several years. Then a Japanese student gave him a card with his name in Japanese. He liked his Japanese name so much that he decided to have it tattooed on his shoulder. He regrets the tattoo now because the wrong name was written on the card; it says 'Sidney'.

3 📟 [T11.2] Ask the students to copy the three sentences into their notebooks with a bigger gap to write in. Play the recording, pausing after the appropriate sentences to give students time to write. Ask them to compare answers in pairs before referring them to the tapescript to check.

> **ANSWERS**
> See tapescript on page 173 of the *Students' Book*.

Analysis

1 Remind students of the Past perfect form (*had* + past participle) and then put them into pairs to discuss the questions. Students should be familiar with the Past perfect used in reported speech and to refer to earlier actions. Most will also have seen the *get something done* form. If they are unsure, go over the use in a later lesson but do not let it distract them from the hypothetical past form at this stage.

> **ANSWERS AND LANGUAGE NOTES**
> a *The cards **had got mixed up** by accident.* (The event happened before Stuart realised the mistake.)
> b *Everyone said it was the best tattoo they'd ever **seen** …*
> c *If I'd just **checked** with a Japanese person before I had the tattoo done!*

2 Set the exercise and read through the sentences with the class, showing them that you have to use the Past perfect to talk hypothetically about the past. Copy the first two example sentences onto the board, showing that there is a direct tense shift between the forms they looked at in Language focus 1 and these ones. Highlight form carefully.

> **ANSWERS AND LANGUAGE NOTES**
> *I wish / If only I **didn't have** this tattoo.*
> wish / if only + Past simple = general/present

*I wish / If only I **had checked** what the card said.*
wish / if only + Past perfect = past

Copy the second set of sentences onto the board and for both clauses of each sentence, ask students if the verb refers to the past or is general/present. Use the first two sentences to show that there is a direct tense shift here, i.e. if the 'reality' is in the past, we use the Past perfect to talk about it hypothetically. If the 'reality' is in the present, we use the Past simple to talk about it hypothetically. Highlight the verb forms carefully, drawing particular attention to *would (n't) have* + past participle.

If + Past perfect = past	*would have* + past participle = past
*If he **had checked** with …,*	*he **would have got** the right name.*
(But he didn't.)	(But he didn't.)
If + Past simple = general/present	*would* + verb = general/present
*If it **wasn't** so expensive …,*	*he **would get** rid of it*
(But it is.)	(But he isn't going to.)

Use the third sentence to show that that these forms can be mixed, so that you can talk about the past and the present/general together.

If + Past perfect = past	*would* + verb = general/present
*If he **hadn't met** the girls,*	*he still **wouldn't know** what the letters said.*
(But he did.)	(But he does.)

Read through *Language summary B* on page 156 with students and explain any further problems before they do the *Practice* exercises.

PRACTICE

1 a Students work individually or in pairs. Do the first example as a whole class, highlighting the tenses and the position of *never*. Ask students to write the complete sentences in their notebooks so that they have space to write the answers. Check that they understand *open my mouth* (= say something) and *set eyes on someone* (= meet someone). Walk round the room helping with verb forms. Go through the answers and language notes with the class. Where there are alternative answers, ask students to explain what the difference in meaning is.

> **ANSWERS AND LANGUAGE NOTES**
> 2 *hadn't done*
> 3 *'d/had bought*
> 4 *hadn't met; would be* (= now) / *would have been* (= in the past)
> 5 *'d/had allowed*
> 6 *'d/had tried*
> 7 *would be; didn't open* (= now) / *would have been; hadn't opened* (= past) / *would be* (= now); *hadn't opened* (= past)
> 8 *'d/had never gone*
> 9 *could*
> 10 *'d/had never set*

o To demonstrate the activity, give a true example of your own or use the example in the *Students' Book*. Then give students a few minutes to think of their situations. If you are short of time, reduce the number of situations students write about. While they are working, walk round the room providing any vocabulary they need and helping with verb forms. When they have finished, either ask students to tell their partner about the situations or select a few students to read their ideas to the rest of the class.

2 a 🔲 [T11.3] Focus students on the pictures and introduce the context and characters. If necessary, pre-teach *antique* (both adjective and noun), *burgle*, *charming*, *gambling*, *row* (= argument). Ask students to read the questions and then to make short notes while they listen. Pause the recording after each section to give students time to write. Get them to compare answers with a partner before eliciting answers from the class.

ANSWERS
See tapescript on page 174 of the *Students' Book*.

b Put students into pairs or small groups and check that they understand *foolishly*. Set the activity and encourage students to explain their opinions. Discuss the questions with the whole class.

c Students work individually or in pairs while you walk round the room helping with vocabulary and verb forms. Select a few students to read a couple of their sentences to the class.

3 a Give students a few minutes to decide on their character, and prompt with ideas if necessary. Make sure students discuss the details of the story before they do the next part of this activity.

b Individually, give students a few minutes to think about their questions or explanations. Then put them back in their pairs to prepare the interview. Walk round the room providing any additional vocabulary they need.

c Set a time limit for each interview and ask students to take a few notes while they listen. Note down any errors with the use of hypothetical language and provide correction when all the interviews are finished.

Practice, exercise 3: alternative suggestions

- If you do not think students will be able to think of a suitable character, bring in some magazine or newspaper articles about something a person regrets. They can read these and then base their character on the person in the article.

- If you have a large class, put students into groups for exercise 3C and follow the procedure as above, or select only a few pairs to act out their interviews.

ADDITIONAL PRACTICE

RB **Resource bank:** 11B I wish he wouldn't do that! (wishes in the past and present), page 153; 11C A nightmare holiday (third conditional and *should have*), pages 154–155

Workbook: Talking about hypothetical situations in the past, page 84; Using auxiliaries with *I wish* and *If only*, page 85

Real life (PAGE 121)

Giving and reporting opinions

1 🔲 [T11.4] Read out the three issues and check any problem vocabulary, e.g. *banned*; *illegal*; *surrogate mothers*. Then introduce the recording and set the activity. Explain that each person talks about just one of the issues. Pause after each speaker to allow students to make notes. Ask them to compare answers with a partner before playing the recording again and eliciting the answers.

ANSWERS
1 surrogate mothers; no, shouldn't be illegal
2 smoking in the workplace; yes, should be banned
3 experiments on animals; should be banned for cosmetics, but not for medical research
4 experiments on animals; should be controlled rather than banned
5 surrogate mothers; yes, should be illegal
6 smoking in the workplace; no, shouldn't be banned

2 Explain the activity and give students a few minutes to complete it. As you check answers, put each phrase into an example sentence so students can see how it is used.

ANSWERS
1 As far as I'm concerned (1)
2 I haven't really thought about it (3)
3 If you ask me (1)
4 I'm absolutely convinced that (1)
5 I've no doubt that (1)
6 It's often said that (2)
7 Many people would say that (2)
8 To be honest (1)

Pronunciation

1 🔲 [T11.5] Play the recording, pausing after each sentence to allow students to write their answers. As you check answers, ask students which words are stressed.

ANSWERS
See tapescript on page 174 of the *Students' Book*.

2 Either play the recording again or read the sentences yourself, exaggerating the stress and intonation a little so that students can hear it. Get students to repeat each sentence, and correct if necessary.

3 This stage can be omitted if you feel students will be overloaded. Or, if you want to increase the challenge, you could play recording 4 again and get students to listen and note the phrases, instead of looking for them in the tapescript.

ANSWERS
See tapescript on pages 173–174 of the *Students' Book*.

ADDITIONAL PRACTICE

Workbook: Real life: Giving and reporting opinions, page 85

Task: Make the right decision

(PAGES 122–123)

See *Teacher's tips: making tasks work* on pages 13–14.

Preparation: reading and listening

1 Explain that the texts are about moral problems in modern medicine and, if possible, elicit a few such cases from the students or give an example yourself. Check that students understand *dilemma*. When they have found the vocabulary in their mini-dictionaries, give them a couple of minutes to read the texts and then, in pairs, to summarise the problems. Check the dilemmas in open class to make sure students have understood the texts, and elicit the meaning of *treatable*.

2 [T11.6] Tell students that this is an authentic, unscripted discussion so there are a few 'false starts', unfinished sentences and interruptions. Emphasise that they do not need to understand everything. Read through the questions and then play the recording. Ask students to make brief notes while they listen and then to compare with a partner.

> **ANSWERS**
> a   the second case.
> b   **Arguments for:** she's aware of the condition she's in; she knows she can no longer do what other people can do; depression probably won't be cured in someone who can't move.
> **Arguments against:** the doctors can and should improve her quality of life; her depression might get better; people can live a full life and do amazing things even though they can't move.

3 [T11.7] Explain that students are just going to hear the phrases. Tell them to write complete answers in their notebooks, as they will have more space. Play the recording, pausing after each sentence to give students time to write. Refer students to the tapescript to check answers.

> **ANSWERS**
> See tapescript on page 174 of the *Students' Book*.

Task: speaking

1 **a** Make sure that every case has been chosen by at least two pairs. If you do not have enough students to do this, limit their choice to just two of the cases. Emphasise that they need to think of arguments for and against, and not just their own opinions. To demonstrate this, give an argument for and against the first question, e.g. *For: it's wrong to let a child die if the technology exists to save him/her. Against: parents may want to select embryos for other reasons – sex, hair colour, etc.*

b Go through *Useful language a* and give students five to ten minutes to write their arguments down. Walk round the class providing any vocabulary they need.

2 Put students into groups with others who discussed the same dilemma, but make sure there are not more than four to six students in each group. Go through *Useful language b* and *c* explaining any problem phrases, and remind students of the phrases from exercise 3 on page 122. Set a time limit and

emphasise that each group should reach agreement by the end of the activity. Walk round the room and note any errors (particularly with the use of hypothetical forms) for correction at the end of the lesson. If some groups finish quickly, ask them to discuss another case.

3 Give students a few minutes to think about how to present their arguments and conclusions to the rest of the class. Discuss each dilemma in turn, bringing in all the groups that discussed that case. Select one of the groups to present their case formally, and ask the other groups to contribute. To round up the activity, ask the class to vote on the most difficult dilemma and the best solution.

Writing (PAGE 124)

For and against essay

1 Introduce the activity by referring to the task on pages 122–123 and telling students that they are going to practise expressing arguments more formally, in writing. Ask students if they think smoking should be banned in public places, but do not encourage too much discussion at this stage. Tell them to read the text and, if necessary, check the meaning of *overwhelmingly*, *outlawed*, *legislation*, *critics*, *enforce*, *sparked*, *chaos* and *passive smoking* in their mini-dictionaries.

> **ANSWERS**
> **In favour:** a ban would cut deaths from lung cancer and heart disease.
> **Against:** a ban would be difficult to enforce.

2 Put students into pairs and set the activity. Check answers as a whole class and ask students to underline any phrases which they think will be useful when writing the essay.

> **ANSWERS**
> a against   b against   c against   d for
> e for   f against

3 Read through the categories and demonstrate the activity by doing one or two examples with the class. Tell students that some phrases can go in more than one category. Check answers as a whole class by writing the categories on the board and eliciting the phrases. If necessary, give examples to show each phrase in use.

> **ANSWERS**
> **Introduction:** Many people nowadays think that / It is certainly true that / Over the last few years
> **Arguments for:** Another point in favour of … is / Firstly, / Secondly,
> **Arguments against:** One argument against … is / On the other hand / Firstly, / Secondly,
> **Conclusion:** It is certainly true that / There are two main reasons why I think / In my opinion / Firstly, / Secondly, / To sum up, / In conclusion,

4 Go through the options and check understanding of any problem words or phrases. Give students a few minutes to choose their title. Tell students to plan their essay by making notes under each category in exercise 3 and to ask you for any additional vocabulary they need. Then ask students to write a first draft and give it to another student to check for spelling, punctuation, etc. They can either write the final draft in class or you can set it as homework.

Writing: alternative suggestions

- If students cannot think of sufficient arguments for and against a particular topic, brainstorm ideas as a class and write them on the board. Alternatively, get students to brainstorm ideas in pairs or small groups.
- If students are not interested in any of the titles provided, give them a list of options more relevant to their culture/context or ask them to think of a title themselves.

ADDITIONAL PRACTICE

Workbook: Improve your writing: Reporting opinions, page 86

Study ... (PAGE 124)

Using the Internet (2): Ideas for using online news

Introduce this section by asking students how often they read English-language websites and what the benefits are. Then read through the introductory paragraph with the class and provide a few suggestions for news websites, e.g. http://news.google.com, www.reuters.com, www.bbc.co.uk, www.ft.com.

   Ask students to read the suggestions in the bullet points and tick the ones they would like to try. In future lessons, ask students which suggestions they have used and if they found them useful.

Practise ... (PAGE 125)

This section can be done independently by students or you can use it for further practice of the language areas covered in Module 11, or as a test.

1–6 For each exercise, make sure students read the instructions carefully. If students find exercises 1–6 very difficult, refer them to the appropriate pages in the *Students' Book* for extra help. Provide the answers either by checking as a whole class or giving students a copy from the *Teacher's Resource Book*.

ANSWERS

1 **Hypothetical situations in the present**
a I'd buy a new motorbike
b I used to go swimming every day
c unfortunately I have to go now
d you started looking for a job
e all the time

2 **Hypothetical situations in the past**
a you'd b I had c would have
d 'd be working e would

---

3 **Giving and reporting opinions**
a concerned b say c convinced d honest
e no f thought g you h said

4 **Verb forms**
a be found b to have c improving
d would be e were frozen

5 **Word building**
a immortality b doubtful c justification
d eliminate e poverty

6 **For and against**
a 2 b 1 c 5 d 3 e 4

Pronunciation spot (PAGE 125)

Rhyming sounds

a Give students a few minutes to find the meaning of unknown words in their mini-dictionaries. Put students into pairs and demonstrate the activity by modelling *bleak*, then reading the three words in the first group and eliciting which word rhymes. Students complete the activity in pairs, taking it in turns to say the words out loud. Encourage them to guess if they are not sure.

b 📼 [T11.8] Play the recording for students to check their answers. While students practise the words, walk round the class correcting pronunciation if necessary.

ANSWERS
a week b mud c keys d sweet e stuff
f bed g part h hear

Remember! (PAGE 125)

Give them a few minutes to tick the boxes, or ask them to do this at home if it is a personal record of achievement.

Mini-check (PAGE 160)

This can be done in class or set for homework. You can refer students to the *Language focus* sections in Module 11 or the relevant *Language summaries* on pages 155–156 for help.

ANSWERS
1 had known 2 could 3 would be 4 made
5 would hurry up 6 would be watching 7 To be
8 be found 9 to get married 10 said 11 On 12 from
13 have 14 for 15 on 16 had 17 doubtful
18 concerned 19 poverty 20 conclusion

module 12

Media mania

Vocabulary and speaking (PAGE 126)

Types of media

1 **a** Start by asking students to describe the pictures. Use the pictures to elicit *magazine, current affairs programme, sitcom* and *live sports coverage*, and ask them if they have similar media in their country. Then ask students to categorise the words/phrases in the box that they know before checking the others in their mini-dictionaries. Tell them some of the words/phrases belong to more than one category. Write the three categories on the board and elicit answers from students, putting each one under the appropriate category.

ANSWERS
1   chat shows, live sports coverage, current affairs programmes, sitcoms, phone-ins, documentaries, soaps, traffic reports
2   tabloids, comics
3   chat shows, live sports coverage, current affairs programmes, sitcoms, phone-ins, documentaries, soaps, traffic reports

b Give students a few minutes to think of more examples and then elicit these and write them on the board, checking meaning as you do so. Ask students to copy all new items into their notebooks.

2 Put students into groups to discuss the questions. They can give an English-language example or one from their own country. If the example they choose is unknown to the other students in their group, tell them to describe it. For feedback, ask students which was the most/least popular type of programme in their group.

3 **a** Students can work individually or in pairs. Encourage them to think of examples for the words/phrases they know before checking the others in their mini-dictionaries.

POSSIBLE ANSWERS
1 **Informative:** current affairs programmes, documentaries, traffic reports
2 **Controversial:** tabloids, current affairs programmes, documentaries
3 **Influential:** documentaries, current affairs programmes, tabloids
4 **Sensational:** chat shows, tabloids, soaps
5 **Often biased:** live sports coverage, tabloids, current affairs programmes, documentaries
6 **Entertaining:** chat shows, live sports coverage, tabloids, comics, sitcoms, phone-ins, documentaries, soaps
7 **Addictive:** chat shows, tabloids, comics, sitcoms, soaps
8 **Harmless fun:** tabloids, comics, sitcoms, soaps

9 **Mindless rubbish:** chat shows, tabloids, comics, sitcoms, soaps
10 **Usually worth watching:** current affairs programmes, sitcoms, documentaries, soaps
11 **Aimed mainly at men:** live sports coverage, tabloids, comics
12 **Aimed mainly at women:** chat shows, sitcoms, soaps

b Students can talk about types of programme, e.g. documentaries, or specific examples, e.g. *The Simpsons*. Many of the answers will depend on students' opinions, so tell them to explain their answers and ask each other for clarification. If some of the opinions expressed are controversial, you could extend the speaking by asking the class to discuss these items.

Pronunciation

[T12.1] Put students into pairs and give them time to mark the stress before listening to the recording. While they are working, write the adjectives on the board. Play the recording, and give students time to change their answers if necessary. Elicit answers and mark the stress on the board. Play the recording again and get students to repeat after each word.

ANSWERS
1 informative   2 controversial   3 influential

4 sensational   5 biased   6 entertaining

7 addictive   8 harmless   9 mindless

ADDITIONAL PRACTICE

Workbook: Vocabulary booster: The media, page 87

Speaking and listening (PAGE 127)

The media game

1 Put students into groups of no more than six. Get them to go through the vocabulary on the board in their groups, helping each other where they can. Then get them to look up any they are not sure about in their mini-dictionaries. Give each group a dice and ask them to use coins as counters. Go through the instructions with the class, and do an example with them. Select a student in each group to time the others as they speak about the topics. If a group finishes quickly, ask them to start the game again. At the end, ask who won in each group.

2 [T12.2] These are authentic recordings, so tell students they may not understand everything but they should note down what they can. Explain that they are going to listen to four people talking about four different topics. Pause after each speaker to give students time to write notes. After you have checked the answers for questions a and b, give students time to think about question c and then to compare their opinions in groups.

ANSWERS AND LANGUAGE NOTE
1 a what she does and doesn't read in the newspaper
  b She doesn't read the financial pages, sports pages or editorials, because they are usually boring; she likes the arts pages, reviews of new books and films, and (in Sunday papers) reviews of the week.
2 a sport on television
  b The best sports programmes are on cable and satellite, which he likes watching in the pub. (Note that he says *down the pub*, a colloquial way of saying *in the pub*.) On his TV at home the matches are not very good, as they feature the lower divisions of English football, or there are sports that he doesn't like, e.g. cricket and bowls.
3 a violence on television
  b There is violence on TV all day on one of the channels, either in cartoons or adverts. She has become more aware of this since she had a child.
4 a television commercials that she really hates
  b She especially hates perfume adverts, because the women in them are supposed to be beautiful and sophisticated, but they wear ridiculous clothes and do stupid things.

Language focus 1 (PAGES 128–129)

Reporting people's exact words

See *Teacher's tips: using a discovery approach in the teaching of grammar* on page 8.

1 Introduce the idea of *unfortunate quotes*, set the activity and read through the introductory paragraph with the class. Students read the quotes individually, and then explain their choice to a partner. If students find some of the quotes impossible to understand, briefly explain the meaning.

2 Establish that the quotes in exercise 1 are in direct speech, and show students the inverted commas. Students underline the differences and then compare with a partner. Elicit the underlined sections and write them on the board.

ANSWERS
a The weather forecaster told viewers that they were unable to report on
  they depended on
  was closed
  He said they did not know
  they would be able to give a
  the next day
  as it depended on
b The newsreader said that traffic was heavy, and that if people were thinking
  leaving home at that moment, they should
c The journalist asked the Prime Minister if he ran
  if he didn't succeed
d She said that smoking kills, and that if you are killed, you have lost

e The President said that
  in America there were roughly
  He said that this was unacceptable
  and that they were going to
f The coach told reporters that the team's main strength
  was that they did not have
  However, he added that their main weakness was that they didn't have

Analysis

If you think students will find this activity difficult, go through the questions with them. Otherwise, put students into pairs and give them time to answer the questions. Check that they understand *interjections* and give 'Folks' in Quote e) as an example. When they have finished, go through the answers and language notes below. Go through *Language summary* A with the class before they do the Practice activities on page 129.

ANSWERS AND LANGUAGE NOTE
1 In reported speech, verbs generally move one tense 'back' into the past, e.g. in quote a: *are/were unable, depend/depended, is/was closed, will/would be able, depends/depended*. (Elicit more examples from the students.)
2 Verb tenses stay the same in quote d, because what the campaigner says is still true/relevant now. A tense change often happens because the action referred to is now in the past, but this is not the case in d, i.e. smoking still kills. (However, we could change the tenses in d into the past if were reporting in a more formal context, e.g. a newspaper.)
3 Quote a: *told, said*. Forms: *tell* + object noun/pronoun (*viewers*) + (*that*); *say* + (*that*) + subject noun/pronoun (*they*).
  Quote b: *said*
  Quote c: *asked*. Form: *ask* + object noun/pronoun (*The Prime Minister*) + *if/when/whether/why*.
  Quote d: *said*
  Quote e: *said*
  Quote f: *told, added*. Form: *add* + *that* + subject noun/pronoun (*their main weakness*).
4 The conjunctions *that* and *if* follow the reporting verbs. (*That* is optional after *say* and *tell*. In quote c, *if* is used after *asked* because the question is of a yes/no type, i.e. *Do you run the risk of failure?* requires the answer yes/no. *Whether* can be used in the same way.)
  That is repeated in quote e to refer back to the reporting verb (*said*) and the speaker (*The President*). *That* could be omitted from the sentence, but then it might not be so clear who the speaker was.
5 The forms are different:
  say + (*that*) + subject, e.g. in quote b: *The newsreader said that traffic was ...*
  tell + object + (*that*), e.g. in quote f: *The coach told reporters that ...*
  (*That* is optional in both these forms. Elicit more examples from the students.)

6 In reported speech, pronouns change to nouns or
other pronouns to show clearly who is speaking. In
quote a, *The weather forecaster* makes it clearer than
he/she who is saying the words; *they* replaces *we*,
otherwise the reported quote would not be true or
make sense. In quote c, *he* is substituted for *you*, as
the quoted journalist is no longer asking the Prime
Minister directly, and so we must describe him in the
third person.

  Time words also change to show the new
situation. In quote a, *the next day* is used instead of
tomorrow, otherwise the reported quote would not be
true or make sense.

7 Interjections like *folks* tend to be omitted from
reported speech because they are specific to the
actual words spoken by a particular person.

8 Reported questions are not real questions, so the
word order is the same as in statements, e.g. in
quote c: *The journalist asked the Prime Minister if **he
ran** the risk.* The auxiliary *Do* is omitted in the
reported version of c, because we do not generally
use it in a positive statement. Hence, there is no
inversion of subject and verb here, as in some other
direct and reported questions, e.g. ***Will you** help me?
/ She asked if **I would** help her.*

PRACTICE

1 Put students into pairs and walk round the class helping
with the verb forms. Elicit the answers and write them on
the board highlighting the changes.

ANSWERS AND LANGUAGE NOTE

g *The news reporter said (that) most cars on our roads
have only one occupant who is usually the driver.* (The
tenses will probably not change in the reported
version because the content is still true/relevant.
However, students are not wrong if they have
changed the tenses.)

h *The news report said (that) Mao Tse Deng's health was
failing at that time, and that many matters had been
passed to Wan Li, who, despite his age, was still alive.*

i *The police said (that) the streets of Philadelphia were
safe, and that it was only the people that made them
unsafe.*

j *The American footballer said (that) the word genius
wasn't applicable in football, and that a genius was a
guy like Norman Einstein.*

k *The England football manager said (that) if history
repeated itself that night, they could expect the same
thing to happen again.*

l *The baseball player said (that) journalists sometimes
wrote what he said and not what he really meant.*

2 Students can do this in pairs. Emphasise that they should
only change the underlined parts, and that they should read
the rest of the sentence carefully to understand the context.

ANSWERS

a asked; if/whether he knew
b told; would; was
c said; the day before / the previous day / that day;
   that
d asked; he would make
e was; that; would

3 a Ask if students can think of a time when something has
not been reported accurately. Focus attention on the
pictures, and read the speech bubbles aloud, dealing with any
vocabulary problems. In each case, elicit what the situation is
and what the people claim was said, in direct speech. Ask
students to speculate briefly about what each person really
said.

b [T12.3] Tell students that they are going to hear the
original conversations and to make notes about what was said
in each case. Emphasise that they do not have to report exactly
what was said, but that the overall content should be the same.
As you check answers, show how the underlined words should
be stressed because they correct what was said before.

POSSIBLE ANSWERS

1 Actually, she said (that) she didn't/doesn't have any
   plans to start a family at the moment.
2 Actually, she said (that) it was quite important and
   asked if her daughter would call her back.
3 Actually, she asked if she'd borrowed any money
   from her purse.
4 Actually, she asked if he wanted to go out for a
   dinner with a group of people, and the man said
   (that) he might go.
5 Actually, she said that the little boy could play for
   ten minutes only, but that after that it was the girl's
   turn.

Pronunciation

1 [T12.4] Explain that students are going to hear two
people saying the same thing but in different ways. Play
the recording and get students to compare answers in
pairs before checking as a whole class.

ANSWERS

A thinks Debbie is telling the truth. The extra stress on
said means that B thinks Debbie is lying. B also puts
slightly more stress on *ill* and exaggerates the
intonation pattern to show he believes the opposite
is true.

2 [T12.5] Students write letters a–h in their notebooks.
Explain that they are going to hear eight people
reporting what other people said, and that they must put
a tick next to the letter if the person thought the speaker
was telling the truth, or a cross if the person thought the
speaker wasn't telling the truth. Check and ask students
how they know which people thought the speakers
weren't telling the truth. (Answer: these people stress the
reporting verbs to show their disbelief.)

3 [T12.5] Refer students to the tapescript to check their answers for exercise 2. Tell them that the stressed reporting verbs are underlined. Then ask them to underline other words that are stressed, e.g. *easy* in sentence c and *early* in sentence g. Put them into pairs to practise saying the sentences.

ANSWERS

See tapescript on page 175 of the *Students' Book.*

ADDITIONAL PRACTICE

Workbook: Reporting people's exact words, page 88

Reading and speaking

(PAGES 130–131)

1 Start by asking students if they like TV, and what kind of programmes they watch. Introduce the phrase *telly addict* and ask students if they know what it means. Go through the questions and check that students understand *give up*. Give students about five minutes to discuss the questions, and then elicit ideas about why someone might give up TV.

2 Go through the sentences, explaining any problem vocabulary. Then give students a maximum of one minute to read the text and compare their answers in pairs. As you check answers with the class, ask if any of their reasons for giving up TV from exercise 1 are mentioned in the text.

ANSWER

sentence c

3 Set a longer time limit than in exercise 2, and pre-teach *Ceefax* (a service with only written text on the television, i.e. no people presenting it). Tell students not to worry about other vocabulary at this stage. Get students to compare answers with a partner before checking as a whole class. Refer to the text for clarification if students give any wrong answers.

ANSWERS

sentences a and b

4 Explain *colourful, figurative language* and *literal meaning*. Students check the meaning individually and then compare answers with a partner. Make sure students have found the correct literal definition. Then give them time to answer the questions in pairs. Tell students they will have to infer from the text and say what they think rather than find set answers. If necessary, do the first question as a whole class.

ANSWERS

a He uses these words to make us think about eating excessively. Excessive eating is often considered a bad/immoral act, and he makes us feel that watching TV is the same.
b The phrase gives the impression that he had no purpose and no energy. The activity was a waste of time, and he put no effort into it.

c He uses this phrase to make us think of strong human emotions and to see how his relationship with the TV was as intense as a human relationship. He is, of course, exaggerating in order to be funny.
d He continues the same 'human relationship' image by making the situation sound as if he was an over-demanding lover, and TV (like a person) needed to take a break from him. More literally he means that TV used to stop broadcasting at certain times of the day, i.e. at night, so he was forced to stop watching.
e He is continuing the 'human relationship' image. If someone starts hating you, it is easy to stop spending time with them; in this case he found it easy to stop spending time with TV. In all these 'human' images, he is comically shifting the blame away from himself and on to TV.
f The comparison is with a lover being unfaithful (sexually and emotionally) to you. Although he loved TV, it never really made him happy.

5 Give students time to think about the questions before putting them into groups. Encourage them to explain their answers and to ask each other questions.

ADDITIONAL PRACTICE

Workbook: Vocabulary: TV programmes, page 87

Wordspot (PAGE 131)

speak and *talk*

1 [T12.6] Put students into pairs and tell them to read each context carefully before completing the gaps. Explain that they will just hear the words that go into the gaps on the recording, not the complete sentences. Play the recording, and give students time to change their answers if necessary. Then go through the answers and, if need be, provide more examples to reinforce the meaning of the phrases.

ANSWERS

See tapescript on page 175 of the *Students' Book.*

2 a The main aim of this activity is for students to process the phrases to help them memorise them. Ask students to copy a bigger version of the diagrams into their notebooks.

b The aim of this further activity is to check that students understand the phrases. Give them time to read the sentences again and to ask questions if they need to. Then refer them to the questions on page 141 and check that they understand *saying* and *host*. Students answer the questions individually before comparing with a partner.

ANSWERS

a open answer
b You don't like them or you don't care about them. (They may have upset you.)
c actions   d open answer   e open answer
f pleased
g open answer (but probably eccentricity, madness, loneliness, forgetfulness)

h open answer
i work (generally with their colleagues)
j open answer
k politicians, peace campaigners, etc.
l parties, etc.
m open answer

ADDITIONAL PRACTICE

Workbook: Wordspot: speak and talk, page 89

Language focus 2 (PAGES 132–133)

Verbs that summarise what people say

Set the activity but do not pre-teach any vocabulary, as this may give students the answers. As you check answers, give the meaning of new words, e.g. *deaf, criticise, achievement.*

POSSIBLE ANSWERS
a the manager of a sports team
b a politician
c a film star / the manager of a sports team / a politician
d the manager of a sports team
e a politician
f a film star
g the manager of a sports team
h the manager of a sports team

Analysis

1 Read through the information and examples as a class, checking that students understand *admitted, accused, refused to*. Put students into pairs to discuss the form while you copy the sentences onto the board. Highlight form as you go through the answers and language notes below. Emphasise that some verbs can use more than one construction, and students should check in their dictionaries if necessary.

ANSWERS AND LANGUAGE NOTE
admit + (*that*) + object. (If we want to show that the speaker admits doing something himself, we use *admit* + gerund, e.g. *He admitted taking the money.* We can also say *He admitted that he had taken the money.*)
accuse + object + preposition + gerund
refuse + *to* infinitive

2 a Give students a couple of minutes to match the verbs to the quotes. Check that they have done this correctly before they do exercise 2b.

b Check that students have correctly identified the form of each verb before they re-write the quotes. While students re-write the quotes, walk round the room helping with the form of the verbs. As you elicit answers from the class, point out the form of each verb again. If need be, copy the answers below onto the board and use this to highlight form. Read through *Language summary B* on page 157 with students before they do the *Practice* exercises.

ANSWERS AND LANGUAGE NOTES
apologise: quote f. (The first sentence of f demonstrates *apologise.*)
Form: *apologise* + *for* + gerund
deny: quotes g and h. (The first sentence of g and the first clause of h demonstrate *deny.*)
Form: *deny* + gerund
insist: quotes g and h. (The second sentence of g and the second clause of h demonstrate *insist.*)
Form: *insist* + (*that*) or *insist* + *on* + gerund
suggest: quotes e and f. (The whole of e and the second sentence of f demonstrate *suggest.*)
Form: *suggest* + (*that*) or *suggest* + gerund
tell: quote d. (The first sentence of d demonstrates *tell.* In this case, *tell* means 'order' and must not be confused with *tell* meaning 'say'.)
Form: *tell* + object + *to* infinitive

Suggested answers for re-written sentences
d The manager told us to speak up because all the shouting he'd done in the second half had made him a bit deaf.
e The politician suggested that we stopped criticising the government and wrote about its achievements (instead).
f The film star apologised for hitting the photographer at the Oscar ceremony, and suggested (that) he had only been doing his job.
g The manager denied swearing at the referee and insisted he had only been giving him a little advice.
h The manager denied what had been written about his future. He insisted that he was very happy at the club and had no intention of leaving.

PRACTICE

1 To introduce the topic, focus students on the picture and briefly discuss the questions as a whole class.

2 Read through the questions and check that students understand *prize* and *role.* Give students time to read and answer the questions before checking answers with the class.

ANSWERS
a Because Martyn had thrown the tickets away several weeks earlier.
b Because the Totts had broken the rules by not reporting their lost tickets within thirty days.
c They told the media about their story.
d The media encouraged the couple to tell their story in the newspapers and on TV, with the aim of confronting Camelot.

3 Students can work in pairs to complete the gaps. Walk round the room helping with form and refer students to their mini-dictionaries if necessary. Check answers as a class.

ANSWERS
a watching / that they watch   b had failed
c wanted   d throwing
e her husband to get in touch / that he should get
   in touch
f to investigate   g the Totts (that) they had
h the couple not to inform   i had broken
j to pay out   k him to leave   l to inform
m to put   n the couple to appear
o for causing   p (that) they had to follow
q Camelot of ruining their lives   r to sue
s making   t the media for raising

4 Put students into pairs and tell them to refer to the text in exercise 3 to guess who said each sentence. If students find this difficult, refer them to *Language summary B* or their mini-dictionaries.

POSSIBLE ANSWERS AND LANGUAGE NOTE
b *Kay suggested having / that they had a quiet night in and watching / watched a video. (You cannot use a combination of gerunds and that clauses in the same sentence. Before watched, it is not necessary to repeat that they.)*
c *Martyn apologised for throwing / having thrown the ticket away a few weeks earlier.*
d *Camelot promised to investigate the matter thoroughly.*
e *Camelot warned the Totts not even to tell their family about the matter.*
f *Camelot refused to answer any questions about the investigation itself.*
g *Kay denied having / that they had had any problems in their marriage before it happened.*

5 a Give students time to think about their answers before putting them into pairs. Encourage them to explain their opinions and to ask each other questions.

b Give students time to choose a character and decide who will be the journalist and who will be the character. Then ask them to prepare the interview in pairs. Walk round the room providing any vocabulary they need. Then give them a few minutes to roleplay their interviews. Note any errors with reported speech for correction at the end of the activity. Finally, ask a few pairs to act out their interviews for the rest of the class.

ADDITIONAL PRACTICE

RB **Resource bank:** 12A Reporting a crime (reporting verbs), page 156; 12B The marriage from hell (reporting verbs; reporting statements and questions), pages 157–158

Workbook: Pronunciation: Verbs that summarise what people say, page 89; Jazz chant, page 89

Task: Prepare a questionnaire about the media (PAGE 134)

Preparation: listening

1 🔊 [T12.7] Start by asking students if they have ever been interviewed with a questionnaire and what it was

about. Set the activity and play the recording, pausing after each section to give students time to write the question. Ask students to compare answers before checking with the class.

POSSIBLE ANSWERS
1 How often do you use the Internet?
2 Do you often listen to the radio?
3 Do you prefer going to the cinema or watching films at home?
4 Do you read a newspaper every day?
5 Do you watch a lot of TV?

2 Read the topics and check that students understand *screen*. Explain that each question answered in exercise 1 relates to one of the topics in the list. Give students a few minutes to answer and then check as a class.

ANSWERS
Films and the cinema: question 3
How people use the Internet: question 1
Newspaper and magazine reading habits: question 4
Radio: question 2
TV viewing habits: question 5

Task: writing and speaking

1 Give students a few minutes in pairs to decide on their topic(s) and the general issue they want to address. If necessary, give the example below:
• **Topic:** films and the cinema
• **General issue:** the popularity of different kinds of film and why / the cinema versus TV or DVD / which movie stars are popular and why?

2 Emphasise that both students need to write the questions. While students prepare their questions, walk round the room providing help. Ask them only to look at the example types of question on page 142 if they need help. Encourage them to ask questions that cover as many aspects of their topic as possible. After about five minutes, go through *Useful language a* and then ask students to complete their questionnaires.

3 Set a definite time limit (e.g. ten minutes) for the interviews and ask students to note down the answers.

4 Before students summarise the results of their questionnaire, go through *Useful language b* explaining any problem phrases. Emphasise that they only need to report on the most interesting things they found out. Set a time limit of five minutes and walk round the room providing help.

5 If you have a small class, all the pairs can present their findings. If not, select only a few pairs to do so. After each report, encourage the other students to ask questions for further information if necessary.

Writing (PAGE 135)

A film review

1 Introduce the topic and set the question. Encourage students to give details about their film and to ask each other questions for more information. For feedback, ask students if they would like to see any of the films they heard about.

2 Check that students understand *review*. Ask if anyone has seen *Bend It Like Beckham* and, if so, to say briefly what it is about. If nobody has heard of the film, get students to guess what it is about from the title. Most students are likely to have heard of David Beckham, captain of the English football team. *Bend It* refers to his famous ability to kick a ball so that it follows a curved path through the air rather than a straight line, making it difficult for the opposition to defend against his shots. Go through the phrases in the box and explain any new vocabulary. Students can work in pairs to complete the text. Check answers with the class.

ANSWERS
a A film I've enjoyed   b What made me want to see it
c It was directed   d it stars   e is set
f The problem is that   g played by   h Eventually
i Things get really complicated
j all ends happily   k there are a number of things
l The soundtrack   m I would recommend this film

3 Go through the headings and check that students understand *plot*. Students work individually and then compare their notes with a partner. Emphasise that they should not simply copy the plot from the text, but write short notes.

POSSIBLE ANSWERS
Title: *Bend It Like Beckham*
Reasons for going to see it: it's a change from Hollywood blockbusters – the title – the cultural background
Director: Gurinder Chadha
Stars: Parminda Nagra and Keira Knightley
Where/when it's set: present-day London
Brief summary of the plot: Jess – traditional Indian family – loves playing football – her family hate it – she plays for a local team – her parents find out – Jess and her friend are in love with same man (football coach) – choice between family and man/sport – but happy ending
Positive points: a lot of humour – amusing characters – warm and colourful scenes – good soundtrack
Negative points: a bit slow-moving – dialogue a bit difficult to understand sometimes
Who it would appeal to: anyone interested in football or family life – anyone who wants a rest from Hollywood blockbusters.

4 Explain that the notes in exercise 3 form the outline of the full film review. Give students a short time to think of a film they have seen and to write their notes. Then give them time in class to write their review, or set it for homework.

5 If your students are reluctant to show everyone their reviews, ask them just to show it to their partner. Give them time to read the reviews and to think about the questions in exercise 5b. Finally, ask which film they would like to see.

ADDITIONAL PRACTICE

Workbook: Improve your writing: Describing a book you have enjoyed, page 93

Consolidation modules 9–12 (PAGES 136–137)

It is primarily intended that you do this in class time, allowing students to work in pairs or small groups. However, we have noted below which of the activities could be set for homework. Emphasise to students that the *Consolidation* activities are for revision purposes and are not tests.

A Speaking: Future forms

1–3 Give students five minutes to choose their topic and prepare the conversation. While they are working, walk round the room providing any vocabulary they need and help them incorporate the phrases in the box. Allow one minute for each pair to act out their conversations. If you have a large class, select a limited number of pairs to act them out. Note down errors and correct these at the end of the activity.

B Grammar and speaking: Modals and hypothetical forms

1 Check students understand *astronaut, vital, penalty shoot-out*. Demonstrate the activity by matching text a to the appropriate situation as a whole class. Tell them not to worry about the gaps at this stage. Check answers as a whole class.

ANSWERS
a what it would be like to have missed in a vital penalty shoot-out
b being in prison for a crime they didn't commit
c they were one of the first astronauts in space, back in the 1960s
d they (or people they know) have won the lottery
e they were one of the first astronauts in space, back in the 1960s
f they (or people they know) have won the lottery

2 Do the first example as a class, and elicit an explanation for choosing *must feel*. When you check answers with the class, ask them to explain their choices.

ANSWERS
a 1 must feel   2 should/could have hit
   3 had put   4 might not / wouldn't have been able
b 5 must be   6 would get
   7 could/might/may even go
c 8 must have been   9 could/might have been
   10 would/might/could have been blown
d 11 must be   12 must feel   13 must/would change
   14 could/might end up
e 15 had been   16 would have been
   17 would have felt

f 18 happened   19 could/might/would be
20 might/could get   21 might/could feel
22 would/might/could happen

3 Give students time to think about themselves in the
situation. Encourage them to explain their answers and to
sk each other questions. While they are talking, note any
rrors with modals and hypothetical forms for correction as the
nd of the activity.

C Listening and grammar:
Reported speech

1 Focus students on the pictures and give them time to
discuss the questions. As you elicit ideas, introduce the
erb *back into* which students need for the next exercise.

POSSIBLE ANSWERS
Picture 1: a hotel receptionist and guest. The guest is
arguing about her bill.
Picture 2: two strangers in a car accident. They are
arguing about whose fault it was.

2 a [C1] Set the questions and play the recording.
Check answers with the class.

ANSWERS
Conversation 1: The guest is refusing to pay $120 for
phone calls made from her room. The problem is
resolved by the receptionist suggesting she speaks to the
manager after his/her lunch.
Conversation 2: One man backed into the other's car
and they're arguing about whether is was an accident
or not. The problem is resolved when one man
recognises the other (Andrew Clark) as a TV celebrity
and asks for his autograph; they calm down.

Students can work alone or in pairs. Do the first example as
whole class. When they have finished, ask students to
ompare with a partner, and then check answers with the class.

ANSWERS
2 the guest (that) she had to pay for the telephone
calls
3 to pay anything until she saw the manager
4 on seeing / (that) she see the manager immediately
5 making / (that) she make an appointment to see the
manager

Remind students that Andrew Clark is the TV celebrity and
heck that they understand *deliberately*, *on purpose* and
utograph, or ask them to use their mini-dictionaries.

ANSWERS
1 angry driver   2 Andrew Clark   3 angry driver
4 angry driver   5 Andrew Clark   6 angry driver

d Do the first example with the class and then put them into
pairs to complete the activity.

ANSWERS
2 Andrew denied doing it on purpose.
3 The angry driver told Andrew (that) his wife thought
he was wonderful.
4 The angry driver asked Andrew for his autograph /
asked Andrew if he would mind giving him his
autograph.
5 Andrew agreed to give the angry driver his
autograph.
6 The angry driver apologised for losing his temper.

D Vocabulary: Alphabet quiz

1 Do the first word with the class and, if necessary, refer
them to Module 10 to find it.

ANSWERS
a   appointment   b biased   c chat show
d   disease   e entertaining   f fits   g Guests
h   housewarming   i influential   j justification
k   Live   l mind   m Neighbours   n put
o   resemble   p stain   q traffic report
r   unsolved   s vaccination   t Weird

2 Tell students to find all five words in Modules 9–12.
Encourage them not to use their dictionaries unless
absolutely necessary. If need be, walk round the room helping
with the clues. Ask each pair to read out their clues for the
others to guess.

Resource bank
Index of activities

Activity	Language point	When to use	Time (minutes)
Learner-training worksheet 1	Making the most of your classroom time	near the start of the course	25–30
Learner-training worksheet 2	Using the mini-dictionary	near the start of the course	40–45
Learner-training worksheet 3	Using a monolingual dictionary with a reading text	after *Learner-training worksheet 2*	35–40
Learner-training worksheet 4	Learning about collocation	near the start of the course	40–45
Learner-training worksheet 5	Making notes in class	near the start of the course	40–45
1A Get to know the *Students' Book*		first day of the course	25–30
1B Me too!	Tenses and question forms	first day of the course or after *Practice*, exercise 2, page 11	15–25
1C Get circles	Expressions with *get*	after *Wordspot*, exercise 4, page 13	15–20
1D Three-person snap	Various uses of auxiliary verbs	after *Practice*, exercise 2, page 15	15–25
2A Which stress pattern?	Stress patterns of verbs, nouns and adjectives	any time in the module	15–20
2B Who am I?	Gerunds and phrases to describe abstract ideas	after *Practice*, exercise 3, page 21	20–30
2C How many schwas?	Schwas in three- and four-syllable words	after *Practice*, exercise 3, page 21	15–25
2D Prefix and suffix dominoes	Prefixes and suffixes with nouns and adjectives	after *Practice*, exercise 3, page 23	15–25
3A Sidney and the circus	Narrative tenses; verb–adverb combinations for travel and movement	after *Practice*, exercise 2, page 35	30–45
3B Continuous snakes and ladders	Simple and continuous verb forms of various tenses	after *Practice*, exercise 2, page 37	30–40
3C Problems, problems!	Language for responding to unexpected problems	after *Real life*, exercise 3, page 38	20–30
4A Passive scrabble	Passive tenses and passive forms	after *Practice*, exercise 2, page 45	25–35
4B It's all in the mind	Expressions with *mind*	after *Wordspot*, exercise 3, page 48	15–25
5A A wonderful life	Present perfect (various uses)	after *Practice*, exercise 3, page 55	30–45
5B Word combinations	Verb–noun word combinations	after *Vocabulary*, exercise 2, page 56	20–30
5C Who's worked for the CIA?	Present perfect simple and continuous	after *Practice*, exercise 3, page 59	20–30

Activity	Language point	When to use	Time (minutes)
6A The genuine article	Use and non-use of articles	after *Practice*, exercise 4, page 66	15–25
6B Where on earth are we?	Ways of adding emphasis; cleft sentences	after *Practice*, exercise 2, page 68	20–30
7A Relative clauses crossword	Defining relative clauses	after *Practice*, exercise 2, page 77	15–25
7B What's buried at the bottom of the garden?	Non-defining relative clauses	after *Practice*, exercise 2, page 77	20–40
8A Fame and fortune	Vocabulary extension (collocations on the topic of fame and fortune)	after *Vocabulary and speaking*, exercise 2, page 86	15–25
8B Gerund and infinitive dominoes	Gerund and infinitive forms	after *Practice*, exercise 2, page 88	20–30
8C Design your own soap opera!	Verbs that take the infinitive or the gerund	after *Practice*, exercise 2, page 88	25–45
9A The maze of terror!	Modal verbs of deduction in the past and present	after *Practice*, exercise 4, page 101	25–35
9B What's wrong with it?	Language for complaining	after *Real life*, exercise 3, page 104	20–30
10A Getting together	Vocabulary extension (word families and dependent prepositions)	after *Reading*, exercise 3, page 106	20–30
10B The Supasaver debate	Ways of expressing the future	after *Practice*, exercise 2, page 109	30–45
10C How about ten thirty?	Future continuous and Future perfect	after *Practice*, exercise 3, page 112	15–20
11A Wishing	Hypothetical situations in the present	after *Practice*, exercise 3, page 119	15–25
11B I wish he wouldn't do that!	Wishes in the past and present	after *Practice*, exercise 3, page 121	20–30
11C A nightmare holiday	Third conditional and *should have*	after *Practice*, exercise 3, page 121	20–30
12A Reporting a crime	Reporting verbs	after *Practice*, exercise 5, page 133	15–20
12B The marriage from hell	Reporting verbs; reporting statements and questions	after *Practice*, exercise 5, page 133	30–45
12C Preposition race	Revision of prepositions	towards the end of the module	20–30

Test one (modules 1–4) pages 161–163   **Test two** (modules 5–8) pages 164–166   **Test three** (modules 9–12) pages 167–169

Instructions for activities pages 96–103   **Resource bank key** pages 170–174
Questionnaire page 175

Instructions

The activities in the *Resource bank* consolidate and extend material covered in the *Students' Book*. The **first** point at which each activity in the *Resource bank* can be used is indicated in the index and at the appropriate point in the teacher's notes. However, teachers may choose to do an activity in the same class as the *Practice* activities in the *Students' Book,* in the following class as a 'warmer' or 'filler', or after a longer time space as a revision exercise.

Learner-training worksheet 1
(Making the most of your classroom time)

You will need: one worksheet per student.

1   Pre-teach any difficult vocabulary and answer any questions. Students should not read the *Commentary* section yet.
2   Give students time to mark whether the statements are true for them. Encourage honest discussion rather than giving the 'answers' yourself. Ask the class for their conclusions on being an active learner.
3   The students now read the *Commentary*. Ask them how their own ideas compare with those in the text.
4   Refer them to the questions, either to discuss in pairs, or as a class. Take a positive attitude to any suggestions they make.

Learner-training worksheet 2
(Using the mini-dictionary)

You will need: one worksheet per student.

The *Mini-dictionary* helps students make the transition from bilingual to monolingual dictionaries. The dictionary **only** includes words used in the *Students' Book*. This worksheet helps them to become familiar with the different types of information the *Mini-dictionary* contains: meanings, grammar, pronunciation, etc.

1   Encourage students to guess meanings before looking up the words. This will help them with the valuable strategy of guessing meaning from context. It may be best to work through this section with the whole class until they are accustomed to the *Mini-dictionary*.
2   Pre-teach any unfamiliar grammatical terms (for example, transitive/intransitive verb, countable/ uncountable noun) and ask for examples. Students now do the exercise.

Learner-training worksheet 3
(Using a monolingual dictionary with a reading text)

You will need: a class set of the Longman Dictionary of Contemporary English; *one worksheet per student.*

This worksheet trains students to use dictionaries to read a text more actively, and to use a monolingual dictionary together with a reading text to expand their knowledge of grammar and vocabulary. This can be done when students are accustomed to using the *Mini-dictionary* and need to consolidate/extend their monolingual dictionary skills. Go through the explanation of the different information which the *Longman Dictionary of Contemporary English* contains with the whole class.

1   Focus students' attention on the title; check the possible meanings of *crossing*, and the meaning of *chaos*. Allow students to read the text silently: they should not look up unknown words at this stage, but should focus on explaining the title of the text.
2   Students do the exercise individually or in pairs, before checking with the whole class.

Learner-training worksheet 4
(Learning about collocation)

You will need: one worksheet per student; the Longman Dictionary of Contemporary English *(optional).*

This worksheet helps students notice and record collocations in written texts. Explain what a collocation is and ask students for examples.

1   Work with the whole class, or students work in pairs. Provide students with monolingual dictionaries if they do not have any ideas.
2   Students work individually or in pairs. Check answers with the whole class (see Resource bank key).
3   Discuss preferences for recording collocations. Avoid saying that any method is always right or wrong – this depends on the vocabulary, and on learning style.
4   Encourage students to keep a record of the collocations in a special notebook.

Learner-training worksheet 5
(Making notes in class)

You will need: one worksheet per student.

This worksheet helps students to keep effective records of lessons by making notes. It can be used on its own, or in conjunction with *Listening and writing: taking notes* on page 69 of the *Students' Book*.

1   Get students to discuss the four statements, either as a class or in pairs/groups. Pre-teach difficult phrases and answer any questions as they read the *Commentary 1* section.
2   Encourage students to discuss each set of notes, listing good points and possible improvements before they read *Commentary 2*. Encourage them to compare their own conclusions with those of the writer.
3   Stress that there is no 'correct' way of taking notes, as much depends on personal preference and learning style.

1A Get to know the *Students' Book*

You will need: one set of cards for each pair of students.

- Shuffle each set of cards and place them face down in piles at the front of the class. Put the students into pairs and allocate one set of cards to each pair.
- A student from each pair takes **one** card only from the top of their pile and goes back to their partner. Then they write the answers to the question **on their card**.
- The student takes a completed card to the teacher to check the answer (see *Resource bank key*). If the answer is correct, the pair keeps the card and takes the next one. If not, the pair must work out the correct answer.
- The first pair to finish all the cards wins.

1B Me too!

You will need: one worksheet per student.

- Give each student a copy of the worksheet. They work individually and write their answers in the second column. Ask them to write short notes, **not** complete sentences. Set a time limit of five minutes.
- Tell students that for each of their answers, they must now find another student with the same, or a similar, answer. Students move around the room asking questions. They cannot look at one another's worksheets.
- When they find someone who has the same, or a similar, answer, they write that student's name in the third column. They must then ask **at least two** follow-up questions on the same topic. For example, if students find that they have visited the same country, they could ask: *When did you go there? Where was the best place you visited?*
- Students can discuss their findings in small groups or with the whole class.

1C Get circles

You will need: one worksheet per student.

- Give each student a worksheet. Make sure they write their answers in **random** order. They should write single words, numbers or short phrases, **not** complete sentences. Set a time limit of five minutes.
- Students work in pairs. They fold their worksheet and swap with their partner. Students have to guess why their partner has written the items in the circles. For example, they could ask: *Is Juan someone you get on well with? Is this the best present you got for your last birthday?*
- Encourage students to find out more by asking suitable follow-up questions. For example, for someone's favourite birthday present, a student could ask: *Who gave it to you? What else did you get?*
- Afterwards, students report back to the whole class.

1D Three-person snap

You will need: one set of Question master cards*, and two*

sets of Auxiliary verb cards *for each group of three students.*

- Students work in groups of three. Give student A a set of *Question master cards*, face down in a pile. Give students B and C a set of *Auxiliary verb cards* each, and tell them to spread them out in front of them, face up.
- Student A turns over the first *Question master card* and reads **only** the question or statement out loud. Students B and C find the correct *Auxiliary verb card* from their set as quickly as possible and give it to student A, saying the answer correctly at the same time. The student who is first takes both cards as a 'trick'. The student with the most tricks at the end wins.
- Students may repeat the activity, with a different student A.
- Finally, students work together and sort the tricks into four groups: *short answers to avoid repetition, correcting, question tags,* and *short questions to show interest.*

2A Which stress pattern?

You will need: one set of stress pattern cards and one set of vocabulary cards for each pair of students.

- Students work in pairs. Give each pair a set of stress pattern cards and ask them to spread them out **face up**.
- Give each pair a set of vocabulary cards **face down** in a pile. Student A turns over a card and places it under the correct stress pattern card, saying the word correctly at the same time. Do an example with the whole class.
- If student B thinks his/her partner is correct, then student A gets one point. If student B thinks the card is in the wrong place, he/she can challenge student A. Student B can then place the word under another stress pattern card and, if correct, wins a bonus point.
- If the students cannot agree, the teacher adjudicates (see *Resource bank key*). If neither student was correct, the vocabulary card is returned to the bottom of the pile.
- Students continue to take turns. The student with the most points at the end is the winner.

2B Who am I?

You will need: one worksheet per student.

- **Before** giving out the worksheets, write a **number** in the box at the top. If you have ten students, for example, write 1 to 10.
- Distribute the worksheets in **random** order. Students work individually. They **must not** write their name on the paper, and are **not allowed** to look at their classmates' papers. They should try to begin each sentence with a gerund, or another phrase used to describe general/abstract ideas (see page 24 of the *Students' Book*).
- Collect the worksheets, shuffle them and put them up around the classroom.
- Students work individually or in pairs. They walk around the class and read the worksheets, then decide which student wrote each.
- The student or pair with the most correct guesses wins.

2C How many schwas?

You will need: one set of Schwa cards *and one set of* Word cards *for each pair of students.*

- Students work in pairs. Give each pair a set of *Word cards* and tell them to spread them out **face up** in front of them. Also give them a set of *Schwa cards* **face down** in a pile. Shuffle both sets of cards beforehand.
- Student A turns over a *Schwa card*, and then tries to find a *Word card* that matches it. **The Word card must match the number of syllables, the stress pattern and the position of the schwas.** If the student is correct, he/she takes the cards as a 'trick'.
- If student B thinks the cards do not match, he/she can challenge his/her partner. If they cannot agree, the teacher adjudicates (see *Resource bank key*). If student A is wrong, the turn passes to student B, who tries to find a *Word card* which matches the pattern on the *Schwa card*.
- Students continue to take turns. The student with the most tricks at the end of the game wins.
- After the activity, the students can group the words together under the same stress and schwa pattern. There are three *Word cards* for each pattern (see *Resource bank key*).

2D Prefix and suffix dominoes

You will need: one set of dominoes for each group of three students.

- Divide your students into groups of three. Give one set of dominoes to each group, and ask them to share them equally **face down**. Each student then places the dominoes **face down** in a pile in front of himself/herself.
- One student turns over the top domino on his/her pile and places it on the desk or floor. The next student turns over the top domino of his/her pile and places it next to the first domino if it makes a word.
- Students must place their dominoes so that the arrows in the centre of the dominoes are pointing **in the same direction** to ensure all the words match. They cannot **rotate** the dominoes.
- Students can place their new domino next to **any** domino already in play. However, if two or more edges of the new domino are in contact with other dominoes, then each edge must make a correct word.
- If a student can't place his/her domino anywhere, he/she puts it back at the bottom of his/her pile and the next student takes his/her turn.
- If one student thinks a word isn't correct, he/she can challenge the other student. The teacher adjudicates. If the word is incorrect, the student has to take back the domino and put it at the bottom of his/her pile.
- Each word must be spelt correctly, and students are not allowed to 'drop' letters. For example, *care-* can match with *-ful* or *-less*, but not with *-ing*.
- The first student to put down all his/her dominoes wins.
- After the activity, students can note the words they created and compare them with those of other groups.

3A Sidney and the circus

You will need: one Student A *worksheet and one* Student B *worksheet for each pair of students. Detach the* Movement verbs *worksheets from the pictures* **before** *the lesson.*

- Divide the students into pairs. Give students A and B a copy of their respective worksheets. Students cannot look at each other's pictures.
- Pre-teach any difficult vocabulary. Students have to describe the pictures on their worksheet to their partner and decide on the correct order of the pictures. Make sure students do **not** look at their partner's worksheets.
- When a pair has decided on the correct order, they may look at both worksheets and check their answers. Check the correct order with the whole class (see *Resource bank key*).
- Give a copy of the *Movement verbs worksheet* to each student. Individually or in pairs, students match each verb with a picture using a dictionary to help them. Check the answers with the whole class (see *Resource bank key*). Note that there can be more than one correct answer for some of the verbs.
- Students then work individually or in pairs, and write the story in the past, using narrative tenses and the vocabulary from the worksheet (see *Resource bank key* for example).

3B Continuous snakes and ladders

You will need: one snakes and ladders board per group of three students; one set of question cards for each group; counters and dice.

- Divide students into groups of three, and give each group a snakes and ladders board, a set of question cards (shuffled, **face down**), counters and dice.
- Students take it in turns to throw the dice. When they land on a square with a question mark on it, they must take a question card from the top of the pile. If the student answers the question correctly, he/she stays on the square and the next student takes his/her turn.
- If one player thinks a student's answer is wrong, he/she can challenge him/her. The teacher adjudicates (see *Resource bank key*).
- If a student lands at the foot of a ladder, he/she must get the question correct **before** he/she can go up it. If a student lands on the head of a snake, he/she **must** slide down to its tail.
- The game continues until one student reaches the *Finish* square (or the group runs out of question cards).
- At the end of the game, students can discuss the cards they got wrong, or go through the question cards they didn't answer.

3C Problems, problems!

You will need: one set of Role cards *for each pair of students.*

- Divide the students into pairs, student A and student B. Give each pair matching *Role cards*, and allow them time to digest the information.

- Students act out the roleplay in their pairs. Encourage them to use expressions for responding to unexpected problems where appropriate (see page 38 of the *Students' Book*). They continue the roleplay until there is a resolution.
- When each pair finishes their roleplay, collect the *Role cards* from them and give them to another pair. Make sure you always give *Role card A* to **student A**.

4A Passive scrabble

You will need: one set of cut-up cards for each group of three or four students. Put each set of cards in an envelope.

- Students work in groups of three or four. Give one envelope to each group, and ask them to take out twelve cards each.
- Students must take it in turns to use the cards to make a correct sentence (or a question) in the passive. One student starts, and the next student must make another sentence which includes one card from the first sentence. The students continue in turn.
- When a student puts down a correct sentence, he/she adds up the number of points on the cards and adds them to his/her score. He/She also takes more cards so that he/she always has twelve cards.
- If the student makes a sentence which adds a word to the beginning or end of another sentence, he/she gets points for **both** sentences.
- Tell students that if they have a card which says *'To be' or Past Participle*, they can use it to form any tense of the auxiliary verb *to be*, or in place of any past participle.
- If a student cannot make a correct sentence, he/she has to collect up any cards he/she put down, and the turn passes to the next student.
- If a student cannot make a sentence, he/she can swap three cards with ones still in the envelope. The turn then passes to the next student.
- The students continue until they run out of cards, or until nobody can make a sentence. They add up the number of points left on the cards they haven't used and deduct this from their score.
- The student with the most points wins.

4B It's all in the mind

You will need: one set of cards for each group of three students.

- Shuffle the cards. Divide students into threes (include one group of four if necessary). Give each group a set of cards, which they place **face down** in a pile.
- Student A turns over the top card and reads out the situation to the student on his/her left (student B), who has to respond using an expression with *mind*. If student B gives a correct response, student A gives student B the card to keep. In order for a response to be correct it **must** include the words in *italics* on the question card.
- If student B cannot answer the question correctly, the question passes round the group. If no student knows the answer, student A reads it out and keeps the card.

- Student B picks up the next card and reads out the situation to student C. The turn passes round the group.
- The student who collects the most cards wins.

5A A wonderful life

You will need: one pair of role cards for each pair of students.

- Give half the class the *TV Interviewer* card, and the other the *Chris Bull* card (if there is an odd number, have an extra interviewer).
- Allow students time to prepare for the interview. Encourage them to think of questions and answers using the Present perfect simple and continuous from the *How long?* and *How many?* prompts on the cards. (This stage could be done for homework.)
- Organise pairs of one 'TV Interviewer' and one 'Chris Bull'. Students do the roleplay. The activity can be repeated by swapping around the interviewers.
- Interviewers report back to the whole class on the most interesting things they found out.

5B Word combinations

You will need: one set of cards for each group of three or four students; one What about you? *worksheet per student.*

STAGE 1

- Students work in groups of three or four. Each group spreads out a set of cards **face down**.
- Each student takes it in turns to turn over two cards. If they find a verb and a noun that match, they keep the cards as a 'trick' and have another turn. If the cards do not match, they go back **in exactly the same place**.
- The activity continues until all the cards are matched. The student with the most tricks wins.

STAGE 2

- Give each student a copy of the *What about you?* worksheet. Make sure they write their answers on a **separate** piece of paper in **random** order. They should write words or short phrases, **not** complete sentences.
- Students work in pairs and swap papers. They ask each other to explain why they have written the items on the paper. For example, students might ask: *Why have you written 'yoga'? Who is (Steve Phillips)?* Encourage them to find out more information by asking follow-up questions, for example, *When did he win his award?*
- Students report back to the whole class on the most interesting thing they found out about their partner.

5C Who's worked for the CIA?

You will need: one Find someone who ... *worksheet per student; one* Role card *per student.*

- Give each student a copy of the *Find someone who...* worksheet. Tell them that the space at the beginning of each line corresponds to a person's name. Students decide whether they should use the Present perfect

Instructions

simple or continuous in the sentence, or whether both are possible (see *Resource bank key*). Check the answers with the class.

- Tell the students they are going to a party with lots of interesting people. Give each student a *Role card* in **random** order, and allow them time to read and digest the information. **They must not look at each others' cards**. Give *Role card 10* (the CIA role card) to one of the stronger students.
- Tell the students they must talk to all the other guests at the party, then write their names in the correct place on the *Find someone who ...* worksheet. Students then mingle and have short conversations with one another. Encourage students to introduce themselves and ask each other about their jobs/lives, rather than just the questions required to complete the worksheet.
- Students check their answers in pairs. If the CIA agent is discovered, this is the end of the activity.
- If the CIA agent **isn't** discovered, students discuss in pairs what they know about the characters and decide who they think the CIA agent is. Finally, the real CIA agent can reveal himself/herself to the class.

6A The genuine article

You will need: one set of cards for each pair of students.

- Divide the students into pairs and give each pair a set of cards. Students divide the cards equally without looking at the cards. Tell students there are **two** mistakes on each card.
- Student A turns over his/her first card, **covers up the answer**, then shows the question to student B, who must correct the mistakes. Student A checks student B's answers, and awards one point for each correct one.
- Students take turns to show each other the questions. They place cards they got wrong in a separate pile. The student with the most points wins. After the activity they can go through the cards they got wrong.

6B Where on earth are we?

You will need: one pair of role cards for each pair of students.

- Students work in pairs. Explain that they are driving to a wedding, and they are lost. Give each pair a matching pair of role cards and allow time to prepare for the roleplay.
- Students act out the roleplay in pairs. Encourage students to use the various ways of adding emphasis in the *Useful language* box.
- The class discusses the outcome of the roleplay.

7A Relative clauses crossword

You will need: one Student A crossword and one Student B crossword for each pair of students.

- Divide the class in half. Give a copy of the *Student A* crossword to each student in group A, and a copy of the *Student B* crossword to those in group B.

- Students work together in groups to check they know all the meanings of the words on their half of the crossword. Students should refer to the *Longman Dictionary of Contemporary English* if necessary.
- Pair one student A with one student B. They are not allowed to look at each other's crossword.
- Students take it in turns to define the words that appear on their half of the crossword to their partner, using defining relative clauses (*It's a place where ...*, *This is a person who ...*). The partner has to guess the words and write them in his/her own crossword.
- Students continue until they both have a completed version of the crossword.

7B What's buried at the bottom of the garden?

You will need: one set of story cards and one set of Extra information cards for each pair of students

- Pre-teach any difficult vocabulary. Students work in pairs. Give each pair a set of story cards. Students have to put these cards in order to produce a logical story. Check the order with the whole class (see *Resource bank key*). Ask a few general comprehension questions to check the students have understood the story.
- Give each pair a set of *Extra information cards* **face down** in a pile. Students turn over the cards one at a time and discuss where to include the information in the story. When they have decided, they place the *Extra information card* next to the appropriate story card. They continue to do this until they have used all the *Extra information cards*.
- Students must then decide what **changes** are required in order to turn the sentences on the *Extra information card* into a non-defining relative clause in the text (which pronoun to use, changes in punctuation, etc). Students can write down their non-defining relative clauses at this stage for checking (see *Resource bank key* for completed text).
- Students check their answers with the whole class.
- Students can discuss in pairs how they think the story ends. They can then write the ending for homework, including some non-defining relative clauses where appropriate.
- The finished versions can be read out or displayed for others to read.

8A Fame and fortune

You will need: one set of cards for each pair of students.

- Students work in pairs (or in groups of three). Give each pair a set of cards and tell them to spread them out in front of them **face down** without looking at them first.
- The students take it in turns to turn over any two cards. If a student finds a collocation in **bold** that matches, he/she keeps the cards as a 'trick' and has another turn. If the cards do not match, he/she must replace them **face down in exactly the same place**.
- The activity continues until all cards are matched up. The student with the most tricks wins.

100

- Students then put down all the pairs and put the sentences in a logical order to complete the story. Check the answers with the whole class (see *Resource bank key*).

8B Gerund and infinitive dominoes

You will need: one set of dominoes for each pair of students.

- Students work in pairs. Give one set of dominoes to each pair, and ask them to share them out equally.
- One student places a domino **face up** in front of himself/herself, and the other student places one of his/her dominoes at either end of the first domino to complete the sentence. The students take it in turns to put down their dominoes at either end of the domino chain.
- If a student thinks his/her partner's sentence is not grammatically correct or doesn't make sense, he/she can challenge the other student. If the students cannot agree, the teacher adjudicates. If the sentence is incorrect, or if a student cannot make a sentence, the turn passes to his/her partner.
- The game continues until one student has used up all his/her dominoes, or until neither student can make a correct sentence. The student who finishes first, or has the fewest dominoes remaining, wins.

8C Design your own soap opera!

You will need: one Design your own soap opera! worksheet for each student; one set of Plot cards for every two or three groups of students; one Verb bank worksheet for each student.

- Divide students into threes. Give each student a *Design your own soap opera!* worksheet and allow them time to do the task at the top of the page. Encourage students to make notes. Students report back to the whole class on their ideas.
- Prepare an envelope of *Plot cards*. (One set is enough for three groups, but extra *Plot cards* will allow students to swap any they do not want to use.) One student from each group chooses three *Plot cards* without looking inside the envelope. They can swap one or two cards if they choose.
- Students work in their groups and decide which character in their soap opera has the problems on the *Plot cards,* and who else is involved. Encourage them to make notes at this stage.
- Students plan what happens in the next episode. Tell them to write their plan **in note form only** at this stage.
- Give each student a copy of the *Verb bank* worksheet.
- Students write what happens next using **at least eight** of the verbs on the *Verb bank* worksheet (followed by either the infinitive or the gerund). Students should write their episode as a narrative, **not** as a dialogue. They can use either the present or the past tense.
- The completed episodes can be read out or displayed.

9A The maze of terror!

You will need: one set of cards for each group of three students (colour-coded if possible).

- Pre-teach any difficult vocabulary.
- Divide students into threes. Explain that they are on holiday together in the USA. Tell them that the aim is for them to get out of the maze by finding somewhere to spend the night.
- Give each group *Card 1*, and explain that every time they see a question **in capitals**, they must make deductions about the situation using modal verbs in the present or past. (For *Card 1*, students might say, *The owner might have gone away* or *There can't be many tourists visiting this area.*) Students then decide amongst themselves which card they want next.
- Students continue through the maze, making deductions from the prompts and discussing the options at the bottom of each card. The teacher moves around the room giving out cards. Make sure you keep each set of cards for each group separate.
- When a group has reached the end of the maze, ask them to go through the cards again in order. Encourage students to evaluate their own decisions (using *should(n't) have* and third conditional sentences), and discuss the options they **didn't** take (using *could have* and third conditional sentences).
- Groups report back to the whole class.

9B What's wrong with it?

You will need: one pair of role cards for each pair of students.

- Divide the class into two. Give one half the *Student A* role card, and the other half the *Student B* role card.
- Give them time to prepare for the roleplays. Encourage them to make notes on the two situations where they need to complain (using phrases from page 104 of the *Students' Book* where possible), and check they have understood the details of the other two situations.
- Arrange the class so that the holder of a *Student A* role card is paired with the holder of a *Student B* role card. Students then do roleplay 1 (*Restaurant*) in pairs. Encourage students to continue talking until there is a resolution.
- Students then move on to roleplay 2 (*Clothes shop*). Allow them a short break so that students can remind themselves of their new roles.
- If possible, rearrange the class again (by asking all those with the *Student A* role card to move round clockwise one seat), and the students do the roleplays 3 (*Department store*) and 4 (*Repair company*) with their new partner.
- Students report back to the whole class.

10A Getting together

You will need: one set of cards for each pair of students; a set of monolingual dictionaries, for example, the Longman Dictionary of Contemporary English *(optional).*

- Shuffle each set of cards. Put students into pairs. Place the sets of cards **face down** in piles at the front of the class and allocate one pile to each pair.
- One student from each pair takes **one card only** from the top of their pile. They go back to their partner, read the question, and write the answers **on their card**, referring to the *Getting together 21st-century style* text on page 107 of the *Students' Book* (or a copy of the *Longman Dictionary of Contemporary English*) to find the answers.
- When a pair have completed a card, they take it to the teacher, who checks the answers. If the answers are correct, the student keeps the card and takes the next card from his/her pile. If the answer is not correct, the student has to return to his/her partner and find the correct answer. (See *Resource bank key* for answers).
- The first pair to finish all the cards wins.

If it is not possible for your students to move around the class freely, follow this procedure:

- Put students into pairs and give each pair a set of cards **face down** in a pile. Students turn over the cards one by one and write the answers on the cards.
- When a pair has finished, they hand their pile of cards to the teacher for checking. The teacher gives back the cards which are not correct, and the students correct their mistakes.
- The first pair to finish all the cards wins.

10B The Supasaver debate

You will need: one newspaper article per student; one set of role cards for each group of six students.

- Give each student a copy of the newspaper article. Allow them time to read, and check they have understood the text and the map. Pre-teach any difficult vocabulary.
- Distribute the role cards as follows: **four students** – omit the head of the school and the head of Supasaver; **five students** – omit the head of Supasaver; **six students** – give one role card to each student; **seven students** – add an extra politician; **eight students** – have two debates with four students (as above); **nine students** – have two debates, one with four students, one with five (as above); **ten students** – have two debates and omit the head of Supasaver; **eleven students** – have two debates, one with all the roles, and one without the head of Supasaver.
- Allow students time to prepare what they are going to say. If possible, put students into 'same-role' groups to discuss their ideas.
- Arrange the class so that they are in a circle. If you have two debates, put them at opposite ends of the classroom. The chairperson begins the debate; let the debate proceed uninterrupted. Ensure that the chairperson gives everybody a chance to speak. The teacher may make notes of mistakes for discussion after the activity.
- At the end of the debate, students take a vote on whether to allow the supermarket to be built.
- Students discuss the outcome with the whole class.

10C How about ten thirty?

You will need: one pair of Role cards *for each pair of students.*

- Students work in pairs. Give *Role card A* to one student, and *Role card B* to the other, and allow them time to read the information. Encourage the publisher (*Role card B*) to make an appointment **as early as possible**, and to use the expressions in the *Useful language* box.
- Students act out the roleplay in pairs and arrange a mutually convenient time for the appointment.
- Students can check their answers with the rest of the class. (The only possible time is 3.00–3.30 on Thursday afternoon.)

11A Wishing

You will need: one Find someone who ... *worksheet per student.*

- Give each student a copy of the *Find someone who ...* worksheet. Pre-teach any difficult vocabulary and check students know how to form the questions.
- Students walk around the room asking each other questions in order to find another student who fits each description. Encourage students to mingle freely and **not** to ask just one or two students all their questions. Each student must try to collect as many different names as possible.
- When they have found someone, they write his/her name in the space provided on the worksheet. Then they ask appropriate follow-up questions and write short notes in the space provided.
- When they have finished, students can compare their findings with their neighbour or with the whole class.

11B I wish he wouldn't do that!

You will need: one pair of Role cards *for each pair of students.*

- Students work in pairs. Give one student *Role card A* and the other *Role card B*, and allow them time to read the information. Pre-teach any difficult vocabulary.
- Elicit from students some questions people in a doctor's waiting room might ask each other to pass the time, and write them up on the board. Include the following questions: *What's the matter with you? What do you do? Have you got any children? Whereabouts do you live? What are your neighbours like? Where did you go on holiday last year?*
- Students do the roleplay in pairs, using the questions

on the board. They should include *I wish ...* or *If only ...* where appropriate. Encourage students to have a 'natural' conversation (rather than just reading out a list of wishes) and to try and persuade each other that their problems are worse than their partner's. They do not have to discuss the topics in the same order as on the *Role card* but they must try to cover all the points.
- Students report back to the class on who had the biggest problems.

11C A nightmare holiday

You will need: one copy of the advertisement per student; one Tourist role card *and one* Travel agent role card *for each pair of students.*

- Introduce the topic of holidays and package tours. Pre-teach any difficult vocabulary.
- Give each student a copy of the holiday advertisement and ask them to decide which three things about the holiday are the best. Discuss the answers with the class.
- Give one half of the class the *Tourist role cards*, and the other the *Travel agent role cards*. Allow the students time to prepare.
- Arrange the class so that each 'tourist' is next to a 'travel agent'. Students do the roleplay in pairs. Encourage students to use the structures in the *Useful language* box on their *role card* where appropriate.
- Students report to the class on how much money each 'tourist' managed to get back from each 'travel agent'.

12A Reporting a crime

You will need: one set of Role cards *for every twelve students in the class.*

- Explain the situation to the students: they are all part of a criminal gang and have been arrested following a bank robbery that went disastrously wrong. They are locked up together in a police cell, waiting to be interviewed by the police. Pre-teach any difficult vocabulary.
- Give each student a *Role card* and allow them time to read the information. Students then walk around the room and have short conversations about what is on their card. They **must start** with the words in the speech bubble.
- Each student must talk to everyone else. They must also try to remember what was said to them. While they are mingling, the teacher can write on the board the reporting verbs they must use in the next stage (see *Resource bank key*), and, if desired, the appropriate students' names next to them.
- Students then sit down and work in pairs. They must now report to each other what everybody else said, using the reporting verbs on the board, and where possible give their reaction. For example: *Juan suggested digging a tunnel so that we could all escape, but I think that's a stupid idea, because ...*
- Discuss the answers with the whole class.

12B The marriage from hell

You will need: one newspaper article for each student; a set of two Movie World reporter *role cards, one* Jim Small *role card and one* Catherine Hunt *role card for each group of four students.*

- Give each student a copy of the newspaper article and ask them to find out what the problems are in the marriage. Check the answers with the whole class.
- Give half the class the *Movie World reporter* role cards, and tell them to work in pairs and prepare questions (if there is an odd number of students, have extra reporters).
- Divide the other half into 'married couples'. Give each couple a *Jim Small* role card or a *Catherine Hunt* role card, and tell them not to look at each other's cards. Allow the class time to prepare for the roleplay.
- Rearrange the class so that one reporter is paired with either 'Jim' or 'Catherine'. Reporters then conduct the interview and make brief notes of the answers.
- Now swap the interviewers around so that the reporter who has interviewed 'Jim' interviews 'Catherine', and vice versa.
- Reporters then tell their new interviewee what their wife/husband said and ask them to respond. Encourage reporters to use reporting verbs and reported questions/statements for example, *When I asked your husband if he was having an affair, he denied it.* Ask the reporters to make brief notes.
- To help students during this stage write the following reporting verbs on the board as prompts: *say, tell, ask, accuse, deny, threaten, warn, decide, urge, promise, offer, assure, order, suggest, blame, refuse, insist.*
- Students report back to the whole class.
- As a follow-up activity, the reporters can write their article for *Movie World*, and 'Jim' and 'Catherine' can write a letter to their lawyers.

12C Preposition race

You will need: one set of cards for each group of students.

- Shuffle the cards. Divide students into pairs or small groups, and make sure they have a large area (e.g. the floor) to work on. Give each group a complete set of cards, and tell them that they have to make twenty-four correct sentences **as quickly as possible**.
- As they are working, the teacher moves around the room, checking the sentences. The activity is best done without dictionaries, but if students are having difficulties, or have got some of the sentences wrong, allow them to use one.
- The first group with a complete set of correct sentences wins.
- After the activity, students can remove the preposition cards from their sentences and test each other.

Learner-training worksheet 1

Making the most of your classroom time

1 In order to improve your English, you should try to make the most of your classroom time. Below are some suggestions about how you might do this. Mark each one:

✔ If this **is** true for you. ✗ If this **isn't** true for you.
? If you aren't sure.

Be honest!

a   Whether or not I make progress with my English depends more on **me** than on my teacher. ☐
b   I try to work things out for myself if I can ... but I always ask my teacher if I'm not sure! ☐
c   Working in pairs or groups is a waste of time; I'd rather listen to the teacher. ☐
d   If I'm asked something, I often say I don't know or answer with one word. ☐
e   I sometimes don't speak because I'm worried about making mistakes. ☐
f   I use my own language a lot during my English classes. ☐
g   I take notes during lessons, and try to review what I've learned after class. ☐
h   I'd like to use resources like the grammar books and dictionaries. ☐

2 Compare your answers with other students, explaining **why** you chose yes or no. What conclusions do you draw about how to make the most of your time in class?

3 Now read the commentary. Were your conclusions the same as the ones in the commentary?

COMMENTARY

1 Of course having a good teacher helps; but good learners know that a teacher can't do everything. To make progress, you must take responsibility for your own learning. It's like learning to ride a bicycle; your parents can show you what to do, but you have to do it!

2 We often remember things better when we work them out for ourselves, rather than when we're simply told. Also, asking questions doesn't mean you're stupid: it's a vital part of the learning process. Try to ask your teacher at least one question in every lesson.

3 Occasionally learners feel that working in pairs or groups is a waste of time; but if you are asked to do this, it gives you a chance to use your English, and to share what you know. There's a saying in English that *two heads are better than one*, but three or four can be best of all!

4 It's important that you do more than give a 'minimum response' – for example, if you are asked if you had a good weekend, say what you did, don't just say yes. This will help you to be more confident with your English – and make the lesson more interesting!

5 No one can learn languages without making mistakes. While you shouldn't worry about every little mistake, learners who ignore them become fluent, but can be hard to understand. Identify important mistakes and work on those; your teacher can help you with this.

6 Although your first language can help you learn English (especially if some words or grammatical structures are similar) you should not rely too much on translation: it's not always helpful to translate everything. The less you rely on translation, the better you will communicate in English!

7 You will find a worksheet on taking notes on pages 110–111. Make time outside class to review your notes, read, listen or even think in English! It'll really help your progress. Always try to do any homework your teacher gives you: check it carefully both before handing it in, and when you get it back. If you don't understand something ... ask!

8 The *Students' Book* has most of the grammar and vocabulary you need, but if you need further help, use a grammar book like *Grammar Practice for Upper Intermediate Students*, or a monolingual dictionary like the *Longman Dictionary of Contemporary English* or the *Longman Language Activator*.

4 a) What do you think you could do to make the most of your classroom time?
b) Make three 'resolutions' to help you to make the most of your classroom time. How would you like your teacher to help you?

© **Pearson Education Limited 2005**

Learner-training worksheet 2
Using the mini-dictionary

> The following exercise is based on the *Cutting Edge Upper Intermediate Mini-dictionary* ('the mini-dictionary').
> Other monolingual dictionaries (for example the *Longman Dictionary of Contemporary English*, and the *Longman Language Activator*) are organised in a similar way. For the mini-dictionary the main difference is that it only contains words and meanings that appear in the *Students' Book*, so is much shorter than other dictionaries.

1 FINDING OUT ABOUT MEANING

a) Look at the following sentences: try to guess the meaning of the words written in bold by using the context to help you.

- I saw Michael **frown** as he read the letter. 'Is there a problem?' I asked.
- Although the sun was very bright, there was a gentle **breeze** which helped to keep us cool.
- We all needed a rest after climbing such a **steep** hill.

b) Now look up the words in the mini-dictionary to see if you were right.

c) Look at the following words. This time there is no context to help you guess their meaning. Look up the words and also read the example sentence for each word.

- stubborn   • shabby   • pant

- Do you now understand from the mini-dictionary what the words mean?
- What helped you most – the definition, the example or both?

d) The mini-dictionary gives you information about **style** (whether the word is formal or informal). Look up the following words in the mini-dictionary. Which are formal and which are informal?

- mate .... • weep .... • quit .... • sibling ....

e) The mini-dictionary also gives you information about the **different meanings** a word has. How many meanings are given for the words in **bold**? Which meaning do the words have in these sentences?

- **Poor** Elizabeth! She's failed her driving test again! ....
- The police advised them to **fit** a burglar alarm to protect their house. ....
- Patrick's going to be late: he phoned to say he's **stuck** in traffic. ....

2 INFORMATION ABOUT GRAMMAR

a) The mini-dictionary tells you whether a word is a noun, adjective, etc. It also tells you whether a noun is countable or uncountable, and whether verbs are transitive or intransitive. Match the abbreviations in column A with a grammatical term in column B. Write the correct symbols next to the words below.

A	B			
adj	uncountable noun	a skill	f snore ....
adv	transitive verb	b traffic	g straighten ....
n [C]	adjective	c ignore	h hooliganism ....
n [U]	preposition	d extreme	i bolt ....
phr v	intransitive verb	e according to	j centre on ....
prep	countable noun		
v [T]	adverb		
v [I]	phrasal verb		

> The mini-dictionary also gives you information about:
> - **irregular verb forms**
> - the correct **preposition** to use after a word
> - common **grammar patterns**, such as whether a verb is followed by a **gerund** or **infinitive**.

b) Look up the underlined words in the mini-dictionary and find the best way to complete each sentence.

    a I was so angry, I *teared/tore* the letter up and threw it away. <u>tear</u>

    b Charles Long is a well-known *expert about/on* Roman history. <u>expert</u>

    c The robbers forced the cashier *handing over / to hand over* the money. <u>force</u>

    d No one seems to agree who was *responsible about/for* the accident. <u>responsible</u>

    e The terrorists are threatening *blowing up / to blow up* the buildings unless their demands are met. <u>threaten</u>

3 FINDING OUT ABOUT PRONUNCIATION

a Phonemic symbols

1) Look at the pronunciation table on the inside cover of the mini-dictionary. Use the table to find out what these words are:

    - /ˈhʌnimuːn/   • /nəˈtɔːriəs/   • /ˌpeɪpə ˈhæŋkətʃɪf/

2) Now look up the following words in the mini-dictionary and use the phonemic spelling to find out how they are pronounced:

    - sew   • weapon   • subtle

b Word stress

Word stress is marked like this in the mini-dictionary: /rɪˈsiːt/

Look up the following words in the mini-dictionary and <u>underline</u> the stressed syllable, as in the example.

    For example: rec<u>ei</u>pt   • rebellion   • opportunity   • predominantly

4 OTHER INFORMATION IN THE MINI-DICTIONARY

With certain words in the mini-dictionary, you can find extra information. This could be information about:

    - **British** and **American English**   • **related vocabulary**   • **opposites**, etc.

Look up the words in *italics* in the mini-dictionary to answer the following questions.

    a What is the American word for *pavement*?

    b What is the difference between a *basin* and a *sink*?

    c What do the letters *PhD* mean?

    d What is another word for *mankind*?

    e What is a word connected to *seafood*?

    f What is the opposite of *plug in*?

     PHOTOCOPIABLE

Learner-training worksheet 3

Using a monolingual dictionary with reading texts

THIS WORKSHEET IS TO BE USED IN CONJUNCTION WITH THE *LONGMAN DICTIONARY OF CONTEMPORARY ENGLISH*

The *Longman Dictionary of Contemporary English* gives you information about words in many different ways. For example, it:

*   guides you through the **different meanings** of a word and gives examples of each use
*   tells you whether a word is a **noun** (*n*), **verb** (*v*), **adjective** (*adj*), etc.
*   informs you whether a word or phrase is **British English** (*BrE*) / **American English** (*AmE*) or **formal/informal**
*   gives the **pronunciation** of a word in the **International Phonetic Alphabet** (see the key on page 1 of the dictionary) and indicates **word stress** with a stress mark (ˈ) before the main stressed syllable, e.g. await /əˈweit/
*   shows **collocations** (words that are typically used with a word) and the **grammatical patterns** that follow a word (e.g. whether a verb is followed by an infinitive or a gerund) in **bold**
*   provides **extra tips** on how and when to use a word (see the grey **USAGE NOTE** boxes and the **graphs** showing the frequency of different patterns).

1 Read the text below quickly: do not look up any words in your dictionary yet. Can you explain the title of the text?

Crossing chaos

A motorcyclist was travelling through Europe when he came to a **level crossing**. The gates were down and so he **waited for** the train to pass. While he was waiting, a local villager came along with a goat in **tow**. He tied the goat to the crossing gate, smiled at the motorcyclist and together they waited for the train to pass. A few moments later, another villager arrived driving a horse and cart, then a man in a sports car arrived to join the **queue**. All was fine until an express train came screaming through and **startled** the horse, which **reared** and bit the motorcyclist on the arm. The motorcyclist responded by **punching** the horse on the nose. Not one to tolerate the abuse of animals, the horse's owner got off his cart and punched the motorcyclist. The fight frightened the horse all the more – so much so that it tried to retreat from the fight but **succeeded only in** crashing the cart into the sports car. The driver of the sports car **leapt** from his vehicle and joined in the fight. At this point, the man with the goat attempted to intervene and calm things down. While he was doing so, he failed to **notice** the crossing gates lifting and his goat being strangled.

2 Now use the *Longman Dictionary of Contemporary English* to look up the words in **bold** in the text and answer the following questions.

a Where would you see a **level crossing**? Is the word used in British or American English?
b Find two differences between **wait for** and **await.**
c What does **in tow** mean? Is it a formal or informal expression? Which of these words rhymes with **tow**?
   • now   • no   • two
d What is the pronunciation of **queue**? What is the American equivalent of this word?
e In this context, does **startled** mean *suddenly surprised* or *slightly shocked*? What verbs commonly follow it, and are they in the infinitive or the gerund form?
f In this case **rear** is a verb: which of the four meanings given does it have here?
g What do you use to **punch** someone? On which page is there a picture to show the meaning?
h How does the word **only** change the meaning of **succeed** here? What preposition follows this verb?
i **Leapt** is the past tense of which verb? What is the pronunciation of the infinitive and past form?
j Which of the six grammatical patterns with **notice** shown in the graph is found in the text? Which is the most common pattern?

Learner-training worksheet 4

Learning about collocation

Learning vocabulary is not just a question of learning new words. Very often, we need to learn common combinations of words, known as **collocations**.

1 TYPES OF COLLOCATION

There are several different types of collocation. In each case, add another example, using the *Longman Dictionary of Contemporary English* if necessary.

  a Verb + noun
     e.g. *make a noise, leave home, have* ....
  b Adjective + noun
     e.g. *heavy rain, a strong accent, a(n)* .... *friend.*
  c Verb + adverb
     e.g. *work hard, will definitely, speak* ....
  d Verb + preposition (including phrasal verbs)
     e.g. *talk about* something, *tell* someone *off, think* .... *somebody.*
  e Fixed or semi-fixed phrases
     Fixed, e.g. *On the other hand …, It seems to me that …, Once upon a* ....
     Semi-fixed, e.g. *What I like/hate about it/him is … It's worth seeing / doing / waiting for.*
     It's/he's/she's one of the .... *-est* .... *in the world/country.*

2 NOTICING COLLOCATIONS

In the text below, <u>underline</u>:

  a A collocation with *lawyer*.
  b A collocation with *childhood*.
  c A phrasal verb which means to refuse an offer.
  d A collocation meaning the place where you were born.
  e The preposition used with *the coast*.
  f The preposition following the verb *to emigrate*.
  g A collocation that means *very sad*.
  h Words that collocate with *have*, *get* and *say*.
  i A fixed phrase meaning *between fifty-five and fifty-nine years old*.
  j An adverb which collocates with *try*.

David Matland, <u>a successful lawyer,</u> has finally married his childhood sweetheart, thirty-three years after he first proposed. When eighteen-year-old Jackie Biham turned him down, he left his home town of Brighton, on the south coast of England, and emigrated to Canada, broken-hearted. Both later married other people, had children and got divorced. But earlier this year, Mr Matland, now in his late fifties, decided to try again. This time she said yes. 'It just shows what persistence can achieve,' Mr Matland said.

3 RECORDING COLLOCATIONS

Almost any text you read will contain a large number of collocations. Here are three ways you can keep note of collocations you find.

a) Write down new items as phrases rather than just as words (with an example/translation as necessary).

> *make up your mind – decide*
> *I just couldn't make up my mind, so in the end I bought both.*

b) Use word diagrams to show collocations with common words, like the one below, and add new examples as you find them.

make + noun = 'do something'
make an arrangement / an appointment
a decision / a plan / a mess / a mistake

Other phrases
make sure

MAKE

make = 'to produce'
a cup of coffee / a sandwich / lunch / a noise
made of plastic / leather / made in Japan

c) Look at the *Longman Dictionary of Contemporary English* to find other useful collocations (remember that the most common collocations are shown first). Then copy the entries into your vocabulary notebook.

> **4   make an appointment / arrangement / date, etc.** to arrange to do something, meet someone etc.
> **5   make a contribution / donation / charge, etc.** to give or ask for money for a particular purpose:
>   *We have to make a small charge for use of the facilities.*
> **6   make an appearance / entrance, etc.** to suddenly appear somewhere or enter a room

4 MAKING NOTES
Make a note of any new collocations in the text using some of the techniques above. For more note-making techniques, see *Learner-training worksheet 5*.

Learner-training worksheet 5

Making notes in class

1 Read the statements below about making notes and discuss with a partner which of them are true for you. Then look at *Commentary 1* on the next page to see how your conclusions compare to those of an expert.

a — *I never make notes during lessons.*

b — *I only copy down what my teacher writes on the board.*

c — *I make notes on what I think is important during the lesson.*

d — *I sometimes find it hard to make sense of the notes I've made, and I often lose them.*

2 Look at the notes made by three students on part of a lesson (Reading and vocabulary on page 62 of your *Students' Book*). What do you think are the good points of each set of notes, and how could they be improved? Then look at *Commentary 2* on the next page.

Student A

MONDAY

to outrun (v) =
to run faster than
something else
/aʊtˈrʌn/

a wound = an
injury

<u>Discussion notes</u>
friend was in
earthquake — very
dangerous —
survived

most frightening
disaster — fire

*a big/great
threat

Student B

22.07.04   Module 6: Getting it right
                        p62

Vocabulary
to outrun = [prześcignąć]
a wound = [rana]
to distract = [rozpraszać]

'The most frightening situation I've ever been
in was when I ...'

Student C

HOW TO GET IT RIGHT
                    RIGHT
                    RIGHT

outrun

Page 62

I don't
understand
this

PHOTOCOPIABLE

3 Look back on your notes on previous lessons (if you have them!) and decide how they could be improved. Choose some of the methods for making notes mentioned on this worksheet and try them out for the next week or two.

COMMENTARY 1

a It may seem unnecessary to make notes during a lesson, particularly when there is a lot of conversation – but in any lesson there are points which you'll forget unless you write them down: getting things on paper can help fix them in your mind. The chances are that if you haven't taken any notes during a lesson, you won't have gained very much from it.

b Many students write down everything their teacher writes on the board: this is generally a good idea, although remember not everything on the board will be useful – and your teacher may not write much up during a lesson! It's a good idea to note down new vocabulary and grammar explanations **if you don't know them already**, but don't waste time copying things you already know.

c The way to get the most out of your lessons is to be active, whether by asking questions, working things out for yourself or by taking notes on things you think could be useful. When you come to look back on what you've learned, at the end of your course or before an exam, notes will be necessary as a record which you can refer to. Different people will find different things useful during a lesson.

d Writing your notes on a loose piece of paper is the best way to lose them – buy a notebook or a file so you can keep all your notes together. If you find it difficult to make sense of the notes you've made when you return to them later, read *Commentary 2* below for extra help.

COMMENTARY 2

Student A's notes have a number of good points. She has noted new vocabulary with a note on meaning, pronunciation and a synonym to help her remember. She has also made some brief notes for the discussion – this is a good idea to help you speak fluently, as long as you don't try and write out every word. In addition, she has made a note of a couple of useful collocations (see *Learner-training worksheet 4*). The only problem is that there aren't many headings, so it's not easy to see how the notes are organised.

Student B has used boxes, headings and different shapes to help him divide and organise his notes: this makes them easier to refer to later. He has also written a translation of the new phrases so he can test himself. Perhaps an example sentence would be helpful too. In addition, he has written down a sentence he heard which he felt could be useful – noting useful phrases you hear during the lesson is a good way to remember language points. Remember you should listen to **how** proficient speakers of English say things, and not just what they say.

Student C's notes really don't make much sense, probably even to the person who wrote them! The vocabulary is written down without a translation, definition or example sentence and so will be difficult to remember. However, she has made a note of something she **doesn't** understand – which she can check or ask about later. Drawings and using different colours can be useful in stimulating your visual memory and they make the notes look more attractive ... just as long as the pictures are relevant to the lesson!

 © Pearson Education Limited 2005

1A Get to know the *Students' Book*

A

Do all the modules have a **Study ... Practice ... Remember!** section at the end?

....

B

On which page is the **Language summary** for Module 5?

Page ....

C

What colour is the **Useful language** box in Module 7?

....

D

How many **Consolidation** sections are there in the *Students' Book*?

....

E

What topic is studied in the **Real life** section in Module 10?

....

F

Where can you find a **Pronunciation** table?

....

G

What colour are the **Analysis** boxes in Module 12?

....

H

On which pages are the **Tapescripts** for the listening exercises in Module 7?

Pages .... and ....

I

On which page is the **Mini-check** for Module 9?

....

J

How many **Pronunciation** boxes are there in Module 3?

....

K

Which words are studied in the **Wordspot** in Module 8?

....

L

On which page is there a list of **Irregular verbs**?

Page ....

1B Me too!

Tenses and question forms

	My answers	Name
Two things you like doing in your free time		
Something you're going to do next weekend		
Two or three interesting countries you've been to		
Something you would do if you had more money		
The length of time you've been studying English		
Two things you've bought recently		
Two interesting things you did last month		
What you were doing at nine o'clock last Saturday evening		
The first thing you'll do when you get home today		
Two films you've seen in the last three months		
Something you hated doing when you were a child		
The length of time you've known your best friend		

© Pearson Education Limited 2005

1C Get circles

Expressions with *get*

Write down **short** answers to the following points in the circles below. Write your answers in any circle you like, but **not** in the same order as the questions. You do not have to answer every question, but try to answer at least **twelve**.

- the name of someone you've got to know recently
- how long it takes you to get ready if you're going out for the evening
- the name of an old friend you would like to get in touch with
- whether you used to get into trouble a lot when you were a child
- the name of someone you get on well with
- the last time you got really annoyed
- the best present you got for your last birthday
- the length of time since you last got your hair cut
- something foreigners would find hard to get used to if they lived in your country
- a reason why people often get to work late
- what you would do to get over your boyfriend or girlfriend leaving you
- something in your house which might get broken if you had a party there
- how long it takes to get home from where you are now
- how you would spend your time if you got stuck in a traffic jam for three hours
- the last time you got your car or bicycle mended
- the best thing to do if you get a cold

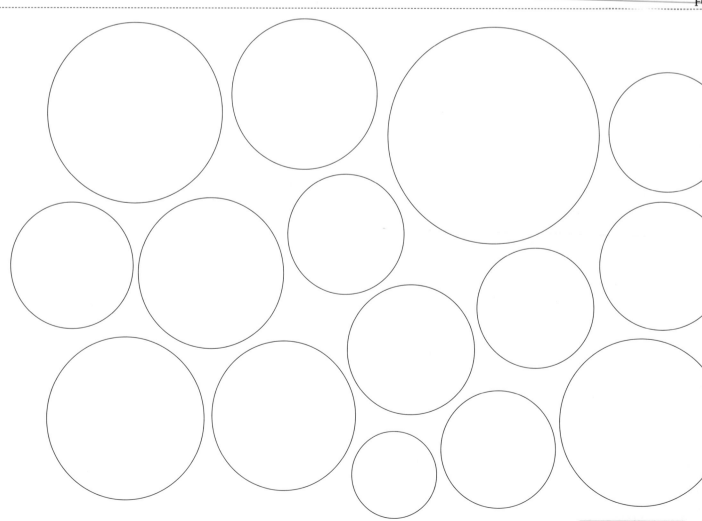

1D Three-person snap

Various uses of auxiliary verbs

Question master cards

Does your sister like watching football? (**Answer:** Yes, she does.)	You've got lots of money. (**Answer:** No, I haven't!)	You haven't been to Argentina, (**Answer:** have you?)
Are you going out tonight? (**Answer:** No, I'm not.)	The other students weren't here yesterday. (**Answer:** Yes, they were!)	My sister was arrested last night. (**Answer:** Was she?)
Has your mother ever been to the United States? (**Answer:** No, she hasn't.)	You're not angry with me, (**Answer:** are you?)	I got the highest mark in the class. (**Answer:** Did you?)
Your father hates watching soap operas. (**Answer:** No, he doesn't!)	Your parents have got a house in London, (**Answer:** haven't they?)	My uncle has climbed Mount Everest. (**Answer:** Has he?)
The other students didn't enjoy themselves at all. (**Answer:** Yes, they did!)	Your father visited you last week, (**Answer:** didn't he?)	I wasn't told about the homework yesterday. (**Answer:** Weren't you?)

Auxiliary verb cards

Yes, she does.	No, I haven't!	have you?
No, I'm not.	Yes, they were!	Was she?
No, she hasn't.	are you?	Did you?
No, he doesn't!	haven't they?	Has he?
Yes, they did!	didn't he?	Weren't you?

2A Which stress pattern?

Stress patterns of verbs, nouns and adjectives

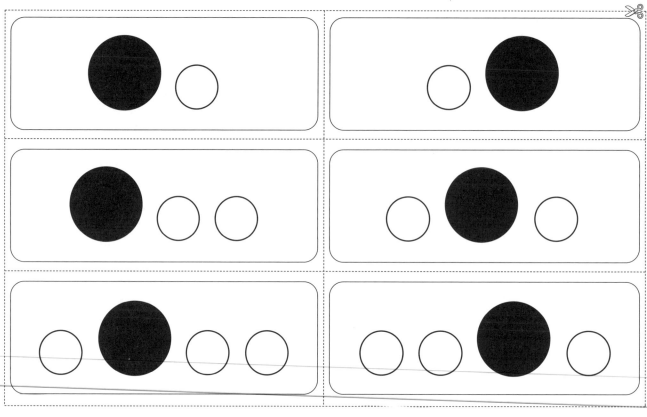

psychology	depress	science	support
psychologist	depression	scientific	supportive
anxiety	depressing	scientist	supporter
anxious	depressed	suffering	involvement
awareness	envy	suffer	involve
aware	envious	sufferer	involved

2B Who am I?

Gerunds and phrases to describe abstract ideas

Who am I?

Student number ☐

.... makes me feel nervous.

.... is my idea of happiness.

.... is something that really annoys me.

.... helps me relax.

.... makes me feel stressed.

.... really frightens me.

.... always makes me laugh.

.... would embarrass me.

.... makes me feel really depressed.

.... sometimes confuses me.

.... is often a disappointment.

.... makes me feel proud.

2C How many schwas?

Schwas in three- and four-syllable words

Schwa cards

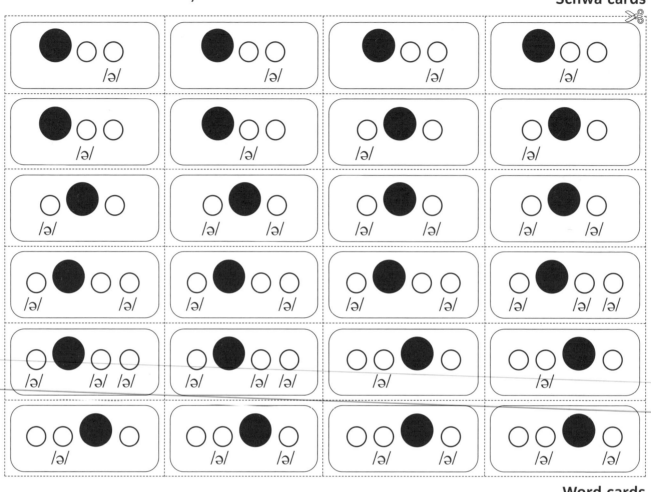

Word cards

happiness	confidence	genius	jealousy
suffering	exercise	genetic	annoying
supportive	contentment	confusion	performance
continuous	certificate	political	dependable
traditional	development	scientific	democratic
disappointed	demonstration	disappointment	politician

2D Prefix and suffix dominoes

Prefixes and suffixes with nouns and adjectives

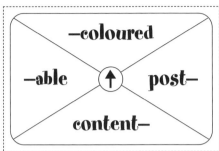

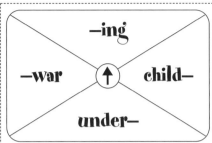

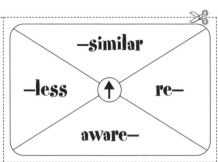

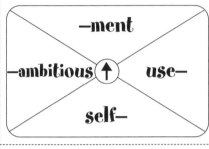

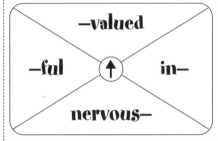

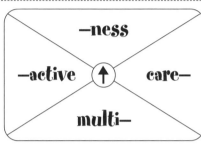

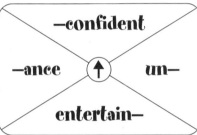

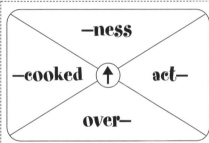

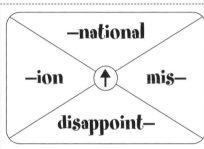

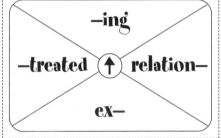

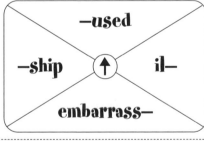

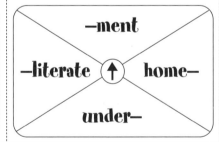

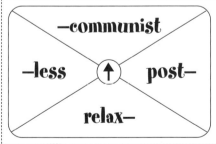

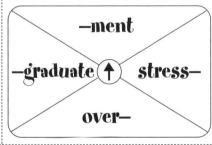

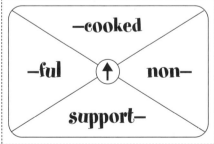

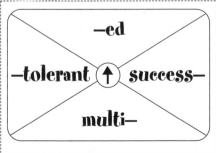

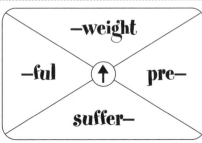

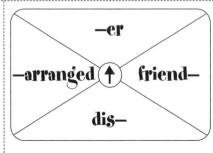

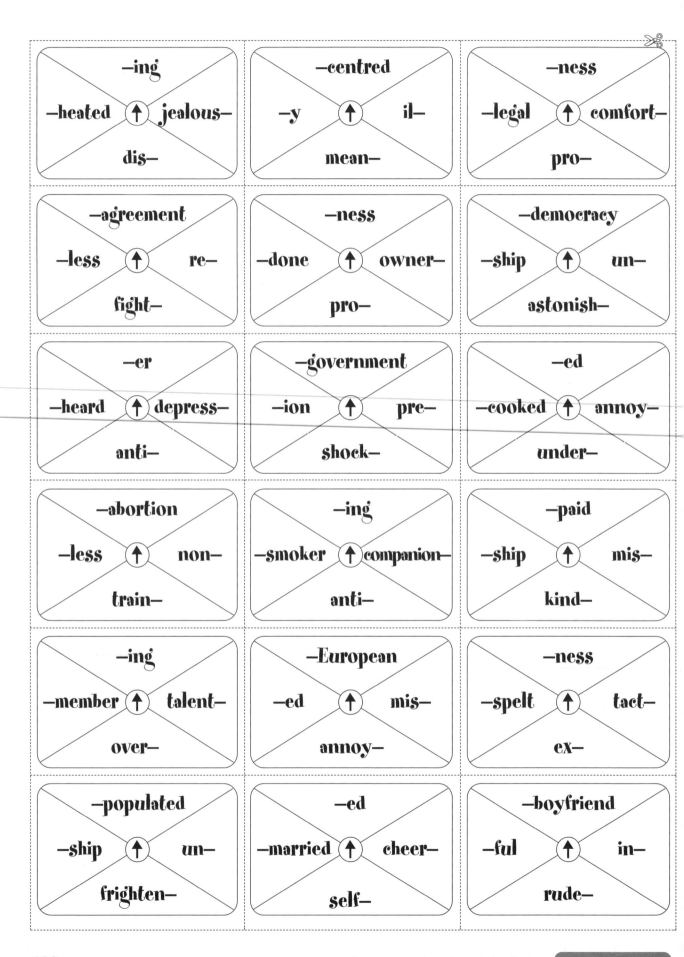

3A Sidney and the circus

Narrative tenses; verb–adverb combinations for travel and movement

Student A

Movement verbs worksheet

With your partner, match these verb–adverb combinations with the pictures.
Use a dictionary, if necessary.

rush home	run up to	walk home	walk up to ....
wander off	walk off	travel around	drive up to ....
walk past	run around	run away	walk along ....

© Pearson Education Limited 2005

Student B

Movement verbs worksheet

With your partner, match these verb–adverb combinations with the pictures.
Use a dictionary, if necessary.

rush home ....   run up to ....   walk home ....   walk up to ....

wander off ....   walk off ....   travel around ....   drive up to ....

walk past ....   run around ....   run away ....   walk along ....

        PHOTOCOPIABLE

3B Continuous snakes and ladders

Simple and continuous verb forms of various tenses

Questions

1 Which tense is correct?

Tom *walked / was walking* home when someone *called / was calling* out his name.

2 Which tense is correct?

When John *phoned / was phoning*, I *wrote / was writing* an essay. I *finished / was finishing* it at midnight.

3 Is this sentence right or wrong? (If it's wrong, correct it.)

When she was getting home, her husband was watching football on television.

4 Is this sentence right or wrong? (If it's wrong, correct it.)

As soon as she was seeing the time, she was jumping out of bed.

5 Which tense – Past simple or Past continuous?

While we (*wait*) for the guests to arrive, Sally (*ring*) to say she couldn't come.

6 Which tense – Past simple or Past continuous?

When he (*arrive*) at the party, everyone (*talk*) and (*laugh*).

7 Which tense is correct?

Sam's friends *had already gone / had already been going* by the time he *got / was getting* there.

8 Which tense is correct?

As soon as Cath shut the car door, she *realised / was realising* she *had left / had been leaving* the keys inside.

9 Which tense is correct?

They *waited / were waiting* until everybody *had left / had been leaving* the bank, then *broke in / were breaking in* through the window.

10 Which tense – Past perfect simple or Past perfect continuous?

When the helicopter finally found us we (*sit*) in the lifeboat for hours and (*eat*) all our food.

11 Is this sentence right or wrong? (If it's wrong, correct it.)

Tom was exhausted because he'd been working too hard.

12 Is this sentence right or wrong? (If it's wrong, correct it.)

By the time the emergency food supplies arrived, thirty people had been dying.

13 Is this sentence right or wrong? (If it's wrong, correct it.)

Before the accident, he'd never been thinking anything like this would happen to him.

14 What's the difference between these two sentences?

a He'd been trying to phone her before she left the country.
b He'd tried to phone her before she left the country.

15 Which tense is correct?

He *is working / has been working* there since he *left / was leaving* university.

Questions

---

16 Which tense is correct?

He *is playing / has been playing* tennis since he *started / was starting* school.

---

17 Which tense – Present perfect simple or continuous?

Oh no! The train (*stop*) again! I (*sit*) on this train for hours, and I (*already miss*) my first meeting.

---

18 Which tense – Present perfect simple or continuous?

You're covered in blood and you (*tear*) your jacket! You (*fight*) again, haven't you?

---

19 Is this sentence right or wrong? (If it's wrong, correct it.)

Careful where you walk. Susie's been breaking a vase, and Johnny's already cut himself.

---

20 Is this sentence right or wrong? (If it's wrong, correct it.)

They've been living next door for years, but we've never spoken to them.

---

21 Is this sentence right or wrong? (If it's wrong, correct it.)

I've been knowing him for a few months, but I've only been meeting his sister once.

---

22 Which tense is correct?

Normally I *get up / am getting up* at eight, but this week I *get up / am getting up* at seven because I have to start work early.

---

23 Which tense – Present simple or continuous?

Peter (*play*) football at the moment. He (*want*) to be a footballer when he grows up.

---

24 Is this sentence right or wrong? (If it's wrong, correct it.)

I'm loving hamburgers! I eat five every day, and I eat one at the moment!

---

25 What's the difference between these two sentences?

a What do you think?
b What are you thinking?

---

26 What's the difference between these two sentences?

a He's very rude.
b He's being very rude.

---

27 Which tense is correct?

This time next week I'll *lie / 'll be lying* on a beach in Spain.

---

28 Which tense is correct?

Don't come round at eight. I'll *put / 'll be putting* the children in bed then.

---

29 Is this sentence right or wrong? (If it's wrong, correct it.)

When I arrive at the station, my parents will wait for me.

---

30 What's the difference between these two sentences?

a I'll be cooking dinner when you get home.
b I'll cook dinner when you get home.

© Pearson Education Limited 2005   **125**

3C Problems, problems!

Language for responding to unexpected problems

Role cards

Language school – Role card A

You have just walked into an English language school to book a four-week intensive course starting next Monday. The classes are every morning from 9.00 to 12.00. You telephoned the school yesterday and they said that there were still some places available. You really need to study English, as you need it for your job (you work in a tourist information office in the afternoon). You are about to talk to the receptionist.

Language school – Role card B

You are a receptionist at an English language school, which has four-week intensive courses in the morning (9.00-to 12.00) and afternoon (2.00-to 5.00). The morning class is now full (you registered the last student ten minutes ago), but there are places available in the afternoon class. There are also part-time courses on Monday, Wednesday and Friday evenings from 7.30 to 9.00. If a class is full, students can join a waiting list.

Clothes shop – Role card A

You work in *BennyTown*, a famous clothes shop. The company has a strict policy on dealing with customers who bring back clothes. If there is a genuine problem with an article of clothing, you can: **a)** refund the money, but only if the customer has a receipt; **b)** exchange the item for a similar one; or **c)** take back the item and give the customer *BennyTown* vouchers, which they can use to buy clothes in the future. The only shirts you have at the moment are bright pink or black.

Clothes shop – Role card B

Last week you bought a beautiful pale blue shirt from *BennyTown*, a famous clothes shop. You wore it for the first time yesterday, and noticed that there was a hole in it. You cannot find the receipt (you're not even sure they gave you one), but there is a *BennyTown* label in the back of the shirt. You have gone back to the shop to exchange the shirt for a new one; you want to wear it tonight when you meet your new boyfriend/girlfriend.

Travel agency – Role card A

You are planning to go on holiday for two weeks. You telephoned a travel agency yesterday, and reserved a seat on the British Airlines flight to New York next Saturday. The flight departs at 9.30 a.m., and you were told that the return fare is £259 including taxes. You are now going to the travel agency to pay for your flight.

Travel agency – Role card B

You work in a travel agency which specialises in flights to the USA. You have just found out that the British Airlines flight to New York at 9.30 a.m. next Saturday has been cancelled because of a strike by pilots. There are still a few seats available to New York on the same day on American Airways, which leaves at 6.30 a.m. The return fare is £299 including taxes. All other flights to New York on that day are fully booked.

Restaurant – Role card A

You are a waiter at *The Garden Restaurant*. Tonight the restaurant is very busy, because a group of American tourists arrived at 8.00 and took all the tables. Your reservation list shows that nobody has booked a table tonight, although someone has already booked a table for four people at 8.30 tomorrow night. It's now 8.35 p.m, and the tourists will probably finish eating at about 9.30 p.m. A customer has just walked in, and you walk over to welcome him/her.

Restaurant – Role card B

You are going out for a meal with three friends of yours to celebrate passing your exams – it is a very special occasion! You phoned *The Garden Restaurant* this morning and reserved a table for four at 8.30 p.m. You have just arrived at the restaurant (it's now 8.35 p.m.). Your three friends will be there in five or ten minutes. A waiter comes to welcome you.

4A Passive scrabble

Passive tenses and passive forms

the two brothers 1	are 2	accused of 4	robbery 4	my house 2	is being 2
looked after 3	by a friend of mine 3	this week 2	AT THE MOMENT 3	she 1	is being 3
followed 3	by a man in a dark suit 3	yesterday 1	my sister 2	was 2	attacked 3
BY A MAD DOG 3	two days ago 1	he 1	was 2	shot 3	by a stranger 3
in the bedroom 4	the students 2	were 2	told 3	to finish it 4	last week 1
when we got there 4	people 2	WERE BEING 3	carried out of the building 4	all the guests 2	have been 2
taken 3	to the station 3	by the manager 2	Mark killed himself because he 4	had been 3	sent to prison for 4

murder **4**	**this year 2**	thousands of people **2**	have been **2**	arrested for **4**	burglary **4**
in London **2**	**when I arrived 3**	all the seats **2**	**HAD BEEN 3**	taken **3**	by foreign journalists **3**
the rest of the family **2**	will be **3**	told the news **3**	**next week 2**	by one of the lawyers **2**	all the staff **1**
MUST BE 3	invited to the conference **4**	**next month 2**	Tom and Alice **1**	**expected to be 3**	picked up **4**
at the airport **4**	**by their aunt 2**	most children **2**	**hate being 3**	told **2**	**what to do 4**
by their parents **2**	everyone **1**	**LOVES BEING 3**	given **3**	money **2**	at Christmas **2**
'To be' or Past Participle **0**	'To be' or Past Participle **0**	'To be' or Past Participle **0**	'To be' or Past Participle **0**	'To be' or Past Participle **0**	'To be' or Past Participle **0**

4B It's all in the mind

Expressions with *mind*

Situation 1
This morning you borrowed your friend's bike without asking. When you see your friend, what do you say?

Response
I hope you don't mind, but I borrowed your bike this morning.

Situation 2
A friend tells you she didn't get any tickets for the concert. This isn't a big problem for you. What do you say?

Response
Oh well, *never mind!*

Situation 3
You want a friend to help you get ready for the party you're having tonight. What do you say?

Response
Would you mind helping me get ready for the party?

Situation 4
Your friend has rented two videos. He asks you which you want to watch first. You think they are both good. What do you say?

Response
I don't mind which one we watch first.

Situation 5
You are showing a friend around your new house. You are going into a room with a very low doorway. What do you say to your friend?

Response
Mind your head!

Situation 6
Someone you don't know very well has just asked you if you've kissed your boyfriend/girlfriend after the first date. What do you say?

Response
Mind your own business!

Situation 7
This morning you arranged to go out with a friend, but now you want to stay at home. What do you say to your friend?

Response
I'm sorry, but *I've changed my mind.*

Situation 8
You are outside a cinema, and your friend can't decide which film to see. The films start in two minutes! What do you say?

Response
Hurry up and *make up your mind!*

Situation 9
A friend of yours has been very quiet recently, and looks worried about something. What do you say?

Response
Have you got something *on your mind?*

Situation 10
Your daughter didn't come home from school today. It's now eleven o'clock in the evening. A friend phones you – what do you say?

Response
My daughter hasn't come home. *I'm out of my mind with worry.*

Situation 11
Your brother is planning to swim across the Atlantic Ocean! What do you say?

Response
You must be *out of your mind!*

Situation 12
You are going to San Francisco on holiday. A friend went there last year, and recommends a good place to stay near the airport. What do you say?

Response
Thanks, I'll *keep it in mind.*

Situation 13
You promised to post a letter for your mother, but you forgot! What do you say to her when you get home?

Response
I'm really sorry I didn't post your letter, *it slipped my mind.*

Situation 14
Your sister has some important things to say to her husband, but knows they might make him unhappy. You advise her to say exactly what she wants to. What do you say?

Response
You should *speak your mind.*

Situation 15
Although your brother seems very fit and healthy, he's certain he has a very serious illness. You think he's just imagining it. What do you say to him?

Response
It's all in your mind.

5A A wonderful life

Present perfect (various uses)

Chris Bull

You are going to be interviewed on a TV programme called *A Wonderful Life*. Decide on the details of your life and make **brief notes** for the ideas below. Do not write complete sentences. If you want, you can base your life on a real person, or a combination of real people.

You're an actor/actress.
- How long?
- How many films?
- Your favourite film?

You are also a director.
- How long?
- How many films?
- Your best film?

You've won some awards.
- How many?
- What for?
- When?

You're making a new film.
- Acting or directing?
- What's the film about?
- Other details about the film?
- How long?

You've got a new hobby.
- What is it?
- How long?

You live somewhere beautiful.
- Where?
- How long?
- Why did you choose to live there?

You're married.
- Who to?
- How long?
- What does he/she do?

You have a famous best friend.
- Who?
- How long?
- How did you meet?
- Your previous marriages?

You've worked in lots of countries.
- How many?
- Your favourite?
- Why?

You're an author as well.
- How long?
- How many books?
- Your most successful book?
- How long?

TV Interviewer

You are going to interview the famous actor, writer and director Chris Bull on your TV programme, *A Wonderful Life*. Before the interview, write down some questions to ask, using the ideas below.

His/Her career as an actor/actress.
- How long?
- How many films?
- His/Her favourite film?

His/Her career as a director.
- How long?
- How many films?
- His/her best film?

He/She is making a new film.
- Acting or directing?
- Title? Plot?
- Other details about the film?
- How long?

Awards and prizes.
- How many?
- What for?
- When?

Famous best friend.
- Who?
- How long?
- How did you meet?

His/Her writing career.
- How long?
- How many books?
- His/Her most successful book?

His/Her marriage.
- His/her partner's name and job?
- How long?
- Married before?

His/Her new hobby.
- What?
- How long?

His/Her home.
- Where?
- How long?
- Why there?

130

PHOTOCOPIABLE

5B Word combinations

Verb–noun word combinations

to achieve	something worthwhile	to overcome	your fear
to achieve	success	to make	a sacrifice
to break	a world record	to show	dedication
to cope with	stress	to take	risks
to cope with	problems	to take over	a company
to overcome	difficulties	to win	an award

What about you?

On a **separate** piece of paper, write down **short** answers to the following questions. Write the answers wherever you want on the page, but **not** in the same order as the questions. You don't have to answer all the questions, but try to answer as many as you can.

- Do you like taking risks?
- Write down the name of a famous person (or someone you know personally) who's achieved something worthwhile in their life.
- What advice would you give to someone who wanted to overcome their fear of snakes?
- If you had enough money to take over a company, which company would you choose?
- What have you achieved some success in?
- Write down the name of someone who's won an award (e.g. for music, acting or writing) in the last three years.

- What sacrifices do parents have to make for their children?
- Think of a problem people have to cope with nowadays that they didn't have to cope with a hundred years ago.
- How do you cope with stress in your daily life?
- Can you name someone who's broken a world record?
- Do you know someone who's overcome a lot of difficulties in their life?

5C Who's worked for the CIA?

Present perfect simple and continuous

Find someone who ...	Name(s)
1 ... has written / has been writing a lot of best-sellers.	
2 ... has made / has been making a film for the last six months.	
3 ... has met / has been meeting the Pope and the queen of England.	
4 ... has learnt / has been learning how to speak seven languages perfectly.	
5 ... has played / has been playing tennis professionally since he/she was eighteen.	
6 ... has been going / has been to the moon.	
7 ... has recently broken / has recently been breaking the hundred-metre world record.	
8 ... has written / has been writing a book about journalism for three years.	
9 ... has won / has been winning an Oscar.	
10 ... has worked / has been working for the CIA for the last five years.	

Role card 1

You are a famous writer of spy stories from England. You've written fourteen best-sellers so far. Your most famous book is called *The Cold War*. At the moment you're not writing anything because you're going to get married. You're going to Moscow for your honeymoon with your Russian wife.

Role card 2

You are a famous film director from the USA. You've already made three films (your most famous film so far is called *Trust Nobody*) and you've been working on your fourth for the last six months. Your new film will be called *Eye Spy*, and is set in Moscow after the Second World War.

Role card 3

You are the ambassador for an Eastern European country (you decide which one). You've met lots of famous people in your job. You met the Pope when he visited your country, and the queen of England last year. You had dinner with her at the American Embassy in London. You've also met Fidel Castro, the president of Cuba.

Role card 4

You are a translator, and you work for the United Nations in New York. You can speak seven languages perfectly (you decide which ones). You have worked all over the world (you decide where). You were born in Cuba, and were in East Germany in 1989 when the Berlin Wall came down.

Role card 5

You are a professional tennis player. You grew up in Eastern Europe (you decide which country), but when you were fifteen your family went to live in the USA because of political problems in your country. You have won a lot of tournaments all around the world, and next week you're playing in a tournament in Germany.

Role card 6

You are a famous American astronaut. You went to the moon on Apollo 16 in 1972, and then worked for NASA (the North American Space Agency). At the moment you are working on the joint American–Russian space programme, which is planning to send a space station to Mars. You've been working in Moscow for the last two years.

Role card 7

You are a famous athlete from Russia. You recently broke the hundred-metre world record at an athletics meeting in Geneva, and are a hero in your country. You recently met the Russian president, who invited you to a dinner at the Kremlin in your honour. Next week you are running in Washington, and hope to meet the American president.

Role card 8

You are a TV reporter, and have travelled all over the world working for CNN (an American news company). You started writing a book about your experiences three years ago, but haven't had time to finish it. You know many politicians very well (you decide who) and tomorrow you're going to Russia to report on the political crisis there.

Role card 9

You are a famous actor/actress from the USA (although your parents were born in Poland). You won an Oscar two years ago for your role in the last James Bond film, which was filmed in Siberia. Next week you are going to Cuba to start making your new film, *Don't Trust Me*, for an American company.

Role card 10

You are the CIA agent! Do **not** tell anyone this! When people ask you about your life, you have to lie! It's a good idea to find out who the other person is **first**, then you can pretend to be someone else on the *Find someone who ...* worksheet. You will need to invent facts about yourself to support your story. Whatever happens, **never** admit you're a CIA agent!

6A The genuine article

Use and non-use of articles

Question 1

A: 'I'm thinking of buying a new bike next week.'
B: 'Have you been to new cycle shop on the Church Street?'

> **Answer**
> A: 'I'm thinking of buying a new bike next week.'
> B: 'Have you been to **the** new cycle shop on ~~the~~ Church Street?'

Question 2

There's a restaurant in centre of Washington that makes a most delicious lasagne in the world.

> **Answer**
> There's a restaurant in **the** centre of Washington that makes **the** most delicious lasagne in the world.

Question 3

I'm reading the interesting book at the moment. It's about a life of Nelson Mandela when he was in prison.

> **Answer**
> I'm reading **an** interesting book at the moment. It's about **the** life of Nelson Mandela when he was in prison.

Question 4

I've got two pets, a cat and a dog. I don't like a cat, because he brings the mice into the house.

> **Answer**
> I've got two pets, a cat and a dog. I don't like **the** cat, because he brings ~~the~~ mice into the house.

Question 5

Mark and Laura got married on twenty-third of December. Few days later, Laura realised she'd made the worst mistake of her life.

> **Answer**
> Mark and Laura got married on **the** twenty-third of December. **A** few days later, Laura realised she'd made the worst mistake of her life.

Question 6

I've started going to a yoga class on Thursdays. A teacher is very good, but I'm worst in the class!

> **Answer**
> I've started going to a yoga class on Thursdays. **The** teacher is very good, but I'm **the** worst in the class!

Question 7

You may now open an examination paper. Write your name and the date at top of the page.

> **Answer**
> You may now open **the** examination paper. Write your name and the date at **the** top of the page.

Question 8

I don't go to the church. In fact, I've only been inside church once, when I went to Russia.

> **Answer**
> I don't go to ~~the~~ church. In fact, I've only been inside **a** church once, when I went to Russia.

Question 9

After leaving school, Janet worked as cleaner in a hospital. She then went to the college to study nursing.

Answer
After leaving school, Janet worked as **a** cleaner in a hospital. She then went to ~~the~~ college to study nursing.

Question 10

His mother is doctor, and she lives in a small village in north of Brazil near the Amazon rainforest.

Answer
His mother is **a** doctor, and she lives in a small village in **the** north of Brazil near the Amazon rainforest.

Question 11

As I was walking along Oxford Street on my way to National Theatre, I found a ten-pound note on a pavement.

Answer
As I was walking along Oxford Street on my way to **the** National Theatre, I found a ten-pound note on **the** pavement.

Question 12

A: 'Welcome home, darling. What do you want for the dinner?'
B: 'Nothing, thanks. I met old friend from school and we had lunch together.'

Answer
A: 'Welcome home, darling. What do you want for ~~the~~ dinner?'
B: 'Nothing, thanks. I met **an** old friend from school and we had lunch together.'

Question 13

While I was staying in the hotel in south of India, I met a man who worked for the CIA.

Answer
While I was staying in **a** hotel in **the** south of India, I met a man who worked for the CIA.

Question 14

Many of the cities in the USA suffer from the crime. The police should be given the money they need to deal with problem.

Answer
Many of the cities in the USA suffer from ~~the~~ crime. The police should be given the money they need to deal with **the** problem.

Question 15

I went to the cinema last night with the friend from work, and we saw a film about Vietnam War.

Answer
I went to the cinema last night with **a** friend from work, and we saw a film about **the** Vietnam War.

Question 16

The last weekend, Janet Morgan went skiing in Alps and then stayed in a hotel by Lake Geneva.

Answer
~~The~~ Last weekend, Janet Morgan went skiing in **the** Alps and then stayed in a hotel by Lake Geneva.

6B Where on earth are we?

Ways of adding emphasis; cleft sentences

Student A

You are on your way to a wedding in your car. You are driving, and your friend has been giving you directions. Now you're completely lost and you're going to be late. You stop the car and discuss what to do. Together you must decide what you're going to do next. You begin the conversation.

These are some points you want to make:
- You have no idea where you are. You've never been to this part of town in your life.
- You didn't leave early enough because your friend was late. You told him/her to arrive at a quarter **to** twelve, and he/she arrived at a quarter **past** twelve.
- You wrote down the directions, and thought they were extremely clear. There was no need to bring a map.
- You think you should have turned left at the crossroads a few minutes ago.
- You think that you must go back to the crossroads to get back on the right road.
- You told your friend yesterday to buy the wedding present, and you want to check he/she has brought it with him/her.
- You didn't want to come to the wedding. Your friend persuaded you to come.
- Your friend always thinks that he/she is right, and this annoys you!

Useful language

I'm absolutely certain that ...

I really do think that ...

What we need is ...

What really annoys me is ...

I told you to ...

It's / It was you who ...

Where / Why / What / How on earth ...?

I really am sorry about ...

Student B

You are on your way to a wedding in your car. Your friend is driving, and you've been giving him/her directions, but now you're lost and you're going to be late. You stop the car and discuss what to do. Together you must decide what you're going to do next.

These are some points you want to make:
- You are sure you know where you are. You and your friend came here together last year for a party.
- You arrived at your friend's house at a quarter past twelve, the exact time he/she told you on the phone.
- You think the directions, which your friend wrote down, aren't very clear. You suggested bringing a map, but your friend said you didn't need one.
- You told your friend to turn left at the crossroads a few minutes ago, but he/she didn't.
- You are sure that if you continue down this street, you will get back on the correct road.
- You didn't buy a wedding present, because your friend said on the phone yesterday that he/she was going to buy one.
- You didn't want to come to the wedding. Your friend persuaded you to come.
- Your friend never believes what you say, and this annoys you!

Useful language

I'm absolutely certain that ...

I really do think that ...

What we need is ...

What really annoys me is ...

I told you to ...

It's / It was you who ...

Where / Why / What / How on earth ...?

I really am sorry about ...

7A Relative clauses crossword

Defining relative clauses

Student A

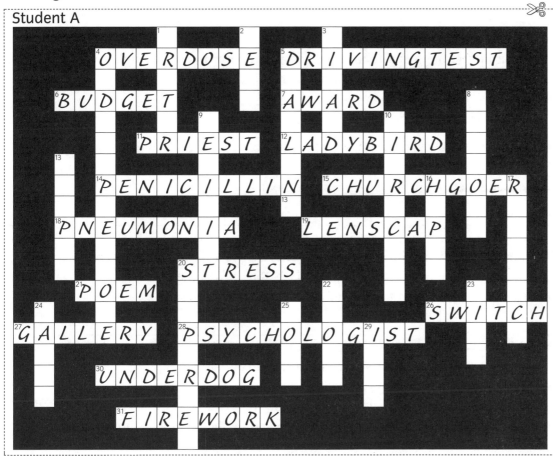

Student B

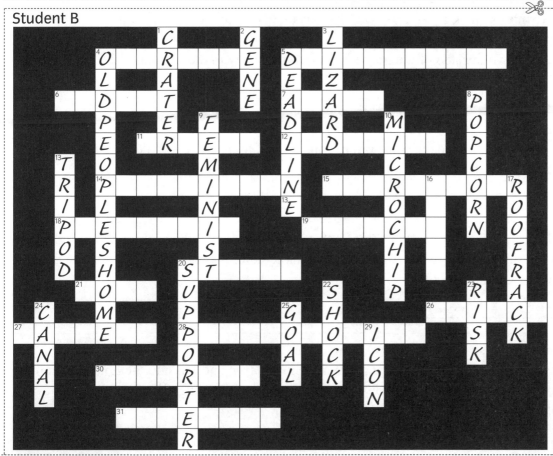

7B What's buried at the bottom of the garden?

Non-defining relative clauses

C   Paul stood outside number twenty-two, Rose Tree Lane, and tried to see if anyone was home. The dark blue curtains in the living room were completely drawn, even though it was still mid-afternoon. There were no cars parked outside the house, and even the garage was completely empty.

F   He took a deep breath and walked up the drive to the front door. As he looked through the letterbox into the hallway, long-forgotten memories came back to him. Now the hallway was dark and empty, and there were letters all over the floor.

H   It looked as though nobody had been home for weeks. 'Does anyone still live here?' he wondered. Perhaps he should have tried to find out before he'd come. Well, it was too late now. He thought for a while, then turned and walked back down the drive.

A   Samantha hurried over to meet him. 'Well?' she asked anxiously.
'There's nobody in,' he said. 'It's now or never.'
He walked back to his car and opened the boot. Inside were two new spades he had bought earlier that day. He handed one to Samantha, then picked up the other and shut the boot.

G   'Let's make this as quick as we can,' said Paul as they hurried back to the house.
'Fine by me,' said Samantha.
They walked down the side of the house and made their way to the bottom of the garden.

B   'It's buried just here,' said Paul, pointing to a space between two large oak trees. He immediately stuck the spade into the ground and started to dig. The rain became heavier and heavier as they worked.

E   They had been digging for nearly an hour before they found what they were looking for. 'There it is!' shouted Paul as he pointed into the large hole. Samantha threw her spade down and looked down into the hole.

D   'Do you mind if I ask you what you're doing in my garden?'
Paul was so surprised by the voice he nearly lost his balance and fell into the hole. Samantha looked round in astonishment and felt her stomach tighten. Standing about ten metres away was an old man in an old brown coat.

 PHOTOCOPIABLE

Extra information cards

1 she had been watching him from across the street

2 the garden was so overgrown it was like walking through a jungle

3 the rain had been falling softly all day

4 her hands were red and sore from the digging

5 he had parked the car round the corner out of sight

6 Paul had lived there over twenty years ago

7 he used to sit and wait for hours in the hallway for his father to get home

8 the door still had the same painted metal numbers screwed into the wood

9 her courage was beginning to leave her

10 he used to keep his bike in the garage out of the rain

11 he had obviously been watching them for some time

12 she grabbed it with both hands

8A Fame and fortune

Vocabulary extension (collocations on the topic of fame and fortune)

Mark Staines knew that his job at the hamburger restaurant would never **bring him**	**fame** and he would never make a lot of money as long as he stayed there.
He did the lottery every week but never bought the **winning**	**ticket** like the people he saw on the television news and in the newspapers.
He dreamt of **making**	**a fortune** but his dreams never came true until he met Cynthia Palmer who worked for a modelling agency in New York.
Cynthia came into Mark's hamburger restaurant one evening and immediately noticed his good looks. 'I could **make you**	**a star**,' she told him and he agreed to go with her to New York.
Mark did his first modelling job and became **an overnight**	**sensation** with the public and media.
After his first photos became known, people stopped him in the street to **ask for**	**his autograph**, which he always gave.
Within months, he was the **centre of**	**media attention**, with everything he did and everything he said reported in newspapers and magazines around the world.
He was so much **in the public**	**eye** that he couldn't leave his house without being followed by the paparazzi.
That was when he started to hate the **loss**	**of privacy** and felt like returning to the obscurity of the hamburger restaurant.
Finally, instead of waiting to make a lot of money, **losing**	**his fortune** was all he could dream of.

8B Gerund and infinitive dominoes

Gerund and infinitive forms

... lift this sofa.	**I need to spend more time ...**	... studying in the library.	**My parents wouldn't let me ...**
... wear make-up until I was sixteen.	He seems ...	... to have been going out with her for years!	It's not worth ...
... seeing that film.	John avoids ...	... eating fatty foods.	**Everybody had better ...**
... try a bit harder than last time.	**All the children were told ...**	... to go home immediately.	It's extremely frightening ...
... to be caught in a hurricane.	The mountaineer managed ...	... to climb to safety.	I don't mind ...
... not going to the party.	**I wish you'd stop ...**	... making that irritating noise!	The burglars must ...
... have been waiting for us to leave the house.	We didn't have enough money ...	... to get into the club.	The children ran around looking for somewhere ...
... to hide.	If you keep driving like that we'll all ...	... be killed!	All the journalists expect ...
... to be told what's happening soon.	At school, he's having trouble ...	... making friends.	It was too expensive ...
... to go to the theatre.	The bank robbers made everyone ...	... lie on the floor.	Bill Gates is believed ...
... to be one of the richest men in the world.	**She's really good ...**	... at playing the piano.	He's so rude! He left without ...
... saying goodbye.	This train's very full. I'd rather ...	... wait for the next one.	I'd like someone to help me ...

8C Design your own soap opera!

Verbs that take the infinitive or the gerund

Design your own soap opera!

All the characters below appear in a soap opera – your soap opera!
With your partner(s), look at the characters and decide:

- who is related/married to who
- what the people do for a living
- who are friends, lovers and enemies

- where your soap opera is going to be set
- what your soap opera is called

Samantha

Laura

Alice

Mark

Richard

Chris

Sally-Ann

Daniel

Notes

Plot cards

Someone is having an affair with someone else's wife/husband/partner	Someone has just found out they are pregnant
Someone has stolen a lot of money	Someone thinks their friend/partner is planning to kill somebody
Someone wants to split up with their boyfriend/girlfriend or get divorced	Someone has just been shot
Someone is in love with two different people	Someone has just met an ex-lover who they thought was dead
Someone has just found out that their partner is the father of someone else's child	Someone is going to kidnap someone else

Verb bank

agree	hope	offer	**promise**
decide	intend	plan	refuse
expect	manage	pretend	threaten
admit	**avoid**	love	risk
consider	enjoy	**miss**	can't stand
deny	hate	imagine	**suggest**

Activities

9A The maze of terror!

Modal verbs of deduction in the past and present

Card 1
You are on holiday in the southern states of the USA. You're driving through a very remote area late at night, and are completely lost! You're looking for somewhere to stay, but have only seen one hotel, which was locked up. (**WHY?**) You have $100 in cash, and are tired and hungry. Finally you come to a junction in the middle of nowhere.
Do you:

• turn left? (**Card 2**)
• turn right? (**Card 3**)

Card 2
Five miles further on you see a big hotel on your left. It's open! You stop and go inside, but the receptionist tells you the hotel is fully booked. A coachload of tourists have reserved all the rooms. However, it's very late and they still haven't arrived. (**WHY NOT?**)
Do you:

• go back to the junction and turn right? (**Card 3**)
• continue along the road? (**Card 4**)
• try to bribe the receptionist to give you a room? (**Card 5**)

Card 3
You drive for ten minutes, then see an old hotel down a narrow turning. There are a lot of cars in the car park, but you can't see any lights on in the bedrooms. (**WHY NOT?**) The receptionist offers you a room for $50.
Do you:

• take the room? (**Card 6**)
• get back in the car and continue driving? (**Card 7**)

Card 4
You drive a bit further, but come to a sign in the middle of the road that says *Road closed – extreme danger!* (**WHY?**)
Do you:

• go back to the junction and turn right? (**Card 3**)
• go back to the hotel and try to bribe the receptionist to give you a room? (**Card 5**)

Card 5
The receptionist takes your bribe, and gives you the key to room 101. When you unlock the door, you see that the room is full of boxes of cigarettes – thousands of them! (**WHY?**) You go back to the receptionist to complain, but he pulls out a gun and tells you to get out.
Do you:

• go back to the junction and turn right? (**Card 3**)
• get back in the car and continue along the road? (**Card 4**)

Card 6
You leave your bags in the room and go to the restaurant – you're very hungry! There are no other guests in the restaurant. (**WHY NOT?**) You order some food, and the waiter offers you free wine with your meal. The atmosphere in the empty restaurant is making you feel a little nervous.
Do you:

• wait for your meal to arrive? (**Card 8**)
• go back to your room without eating? (**Card 9**)

Card 7
You drive for a while and come to a nice-looking motel. Sitting at reception is a man wearing an old-fashioned army uniform. (**WHY?**) There are lots of candles everywhere, and none of the lights are on. (**WHY NOT?**) He tells you there's only one room free – it costs $40.
Do you:

• take the room? (**Card 12**)
• continue driving? (**Card 13**)

Card 8
Your meal arrives, along with two large glasses of red wine. You start eating, but the meat you ordered tastes terrible. (**WHY?**) Also, the wine doesn't taste like any wine you've ever tasted.
Do you:

• leave the food and go up to your room? (**Card 9**)
• complain to the waiter? (**Card 10**)

Card 9
You are now back in your room. You get undressed and try to go to sleep. However, in the next room you hear a woman scream, then a loud noise. (**WHAT'S HAPPENED?**)
Do you:

• go and see what's going on next door? (**Card 11**)
• get back in your car and drive away? (**Card 7**)

Card 10
You make a complaint, and are taken to see the chef. In the kitchen you notice a human finger on the floor. There's also a bag of toes under the table! (**WHAT'S BEEN HAPPENING?**) You run out of the building, chased by the chef waving a large knife! You get in your car and drive away.
Do you:

• go back to the junction and turn left? (**Card 2**)
• continue driving along the road you're on? (**Card 7**)

144 © Pearson Education Limited 2005 **PHOTOCOPIABLE**

Card 11
You go into the room next door and see a woman lying on the bed. She isn't moving. There's a man standing next to her wearing a tall white hat. (**WHO IS HE? WHAT'S HAPPENED?**) You turn and run out of the building, chased by the man. You get in your car just in time.
Do you:

• go back to the junction and turn left? (**Card 2**)
• continue driving along the road you're on? (**Card 7**)

Card 12
You go into the room, light the candles and look around. The room seems very clean and comfortable. You are just about to go to bed when a woman starts banging loudly on your door and asking you to help her. (**WHY?**)
Do you:

• open the door? (**Card 14**)
• pretend you can't hear her and hope she goes away? (**Card 15**)

Card 13
You continue driving, and see an old man sitting at the side of the road. You get out of the car to ask if he knows a hotel nearby. His clothes are torn and his head is bleeding. He looks very frightened. (**WHY?**)
Do you:

• try and help him? (**Card 20**)
• get back in the car and leave? (**Card 22**)

Card 14
You open the door and let her in. She tells you her name is Sally, and her boyfriend is looking for her. If he finds her, he's going to kill her! (**WHY?**) She wants you to drive her away from the motel immediately.
Do you:

• tell her to go away? (**Card 16**)
• help her by driving her away from the motel? (**Card 17**)

Card 15
She kicks down your door and comes in anyway! She tells you her name is Sally, and her boyfriend is looking for her. If he finds her, he's going to kill her! (**WHY?**) She wants you to drive her away from the motel immediately!
Do you:

• tell her to go away? (**Card 16**)
• help her by driving her away from the motel? (**Card 17**)

Card 16
Sally pulls out a gun and tells you to get in your car – now! This time you don't argue! You drive for half an hour, then she tells you to stop. She gives you a thousand dollars, then runs off. (**WHERE DID SHE GET THE MONEY FROM?**) By now you're extremely tired.
Do you:

• go back to the motel? (**Card 18**)
• continue driving? (**Card 13**)
• go to sleep in the car? (**Card 19**)

Card 17
You get in the car and drive off, with Sally in the back seat. You continue driving for half an hour, then she tells you to stop the car. She gives you a thousand dollars, then runs off. (**WHERE DID SHE GET THE MONEY FROM?**) By now you're extremely tired.
Do you:

• go back to the motel? (**Card 18**)
• continue driving? (**Card 13**)
• go to sleep in the car? (**Card 19**)

Card 18
You go back to the motel, but the door to your room is locked from the inside. (**WHY?**) You can't find the man in the army uniform anywhere. (**WHERE HAS HE GONE?**)
Do you:

• continue driving? (**Card 13**)
• go to sleep in the car? (**Card 19**)

Card 19
You go to sleep in the car, but then a loud noise and a bright light wake you up. When the light disappears there is an old man standing in front of your car, looking confused and frightened. (**WHAT'S HAPPENED TO HIM?**) He knocks on your window.
Do you:

• try to help him? (**Card 20**)
• drive off immediately? (**Card 13**)

Card 20
The old man says he's been on an alien spaceship for three days. (**WHAT DO YOU THINK?**) He also says he lives in the next town, and if you give him a lift you can stay the night in his house.
Do you:

• give him a lift? (**Card 21**)
• leave him there and drive off? (**Card 22**)

Card 21

You drive off with the man in the back seat. He says he used to work for the government, but he can't tell you what he did. (**WHY NOT?**) When you get to the next town he invites you to stay in his house. He says there are no hotels in the town.

Do you:

• accept his offer and stay with him? (**Card 23**)
• look around the town yourself? (**Card 24**)

Card 22

Before you can leave he collapses, so you carry him to your car. He says he used to work for the government, but he can't tell you what he did. (**WHY NOT?**) When you arrive at the town he invites you to stay in his house. He says there are no hotels in the town.

Do you:

• accept his offer and stay with him? (**Card 23**)
• look around the town yourself? (**Card 24**)

Card 23

You drive up to his house, and you have to climb in through the window. (**WHY?**) You're extremely tired, so he shows you to your bedroom. You get lost and open the wrong door. The room is full of guns and other weapons! (**WHY?**)

Do you:

• drive away from the house immediately? (**Card 24**)
• go back to your room and go to sleep (**Card 25**)

Card 24

You drive round the town and discover that there is a hotel. The receptionist is wearing a Mickey Mouse costume! (**WHY?**) The hotel looks *very* luxurious, but the rooms only cost $70.

Do you:

• stay in the hotel? (**Card 26**)
• continue driving? (**Card 27**)

Card 25

While you are asleep, the army surround the house. You are arrested for terrorism – the man used to work for the FBI, but is now fighting against the American government. You spend the next three weeks in prison trying to convince everyone that you're innocent! You have reached the end of the maze.

Now go back through the cards and discuss with your partner(s) the decisions you made.

Card 26

You go into your room – it's beautiful! You are just about to go to bed when you open a cupboard to get an extra pillow. Inside is a man – and he's dead! (**WHEN DID HE DIE?**)

Do you:

• close the cupboard and go to sleep? (**Card 28**)
• leave the hotel quietly and get back in your car? (**Card 27**)

Card 27

You drive out of the town and see an old man hitch-hiking at the side of the road. He looks very dirty and untidy, and is standing next to two large suitcases. (**HOW LONG HAS HE BEEN TRAVELLING?**)

Do you:

• give him a lift? (**Card 29**)
• keep driving? (**Card 30**)

Card 28

In the middle of the night the police arrive and search the room. They find the body and arrest you on suspicion of murder! You are taken to the police station and spend two nights in the cells before you can prove your innocence. You have reached the end of the maze.

Now go back through the cards and discuss with your partner(s) the decisions you made.

Card 29

You give the old man a lift to his house – and it's the biggest house you've ever seen! The old man tells you he's a millionaire, and because you've been so kind to him he invites you in. You spend the rest of the holiday as his guest, and have the time of your life! You have reached the end of the maze.

Now go back through the cards and discuss with your partner(s) the decisions you made.

Card 30

Twenty minutes later you run out of petrol! You are a long way from the nearest town, and it's 3 a.m. You decide to go to sleep in the car, and have a very cold and uncomfortable night. In the morning you have to walk for three hours to find some petrol! You have reached the end of the maze.

Now go back through the cards and discuss with your partner(s) the decisions you made.

9B What's wrong with it?

Language for complaining

Student A

Read the following four situations carefully. In the **Restaurant** and the **Department store**, you have a problem you want your partner to solve. In the **Clothes shop** and the **Repair company**, you must respond to what your partner says.

1 Restaurant
You and your father are in a very expensive restaurant, *The Ratz*, to celebrate your birthday. Your food has just arrived (you ordered the steak, your father ordered the fish) but neither of you are happy with it. Decide what's wrong with the food (yours and your father's), and what you want the waiter to do about it.

2 Clothes shop
You are a shop assistant at *Last*, a fashionable clothes shop. If a customer wants to bring back an item of clothing, he/she must have a receipt, and a good reason to return it. You can give customers a refund, or exchange the item for something else in the shop if the item was bought less than a month ago.

3 Department store
You bought a set of china tea cups yesterday, from the famous department store *Herods*, as a Christmas present for your mother. When you got home you found there was a problem with them (you decide what the problem was). You are now going back to *Herods* to complain (you still have the receipt). Decide what you want the store to do about it.

4 Repair company
You are a secretary for a washing-machine repair company, *Fixit and Runn*. You work in the office, and know nothing about how washing machines work. At the moment all the service engineers (the people who repair washing machines) are out. If anyone phones, you must write down their personal details and find out what the problem is with their machine. The earliest available appointment is next week.

Student B

Read the following four situations carefully. In the **Clothes shop** and the **Repair company**, you have a problem you want your partner to solve. In the **Restaurant** and the **Department store**, you must respond to what your partner says.

1 Restaurant
You are a waiter in an expensive restaurant, *The Ratz*. You have just taken two main courses to one of the tables (they ordered the steak and the fish). You are always very polite – this is a very expensive restaurant! – and will do anything to help the customers enjoy their meal. However, your chef has just told you there is no more fish.

2 Clothes shop
You bought a pair of smart trousers two months ago from *Last*, a fashionable clothes shop. You've only worn them twice (for job interviews). However, you have just noticed there is something wrong with them. Decide what the problem is, and what you want the shop to do about it. You still have the receipt.

3 Department store
You are the manager of the china department in the famous department store *Herods*. You personally check every item when it is sold to make sure it's in perfect condition, so you get very few customers complaining. (Usually when they do it's because they've broken it themselves!) When you deal with customers, you never get angry!

4 Repair company
Last week you had a problem with your washing machine (you decide what the problem was), so you called a repair company, *Fixit and Runn*. Someone came to repair it yesterday, and the bill was £70. Now your washing machine is worse than ever! (you decide what else is wrong with it, and what you want the company to do). You're going to telephone the company to complain.

10A Getting together

Vocabulary extension (word families and dependent prepositions)

1a Find a **noun** in the section on Speed dating that
means *a feeling of liking something.*
Write it here: .... and mark the stress.

b Complete the **word family** and mark the stress.
Verb: ....
Adjective: ....

2a Find an **adjective** in the section on Speed dating that
means *dealing with something in a sensible way instead of
following a set of ideas or rules.*
Write it here: .... and mark the stress.

b Complete the **word family** and mark the stress.
Person: ....
Noun: ....

3a Find a **verb** in the section on Arranged marriages that
means *to make a connection in your mind between one thing
and another.*
Write it here: .... and mark the stress.

b What **preposition** is it followed by? ....

c What's the **noun**?
Write it here: .... and mark the stress.

4 Find words in the sections on Speed dating and
Arranged marriages which are **collocations** of
the following:
a to tell your life ....
b to synchronise your ....
c to be alive and ....
d to celebrate a.....................................
e to be happy to ....

5 Find the **prepositions** missing from these expressions
in the sections on Speed dating and Arranged marriages.
a to start ....
b to have conversations with .... fifteen people in one
evening
c to fill .... a card (or a form)
d to be prepared .... live abroad
e to have no problem .... that

6a Find an **adjective** in the section on Friends Reunited
that means *wanting to know something.*
Write it here: .... and mark the
stress.

b What's the **noun**?
Write it here: .... and mark the
stress.

7a Find a **noun** in the section on Friends Reunited that
means *something that is done as a reaction to something
that has happened or been said.*
Write it here: .... and mark the stress.

b What's the **verb**?
Write it here: .... and mark the stress.

8a Find an **adjective** in the section on Reading groups that
means the *size or number of something is guessed without
counting exactly.*
Write it here: .... and mark the stress.

b What's the **verb**?
Write it here: .... and mark the stress.

9 Find the words in the sections on Friends Reunited and
Reading groups which are collocations of the following:
a school .... or ....
b to visit a ....
c old ....
d leisure .... or ....
e a waiting ....

10 Find the **prepositions** missing in these expressions
in the sections on Friends Reunited and Reading
groups.
a to find (something) ....
b to set (something) ....
c to sweep ....
d to meet .... with people
e to have a few hours .... myself

© Pearson Education Limited 2005 **PHOTOCOPIABLE**

10B The Supasaver debate

Ways of expressing the future

Supasaver development to be debated today

The future of Shelbyville's proposed new supermarket will be decided today during a meeting at the town hall. The plan to build a Supasaver in South Park has caused a great deal of discussion since it was announced two months ago. Supporters of the project claim that it will lead to more jobs and greater choice, while opponents say that South Park is important to the town, and that a supermarket will be bad for other businesses in the area.

The meeting will be chaired by the head of the town planning committee, and representatives from both sides of the local community will also be attending. With supporters and opponents of the plan both feeling confident of victory, there is sure to be a lively debate in the town hall this afternoon.

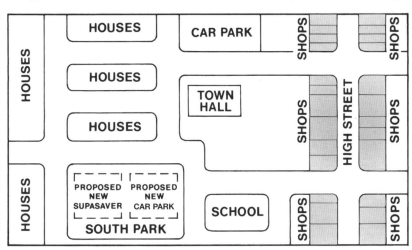

Jack/Janet Charlton

You are the chairperson of the town planning committee. Your job is to control the meeting and organise a vote at the end. Everyone at the meeting is allowed to vote, including you. You are not sure how to vote at the moment. Before the debate begins, decide what the advantages and disadvantages might be:

- put other shops out of business (what kind of shops?)
- the local school (what effect would the supermarket have?)
- South Park is the only park in the town and is popular with local residents (why?)
- attract people (and lots of traffic) from nearby towns (benefits? problems?)
- the effect on jobs (in the short term? in the long term?)
- the effect on local residents (during the day? at night?)
- the supermarket will pay taxes (what could they be spent on?)
- any other advantages and disadvantages you can think of.

Allow everyone to introduce themselves briefly. **Make sure everyone takes turns in speaking**.

Ray/Jane Wilson

You are head of the local council. Unemployment is high in Shelbyville, and you have been trying to attract investment from outside the town for years. You are therefore in favour of the plan for the following reasons:

- more jobs (what kind?)
- attract people from nearby towns (benefit to Shelbyville?)
- convenient (who for?)
- Supasaver will pay local taxes (what could you spend the money on?)
- any other benefits you can think of.

These are some arguments against the plan. Think how you can argue against them:

- near the school
- increased traffic and pollution
- South Park is the only park in the town and is popular with local residents
- other businesses in the town will suffer.

Gordon/Susan Banks

You are head of the Shelbyville Business Association, which represents 140 small businesses in the town. You own a bakery in the High Street, which might have to close if the supermarket is built. You are against the new supermarket for the following reasons:

- many shops will go out of business (what kind of shops?)
- create unemployment (how many people will lose their jobs?)
- destroy the local community (why?)
- local farmers will suffer (why?)
- extra traffic (what problems will it cause?)
- any other problems you can think of.

These are some arguments in favour of the plan. Think how you can argue against them.

- create jobs
- more choice for customers
- attract people from neighbouring towns
- more convenient for local residents

Bobby/Sally Moore

You are a local politician. You are not sure how to vote at the moment; you will decide at the end of the debate. Before the debate begins, decide what the advantages and disadvantages might be:

- put other shops out of business (what kind of shops?)
- the local school (what effect would the supermarket have?)
- South Park is the only park in the town and is popular with local residents (why?)
- attract people (and lots of traffic) from nearby towns (benefits? problems?)
- the effect on jobs (in the short term? in the long term?)
- the effect on local residents (during the day? at night?)
- the supermarket will pay taxes (what could they be spent on?)
- any other advantages and disadvantages you can think of.

Martin/Molly Peters

You are head of the local primary school. Your school has 300 children between the ages of five and eleven. You are against the new supermarket for the following reasons:

- too close to your school (why is this a problem?)
- the children do sports in South Park – it's the only green space in the town
- increased traffic – lorries and cars (what problems will this cause?)
- dangerous for children during construction (why?)
- the town would lose a beautiful park (what effect would this have?)
- any other problems you can think of.

These are some arguments in favour of the plan. Think how you can argue against them.

- good for local economy
- better quality, cheaper food
- create jobs
- more convenient for local residents

Geoff/Rita Hurst

You are head of the Supasaver Corporation. You feel that a Supasaver store in Shelbyville would be extremely profitable for your company, and for you personally. These are some points in favour of the plan:

- cheaper prices, better products, more choice (of what?)
- more jobs (what kind?)
- attract people from neighbouring towns (benefit to town?)
- pay local taxes (benefit to town?)
- any other benefits you can think of.

These are some arguments against the plan. Think how you can argue against them.

- more traffic and pollution
- the effect on jobs in other shops and businesses
- South Park is popular with local residents
- very near a school.

10C How about ten thirty?

Future continuous and Future perfect

Role card A

You are the secretary for Kenny McCormick, the famous tennis player. He is away today, but he said that if anyone from *Ego Publishing* called, you should try to make an appointment with him/her – he is trying to get someone to publish his autobiography.

Below is his diary for the next three days. It is not possible to cancel any of his appointments, and you cannot make an appointment before 8 a.m. If he is not available at any time, say why.

Tuesday 26th November

8.00–9.00	– run
9.00–11.00	– practice
11.00–12.00	– have massage
12.45–1.30	– lunch with shoe sponsors
2.30–3.15	– have meeting (accountant)
4.00–5.30	– practice match
6.30–7.45	– appear on TV quiz programme
7.45–10.00	– attend tennis club dinner

Wednesday 27th November

8.00–9.00	– run
9.00–11.00	– training in gym
12.00–1.00	– dentist
2.00–4.00	– make advertisement (Noke shoes)
4.45–5.45	– meeting; computer games manufacturer
6.30–8.00	– record interview (BBC)
8. 00–10.00	– dinner with clothes sponsor

Thursday 28th November

8.00–9.00	– run
10.00–11.30	– have photo taken for new advertising campaign
12.30–1.30	– lunch with journalist
2.00–3.00	– training
3.30–4.00	– have massage
4.45–6.00	– travel to airport
7.00–9.00	– fly to Paris

Useful language

I'm sorry, he'll be (verb + -*ing*) ... then.

I'm afraid he'll be in a meeting with ... then.

He'll have finished/left by ...

He won't have finished/left ... by then.

Are you free at ...?

Role card B

You work for *Ego Publishing*. Last week Kenny McCormick, the famous tennis player, sent you his autobiography, which he wants you to publish. You are very interested, and are now going to phone his office to make an appointment. You need at least **half an hour** with him.

Below is **your** diary for the next three days. It is not possible to cancel any appointments, or to arrive late. If you're not available at any time, say why. You want to make an appointment **as soon as possible**.

Tuesday 26th November

9.00–9.30	– doctor
10.15–11.30	– meeting with advertising manager
11.30–12.45	– visit Dylan's bookshop
1.30–3.00	– interview applicants for new secretarial job
3.00–400	– meeting with printer
5.30–7.00	– attend book launch, National Gallery

Wednesday 27th November

9.00–9.30	– pick up car from garage
10.30–12.00	– computer training course
12.45–2.00	– lunch with boss
2.30–3.30	– phone New York office
3.30–5.00	– prepare talk for Publishers' Conference
5.30–6.45	– choose covers for new books

Thursday 28th November

9.00–10.30	– meeting with marketing
11.00–12.00	– record interview for 'The Book Programme'
12.30–1.00	– travel to Publishers' Conference
1.15–1.45	– give talk at Conference
2.30–3.00	– lunch (John)
4.00–5.00	– interview new secretary
5.30–6.30	– attend meeting on time management

Useful language

Is Mr McCormick free at ...?

What will he be doing at ...?

Will he have finished by ...?

I'm sorry, I'll be (verb + -*ing*) ... then.

I'm afraid I'll be in a meeting.

I won't have finished/left ... by then.

11A Wishing

Hypothetical situations in the present

Find someone who ...	Name(s) and notes
... wishes the weather were different at the moment.	
... wishes they didn't have to work so hard.	
... has ever wished they didn't live where they do.	
... has ever wished they were someone else.	
... wishes they could see into the future.	
... wishes the weekends were longer.	
... has ever wished they could win the lottery.	
... wishes they could meet someone famous.	
... has ever had a day when they wish they hadn't got out of bed.	
... wishes they were good at a particular sport.	
... wishes they could stop doing something they do all the time.	
... wishes they were older.	

 PHOTOCOPIABLE

11B I wish he wouldn't do that!

Wishes in the past and present

Role card A

Your name is Derek/Doris, and you're sitting in **a doctor's waiting room**. You are fifty years old and married, and there are lots of things in your life you're not happy about! Start a conversation with the person next to you, and ask them questions about their life. During the conversation, tell them about the problems and regrets below. Try to convince your partner that your problems are **worse** than his/hers.

Health
- You have terrible asthma.
- You are allergic to cats.
- You ate some fish yesterday and were sick all night.

Holidays
- You went to the seaside on holiday last year, and it rained all the time.
- You're going back there again this year because your husband/wife wants to.
- You would like to go to Australia, but you can't afford it.

House/Job
- You live in a small flat near a busy motorway.
- You would like a bigger flat, but you can't afford to move.
- You have a boring part-time job at a supermarket checkout.

Family
- Your husband/wife is too lazy to look for a job.
- Your three grown-up sons still live with you – you have no space for yourself.
- Your brother never phones you.

Neighbours
- The baby in the flat upstairs cries all the time.
- The people in the flat below always shout at each other.
- Their cat keeps coming into your flat.

Role card B

Your name is Albert/Alice, and you're sitting in **a doctor's waiting room**. You are fifty years old and married, and there are lots of things in your life you're not happy about. Start a conversation with the person next to you, and ask them questions about their life. During the conversation, tell them about your problems and regrets below. Try to convince your partner that your problems are **worse** than his/hers.

Health
- You have very bad headaches.
- You can't get to sleep at night.
- You picked up a television yesterday and hurt your back.

Holidays
- You went to India on holiday last year, and were extremely ill.
- You can't go on holiday this year, because you haven't got the time.
- You want your daughter to come and visit you, but she is terrified of flying.

House/Job
- You live in a big house very close to a chemical factory.
- You run your own business, so you don't have any spare time.
- You want to live in the country, but your husband/wife doesn't want to move house.

Family
- Your husband/wife has to work every weekend.
- Your daughter lives abroad – you haven't seen her for years.
- Your sister phones you every night – it drives you crazy!

Neighbours
- Your neighbour's dog barks all night.
- Your other neighbour throws his rubbish into your garden.
- He also plays very loud music every evening.

Activities

11C A nightmare holiday

Third conditional and *should have*

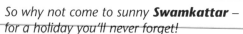

Swamkattar — for the holiday of a lifetime!

Two wonderful weeks on this island of paradise for only **$395** per person! (flight included)

Stay in the beautiful **Palace Hotel**, which offers you:
- luxurious rooms with en-suite bathrooms
- breathtaking views of the surrounding scenery
- private swimming pools
- wonderful food, including local specialities
- three lively bars open all night
- two beautiful beaches close to the hotel.

And our **all-in-one** price includes:
- bus from the airport to the hotel
- excursions to local beauty spots
- a local guide who is fluent in English
- horse riding in the mountains.

*So why not come to sunny **Swamkattar** – for a holiday you'll never forget!*

Tourist role card

You've just come back from Swamkattar, and it was the worst holiday of your life! You are now going to complain to the travel agent who sold you the holiday. Try to get at least some of your money back! Here are some things that went wrong with your holiday.

- You had to share your room (and bathroom) with another family.
- All you could see from your window was a nuclear power station.
- The swimming pools were half empty.
- The food was disgusting, and sometimes there were insects in it! You had to eat in the restaurant next door, and spent over $200 there.
- None of the bars served alcohol.
- The beaches near the hotel were covered in oil.
- There was no bus to meet you at the airport. You had to take a taxi, which cost $50.
- You only went on one excursion – to the nuclear power station!
- The guide was eighty-six years old – and deaf!
- There were no horses, only one very old donkey (which died).

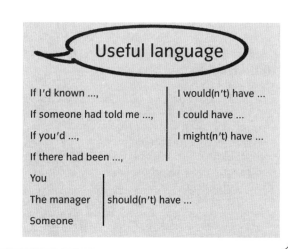

Useful language

If I'd known ...,
If someone had told me ...,
If you'd ...,
If there had been ...,

You
The manager
Someone
should(n't) have ...

I would(n't) have ...
I could have ...
I might(n't) have ...

Swamkattar — for the holiday of a lifetime!

Two wonderful weeks on this island of paradise for only **$395** per person! (flight included)

Stay in the beautiful **Palace Hotel**, which offers you:

- luxurious rooms with en-suite bathrooms
- breathtaking views of the surrounding scenery
- private swimming pools
- wonderful food, including local specialities
- three lively bars open all night
- two beautiful beaches close to the hotel.

And our **all-in-one** price includes:

- bus from the airport to the hotel
- excursions to local beauty spots
- a local guide who is fluent in English
- horse riding in the mountains.

*So why not come to sunny **Swamkattar** – for a holiday you'll never forget!*

Travel agent role card

You sell cheap holidays to Swamkattar, but you've heard from the manager of the Palace Hotel that there have been a lot of problems on the island. You are going to talk to someone who's just returned from their holiday. Explain why things went wrong with his/her holiday. You are allowed to give him/her **some** money back, but **not all** of it.

Here are some problems the hotel manager told you about.

- On Swamkattar it is the local custom for guests to share rooms.
- Only the windows on the **left** side of the hotel have good views.
- It hasn't rained for six months, so there is a water shortage on the island.
- The chef died (of food poisoning!) so his brother did the cooking. Fried insects are a local speciality.
- There has recently been an election on Swamkattar. The new government has banned alcohol.
- Two weeks ago an oil tanker crashed near the hotel.
- There are two exits to the airport. The bus usually waits outside the **back** exit.
- Your most popular excursion is to the nuclear power station. All other excursions started at 5 a.m.
- The guide had a car accident recently, so his father took his place.
- The military police took all your horses.

Useful language

If you'd ...,	you would(n't) have ...
If ... hadn't ...,	you could have ...
If that hadn't happened,	there would(n't) have ... been ...
	you might have ...
You	
The manager	should(n't) have ...
Someone	

12A Reporting a crime

Reporting verbs

Role card 1
You think the best thing to do is to tell the police everything that happened – that way you'll get a shorter prison sentence. Try to persuade everyone else to do the same.

'I really think you should ...'

Role card 2
You think it was everybody else's fault you were caught (but not yours, of course!). Go round the police cell and tell everyone this.

'It's your fault that ...'

Role card 3
You don't think anyone should say anything to the police. In fact, you will kill anyone who does!

'If you ..., I'll ...'

Role card 4
You think it would be a good idea to start digging a tunnel so you can all escape. Suggest this idea to everyone.

'Why don't we ...?'

Role card 5
You think the police might be listening to everything you are saying. Warn everyone not to say anything about what happened.

'Don't ..., because ...'

Role card 6
You are absolutely certain everything is going to be all right, and you'll all be home soon. Tell everyone else there is nothing to worry about.

'Don't worry, ...'

Role card 7
Your friends think **you** told the police about the robbery! Tell your friends that this isn't true.

'I know what you think, but I didn't ...'

Role card 8
You're very rich – because of your last bank robbery! – and you want to pay for a top lawyer for everyone.

'I'll ..., if you want.'

Role card 9
You've decided to tell the police everything they want to know. Tell your friends about your decision.

'I've made a decision. I'm going to ...'

Role card 10
You are the leader of the group. Order them all to sit down and shut up!

'I'm the boss here, so ...!'

Role card 11
You weren't involved in the robbery – you were just walking past the bank when the police arrived! Tell everyone this, and insist that they believe you.

'You probably don't know who I am, because ...'

Role card 12
You know that someone hid the money before the police arrived. You're not sure who it was, so you're going to congratulate everyone!

'Well done! You ...'

12B The marriage from hell

Reporting verbs; reporting questions and statements

Hollywood marriage to end in divorce?

The dream marriage between the fifty-five-year-old film director Jim Small and this year's brightest star, Catherine Hunt, is quickly turning into a nightmare! Small has told Catherine, twenty-six, never to return to their two-million-dollar home in Beverly Hills. Apparently, the couple are already talking to their lawyers about a possible divorce.

Two days ago, Small, who earlier this year cast his wife in the leading role in his new film, *My Life Story*, shocked Hollywood by stopping all work on the movie. He is refusing to continue unless his wife is replaced by 'someone who knows how to act' – although other people have suggested that there are financial problems with the film.

There are also rumours that Catherine's co-star Peter Rickman, who was recently voted 'the sexiest man on screen' by our readers, has been ordered to leave the film too. Is this anything to do with photographs of Catherine and Peter leaving the exclusive new *Fresh Earth Restaurant* on Sunset Boulevard together?

Rising young star Natasha O'Brien, twenty-two, is being lined up to replace Catherine when – and if – filming restarts, and many people are already asking about Jim Small's relationship with the beautiful young actress.

Watch out for our exclusive interviews with both Jim and Catherine in next week's issue of *Movie World* !

Movie World reporter

You are going to interview both Jim and Catherine. Look at the article again, and prepare **at least twelve** questions to ask them. Make sure you cover the following topics:

- why filming was stopped on *My Life Story*
- financial problems with the film
- Catherine's relationship with Peter Rickman
- Peter Rickman's future on the film
- Jim's relationship with Natasha O'Brien
- why Catherine left the house
- where Catherine is living now
- their marriage
- divorce
- any messages they have for each other
- any other questions you have.

During the interview, **make brief notes** of your answers. You will need them later.

© Pearson Education Limited 2005

Jim Small

You are going to be interviewed by a journalist from *Movie World*. Here are some of the main points you want to make during the interview.

- You know the reasons why Catherine left the film. (**What are they?**)
- There are no financial problems with the film. *My Life Story* will definitely be made.
- Your wife's having an affair with Peter Rickman – you're certain of this. (**Why?**)
- You didn't tell Peter to leave the film; he chose to leave. (**Why?**)
- Natasha O'Brien is a wonderful actress – perfect for the film. (**Why?**)
- Natasha is a friend of yours, nothing more.
- Your wife said she would kill Natasha if she took her place on the film.
- Catherine decided to move out of your house. (**Where is she living now?**) You asked her to stay and talk about the situation, but she refused.
- The marriage has been a disaster ever since the honeymoon, and it's all your wife's fault. (**Why?**)
- You want to get a divorce. Your lawyers said that it would be dangerous to say anything about it before you go to court. (**Why?**) You won't give her any of your money!

Now think of a final message for your wife: ....

Catherine Hunt

You are going to be interviewed by a journalist from *Movie World*. Here are some of the main points you want to make during the interview.

- You're not having an affair with Peter Rickman – you're just good friends.
- Filming on *My Life Story* was stopped because your husband was jealous of your friendship with Peter. (**Why?**)
- You've heard that there is no money left to make the film. (**Who told you?**)
- Your husband is having an affair with Natasha – you're absolutely certain of this. (**Why?**)
- Your husband ordered you to leave the house. (**Why?**) He said he would kill you if you didn't.
- You went back two days later to collect your clothes, but he wouldn't answer the door. (**Why not?**) You'll report him to the police if he doesn't let you have your clothes soon.
- You're now living with your mother!
- The marriage has been a disaster ever since the honeymoon, and it's all your husband's fault. (**Why?**)
- You want to get a divorce. You are going to insist that you get half of his money. (**Why?**) You'll meet your husband at any time to talk about it.

Now think of a final message for your husband: ....

PHOTOCOPIABLE

12C Preposition race

Revision of prepositions

A		
I've been trying to **get in touch**	**with**	12 Sam for days, but he's never at home.
B		
I used to **suffer**	**from**	5 stress until I started doing yoga.
C		
I really don't want to **be late**	**for**	19 my doctor's appointment.
D		
I'm not really **sure**	**about**	13 the answer to question two.
E		
I think you should **forget**	**about**	24 work for a while and relax.
F		
The teachers find it difficult to **cope**	**with**	6 such a large class.
G		
His new film **is set**	**in**	22 Europe in the nineteenth century.
H		
All new pupils have to **stick**	**to**	14 the school rules.
I		
The chief accountant **deals**	**with**	20 all the financial problems of the company.
J		
Mark walked into the room **dressed**	**in**	7 a gold football shirt and black shorts.
K		
Sir Edmund Hillary is **famous**	**for**	18 being the first man to climb Mount Everest.
L		
The members of parliament voted **in favour**	**of**	3 increasing taxes on cigarettes.

M	The head of the police force has been **accused**	of	11 taking bribes from politicians.
n	A lot of people **worry**	about	16 what life will be like when they're old.
0	Three of the students **confessed**	to	4 cheating in the exam.
p	Nowadays almost everyone **is aware**	of	17 the dangers of smoking.
Q	Last month I **applied**	for	10 twelve jobs, but I didn't get any of them.
R	The football supporters who started the trouble were **removed**	from	8 the stadium by the police.
S	Tom and Emma decided **to get rid**	of	15 their old sofa and buy a new one.
T	*Game Over!* is a new TV programme **aimed**	at	1 teenagers interested in computer games.
u	It's easy to get **addicted**	to	21 hard drugs like heroin and cocaine.
V	After the match the manager **blamed** his goalkeeper	for	23 letting in the winning goal.
W	I phoned Jack and Sally to **congratulate** them	on	2 their engagement.
X	I'd like to **change** 500 American dollars	into	9 Italian lire, please.

Test one TIME: 45 MINUTES

modules 1–4

A Tense review

Complete the gaps in the following sentences with a suitable form of the verb in brackets.

1 Nadia is one of my best friends; we .... (*know*) each other since we .... (*be*) at primary school.

2 The roads were so empty, we .... (*drive*) for several hours before we .... (*see*) another car.

3 Fewer people .... (*take*) foreign holidays nowadays: and until the economic situation .... (*improve*), the travel industry will continue to suffer.

4 I .... (*wake up*) suddenly: someone .... (*knock*) loudly on my door.

5 When I .... (*arrive*), there was nobody at the house; they .... (*leave*) earlier that day.

6 It .... (*not rain*) once since I .... (*arrived*) here six weeks ago.

12

B Word order

Arrange the words underlined so they are in the correct order.

1 My neighbour has invited me round to his house on Saturday. He *show / his new computer / wants / me / to*.
....

2 Sorry, but I don't know *coming back / is / James / when*. Can I take a message?
....

3 It's strange how every time we go out we *enough / have / money / never* to take a taxi home!
....

4 Perhaps it's none of my business, but *were / talking / to / who / you* when I came in?
....

5 A lot of people don't trust Carlo, but I think he's *a / man / pleasant / quite / young* really.
....

6 Denise *early / home / enough / usually / is* to see her favourite soap opera on TV.
....

6

C Vocabulary: prefixes and suffixes

Use a prefix to make a word which fits the definition.

For example:
To understand something incorrectly (*v*) *mis*.understand

1 Not paid enough for the work you do (*adj*)
.................paid
2 Food that is cooked before it is sold (*adj*)
.................cooked
3 Against the government (*adj*)
.................-government
4 To write something again (*v*) ....write
5 To understand your own personality (*adj*)
.................aware
6 A person studying at a university after finishing their first degree (*n*) ....graduate
7 A hotel room where you cannot smoke (*adj*)
.................smoking
8 To sleep for longer than you wanted to (*v*)
.................sleep

8

D Verb forms

Circle the correct form of the verb in the following sentences.

1 Waiting ages for a bus makes me *feel / feeling / to feel* so frustrated!
2 As I went to bed, I could hear the people next door *have / having / to have* a row.
3 OK, I'd better *get back / getting back / to get back* to work now.
4 Sorry *disturb / disturbing / to disturb* you.
5 You can receive your e-mail by *click / clicking / to click* on the 'Mail' icon on your computer screen.
6 Try *not to worry / not worry / not worrying* too much!
7 There's no point in *revise / revising / to revise* for your exams now: just get some rest!
8 You must *be joking / joke / to joke*!
9 Would you mind *lend / lending / to lend* me your umbrella?
10 I really hate *being followed / following / to follow* by a police car!

10

© Pearson Education Limited 2005

E Pronunciation: word stress

Put the words below in the correct column of the table according to their word stress.

~~luxury~~ involvement impression embarrassing operation dependable confident sensitive sympathetic ambition government disappointed aggressive ridiculous intelligence practical undervalued

● ○ ○	○ ● ○	○ ● ○ ○	○ ○ ● ○
luxury			

8

F Auxiliary verbs

Complete the gaps using a suitable form of the auxiliary verbs *will*, *do* or *have*.

1 A: I've heard you don't eat meat: is that right?
   B: Yes, I'm a vegetarian, but I .... eat fish.
2 A: Linda's lost a lot of weight, ... she?
   B: Yes, she looks a lot slimmer now.
3 It's a lovely day, ... it?
4 A: You must be hungry after such a long drive. Did you stop for lunch?
   B: No, we .... We're absolutely starving!
5 Most people prefer summer to winter but I .... : I'm really keen on skiing!
6 A: Did you know my sister's gone on holiday to the Himalayas?
   B: .... she? That sounds quite an adventure!

6

G Vocabulary

Complete the gaps in the following sentences with the correct word (*on*, *away*, *around*, etc.).

1 After driving .... the motorway for an hour, we realised we were going in the wrong direction.
2 Stephanie looks so worried: she must have something .... her mind.
3 My friends spend a lot of time talking .... the past.
4 Sorry we're late. We've been driving .... for ages looking for a parking space!
5 I don't watch much TV but I like going to the cinema .... time to time.
6 She likes to have plans and know what she's doing and when she's doing it. She hates feeling .... of control.
7 He can't make .... his mind whether to go to the party or not.
8 Now stop shouting everybody, and try to calm ....
9 Young children often fall .... when they first try to walk.
10 If I feel .... too much pressure, I sometimes get a headache.

10

H Vocabulary: collocations

Cross out the word or phrase which is incorrect.

For example:

go to — the cinema / ~~home~~ / school / a party

1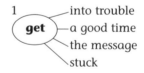
5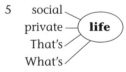

2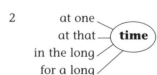
6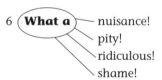

3 lose — your ticket / sleep / your train / your keys
7 change your / make up your — **mind** / get someone's / speak your

4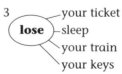
8

8

I Vocabulary: word building

Complete each sentence with the correct form of the word in capitals.

For example:

What do you think has been the most important *scientific* discovery of the last ten years? SCIENCE

1 James soon got over the physical effects of the accident, but the .... effects lasted much longer. PSYCHOLOGY
2 We had a wonderful time on holiday. It was a really .... two weeks. ENJOY
3 Watson is one of our most .... employees. He always finishes his work on time. DEPEND
4 Lots of exercise and a balanced diet is very .... to your health. BENEFIT
5 My husband isn't very .... when he eats out. He always orders the same thing! ADVENTURE
6 I'm usually very good at taking .... from my boss, even if she says something I don't like. CRITICISE
7 He looked through the window but there was no .... Everything was still and quiet. MOVE
8 It is important to deal with problems of this kind with a great deal of .... SENSITIVE

☐ 8

J Active or passive?

Put the verb in brackets in the correct active or passive form. Make sure that you use the correct tense.

1 Stonehenge, the famous stone circle in the south-west of England, ... (*build*) about 5,000 years ago. Some of the stones .... (*weigh*) as much as fifty tonnes. Although visitors .... (*not / allow*) to approach the stones themselves since the 1980s, the historic site .... (*visit*) by thousands of tourists every year.
2 Director Marty Elmore's latest film *The Midnight Road* .... (*release*) next month. The film .... (*feature*) new Hollywood sensation Courtney McCray and .... (*shoot*) entirely on location in Mexico. It .... (*describe*) by its director last week as 'a romantic comedy with car chases'.
3 Motorists .... (*experience*) delays of up to an hour on the capital's roads this week. Traffic jams are particularly heavy at the moment while the city's new underground system .... (*build*). Work on the new system should .... (*complete*) by May next year. In the meantime, drivers .... (*advise*) to leave their cars at home and use public transport.

☐ 12

K Writing formally

In each of the sentences below, replace the word in **bold** with a more formal word or phrase. (You are given the first letters.)

1 **After** our telephone conversation yesterday, I am writing to complain about the product you sent me. f.....................
2 I **bought** the item two weeks ago. pur.....................
3 I am very **unhappy** with the service you provide. dis.....................
4 I want you to **give me back** my money. r.....................
5 I do not **understand** why your receptionist was so rude. com.....................
6 When I opened the box, I **saw** that the machine was broken. dis.....................

 6

L Phrases

Complete the following phrases with *a*, *an*, *the* or – (no word).

1 Things are getting better in .... long term.
2 Oh, for .... goodness' sake! Don't be so stupid!
3 That's .... shame!
4 They left more than .... hour ago.
5 Carol is suffering from .... stress.
6 .... next thing is to switch on the camera.

☐ 6

TOTAL ☐ 100

Test two TIME: 45 MINUTES

modules 5–8

A Perfect tenses

Complete the gaps in the following sentences with the correct form of the verb in brackets.

1 You really should go and see *Trouble in Paradise*. It's one of the best films I .... (*see*) this year.
2 I was especially careful because I .... (*never / drive*) abroad before.
3 I .... (*try*) to get in touch with Chris all week.
4 I'll phone you after ten: my parents .... (*go*) out by then, so we can have a long chat!
5 Ellis .... (*steal*) money from the company for several months before anyone realised.
6 'What's the matter? .... (*hurt*) yourself?'
7 'Good morning, Mr Lett. .... (*wait*) long?'
8 By the time he celebrates his seventieth birthday, Garcia .... (*be*) president for five years.
9 By nine o'clock, everybody was getting impatient. They .... (*wait*) over an hour for take-off.
10 I really don't know what happened to Christina. We .... (*see*) each other for years.

| 10 |

B Vocabulary: word building

Complete each sentence with the correct form of the word in capitals.

For example: She is now one of the most *successful* business people in the world. SUCCESS

1 The .... of oil has transformed the economic situation in the region. DISCOVER
2 It's my grandmother's ninetieth birthday on Sunday, and we're having a huge .... CELEBRATE
3 The dictionary, printed in the early 1900s, was one of the most important .... of its time. PUBLISH
4 The government continues to talk about .... issues, but does very little! ENVIRONMENT
5 The rapid .... of new computer technology is sure to continue in the next decade. DEVELOP
6 Winning a gold medal at the Olympics was an amazing .... because she was only sixteen years old. ACHIEVE
7 The government is unlikely to spend more money on space .... in the near future. EXPLORE
8 Senator McGuire is widely regarded as a very skilful .... POLITICS

| 8 |

C Vocabulary: collocations

For each verb below, choose two words or phrases from the box that can go with it.

> dressed up   an Olympic medal   great   a risk
> someone a challenge   through your notes
> progress   a competition   a world record
> off to a great start   a talk about something
> something possible   a reason for something
> part in a demonstration

For example:

1 to get — *dressed up* ....
....

2 to win ....
....

3 to make ....
....

4 to take ....
....

5 to look ....
....

6 to set ....
....

7 to give ....
....

| 6 |

D Quantifiers

Complete the gaps in the following sentences with an appropriate quantifier (*some, any, enough, plenty, etc*).

1 We had a couple of hours free, so Alex and I decided to do .... shopping.
2 If you order your taxi for ten o'clock, you'll have .... of time to buy your ticket.
3 Don't wait to be asked, come round .... time!
4 Unfortunately, not as .... people came to the show as we'd hoped.
5 Are there .... other questions, or can we move on to the next item?
6 Maria didn't know .... English, only a few phrases she'd learned from the TV.
7 There isn't .... space in the back for three people. You'll have to walk!
8 In general, I agreed with what he said, although I didn't agree with .... points.

. 8

E Pronunciation: Word stress

Underline the stressed syllable in each of the following words.

For example: demonstr<u>a</u>tion

1 political   5 emergency   9 participant
2 possession   6 traditional   10 procession
3 stamina   7 decoration   11 recommend
4 atmosphere   8 dedication   12 politician

6

F Vocabulary: definitions

Read the definitions, and write a suitable word in the example sentence. (You are given the first letter.)

For example:

phr vb to finish a telephone conversation by putting the telephone down: *After I h.ung. up., I realised I forgot to ask him his telephone number.*

1 *n* someone who is watching an event or game. *The match attracted over 40,000 s................. .*
2 *adj* extremely tired and having no energy: *Jill lay on the grass, e................. after her long run.*
3 *n* an exact copy of something: *in some shop windows they use wooden r.................s instead of real food.*
4 *n* a prize that someone gets for something they have achieved: *Brad Pitt won the Best Actor a................. .*
5 *n* clothes that make you look like a famous person, character from a story, etc.: *At carnival time, lots of people wear f................. d................. .*
6 *v* to throw something with a lot of force: *The demonstration became violent and some people were h................. bricks through windows.*

7 *n* the state of not being known or remembered: *For many years she was one of the most famous actors in Hollywood but now she lives in total o................. .*
8 *n* a short form of a word or expression: *Dr is the written a................. of Doctor.*
9 *adj* very wet or wearing very wet clothes: *After the storm, we were all absolutely s................. .*
10 *v* to shout as a way of showing happiness, approval or support of someone: *When the concert ended, the crowed clapped and c................. .*

10

G Relative clauses

Read the sentences below, and decide whether the relative pronoun underlined is correct or incorrect. (ø means no word.) Mark the four correct sentences with a tick (✔) and the four incorrect sentences with a cross (✘).

1 June, <u>that</u> is slightly cooler than July and August, is probably the best time to visit. ☐
2 This is the Chinese vase <u>which</u> I told you about. ☐
3 Isobel Ford, <u>whose</u> husband is the racing driver Jacques Monet, is currently visiting our town. ☐
4 For our anniversary, we're going back to the restaurant <u>which</u> we had our first date. ☐
5 Who's that man <u>ø</u> watching us so intently? ☐
6 Is there a shop near here <u>what</u> sells cosmetics? ☐
7 The magazine, <u>ø</u> is published monthly, has become increasingly popular. ☐
8 He offered to give me a lift home, <u>which</u> I thought was very nice of him. ☐

8

H Vocabulary

Complete the gaps in the following sentences with the correct word (*for, after, up, etc*.).

1 John really takes .... his father. He looks like him, he speaks like him, he even does the same job.
2 I sometimes get embarrassed when I have to refuse an invitation .... a party.
3 Oh, I'm sorry, I've spilled my drink. That was very clumsy .... me.
4 He knows Jane quite well. They've been .... first name terms for a few months now.
5 My life gets very busy sometimes and I find it difficult to cope .... a lot of problems at the same time.
6 Richard was very unfit and his doctor advised him to take .... jogging.
7 Everybody agrees that smoking is very bad .... you.
8 The people were standing so far .... that we couldn't see their faces or hear what they were saying.
9 I love sleeping and can stay in bed for hours at the weekend. So, during the week I have to really make an effort .... get up in time for work.
10 It's very hot in here. I think I'm going to take .... my jacket.

10

I Linking words

Write a suitable linking word or phrase (*however*, *what is more*, etc.) in the gaps. Do not use *and*, *but*, or *so*.

For example:
Being rich means you never have to worry about paying the bills. *..However...*, there are still plenty of other things to worry about!

1 .... she's nearly ninety years old, my grandmother still drives to the shops every day.
2 Vincent is clearly the best-qualified candidate for the job. .... he has plenty of experience in this field.
3 .... the bad weather, we had a very enjoyable holiday.
4 The east of the country is mainly industrial, ... the western part is more rural.
5 She assured me that my ticket was valid. ...., I still felt a little anxious.
6 There are plenty of good beaches on the island, ... they do get rather crowded in summer.

[6]

J Verb forms

Circle the correct form of the verb in the following sentences.
1 Brazil is still the only country to *be winning / to have won / to win* the World Cup four times.
2 Would you rather *eat out / eating out / to eat out* or stay at home this evening?
3 It took a little time to get used *to have driven / to drive / to driving* on the left, but I'm fine now!
4 Restaurants in my city tend *close / to close / to be closing* about midnight.
5 With record temperatures reported all over the world, global warming seems *have / to be having / to have* a dramatic effect on the world's climate.
6 The one person from this century who I'd most like *to be meeting / to have met / to meet* is Elvis Presley.
7 It's no good *argue / arguing / to argue* with her: she'll never change her mind.
8 As long as I have enough money *for pay / to pay / to have paid* the bills, I'm perfectly happy.
9 The kidnappers agreed to let the hostages *go / to go / going* when the ransom was paid.
10 I'm really looking forward *seeing / to see / to seeing* my family again!
11 I'd advise you *not to travel / to not travel / to don't travel* by third-class carriage – it's so uncomfortable!
12 The only film that's worth *see / seeing / to see* at the moment is *Perfect Strangers*.

[12]

K Adding emphasis

Add emphasis to the following sentences by re-writing them using the word in capitals.
1 Look at the mess in here! What have you been doing? EARTH
....
2 I admire his honesty most of all. WHAT
....
3 Beethoven wrote the 'Moonlight Sonata'. IT / WHO
....
4 He means what he says. DOES
....
5 He is more intelligent than he looks. FAR
....
6 I didn't want to walk home, you did! NOT / ME
....

[6]

L Articles

Complete the following phrases with *a*, *an*, *the* or – (no word).
1 Bilbao is a city in .... north of Spain.
2 George is still in .... hospital, recovering from his operation.
3 Thousands of new jobs have been created, so there is now .... little unemployment in the region.
4 If you don't mind, there are .... few details I'd like to ask you about.
5 We had a wonderful picnic on the banks of .... River Danube.
6 Julia's birthday isn't until .... end of July, so we've plenty of time to buy a present.
7 Christmas Eve is the name given to .... night before Christmas.
8 Usually, I'm in too much of a hurry to have .... breakfast.
9 I've never really liked .... jazz. Have you?
10 Who was your teacher .... last year?

[10]

TOTAL [100]

Test three TIME: 45 MINUTES

modules 9–12

A Future forms

Circle the most appropriate future form in the following sentences.

1 It's better if you don't ring me between 1.30 and 4.30 this afternoon. *I'll have taught / I'll be teaching / I'll teach* at that time.
2 The prime minister has been suffering from ill health recently, and as a result he *may well be / is / will have been* forced to resign.
3 In ten years' time, everyone *has forgotten / is forgetting / will have forgotten* about the current financial scandal.
4 'Good morning everybody, this is your captain speaking. In a few moments, the cabin crew *serve / will be serving / will have been served* breakfast ...'
5 A cold night is expected everywhere, and there *is due to be / is likely to be / might be* some snow on the hills.
6 The spread of information technology *is certainly continuing / will almost certainly continue / will almost certainly be continuing* for the next few decades.
7 The next time *I'll be seeing / I'm seeing / I see* Barbara, I'll pass on the message for you.
8 The 20.30 Super-Express train from Paris *could possibly arrive / is due to arrive / might arrive* on platform one in approximately ten minutes' time.

[8]

B Vocabulary: verbs

Write the missing verb to complete the sentences.

1 If something gets smaller because it has been washed, it ....
2 If you tell someone that something bad will happen so that they can stop it happening, you .... them about it.
3 If someone asks you to do something, and you say no very firmly, you .... to do it.
4 If something disappears suddenly and you cannot explain why, you say it has ....
5 If the police take someone away because he/she has done something illegal or wrong, they (the police) .... him/her.
6 If you can say that something will happen before it actually happens, you can .... it.

[6]

C Hypothetical situations

Complete the gaps in the following sentences with a suitable form of the verb in brackets.

1 I miss my boyfriend so much. If only he .... (*be*) here with me now.
2 It's all your fault. If you .... (*not leave*) the map at home, we .... (*not drive*) around lost now.
3 I wish Petra .... (*tell*) me what's wrong. If I .... (*know*) what the problem was, maybe I could help.
4 It's no good sitting around the house all day. It's time you .... (*start*) looking for a job!
5 Suppose you .... (*can*) meet any famous person in the world, who would it be?
6 I wish it .... (*not rain*) so hard. If it .... (*be*) sunny we could all go to the beach for the day.
7 Everyone told me it was a really great show. I wish I .... (*buy*) some tickets!
8 I'm sure Frank .... (*not be*) so popular if he .... (*not have*) so much money.

[12]

D Vocabulary: collocations

Match a verb in column A with a word in column B.

	A	B
1	make	wrong
2	get	a party
3	go	shop
4	break	a decision
5	have	your mind
6	leave	stuck
7	speak	the rules
8	talk	a message

1 .... 2 .... 3 .... 4 ....
5 .... 6 .... 7 .... 8 ....

[8]

© Pearson Education Limited 2005   **167**

E Vocabulary

Complete the gaps in the following sentences with the correct word (*up*, *of*, *round*, etc.)

1 I'm getting a bit fat so I really need to go .... a diet.
2 I was so pleased to hear that you and George are going to get married. I'm absolutely delighted .... you.
3 Your voice is very faint, would you mind speaking .... a bit?
4 Kreutzer Electronics, can I help you? Can you put me .... to the sales department, please?
5 I telephoned Mary but she was very busy, so I said I'd call her .... later.
6 It didn't rain all summer and as a result .... this all the flowers in the garden died.
7 He got dressed so quickly this morning that he put his T-shirt on the wrong way .... The front was at the back and the back was at the front.
8 I've got something to tell you, I'm afraid. It's .... your flights to New York.
9 I've got a car so I can pick you .... at nine o'clock and we can go to the party together.
10 She didn't think there would be any problems with her new job but it all turned .... badly and she hated it.

`10`

F Pronunciation: word stress

Put the words below in the correct column of the table according to their word stress.

emergency dictionary supermarket economy entertaining epidemic ceremony traditional consequences technology engineering education sensational

●ooo	o●oo	oo●o
	emergency	

`6`

G Verb patterns: infinitive or -ing

Complete the gaps in the following sentences with the infinitive or -ing form of the verb in brackets.

For example:
Julia promised ....*to give*.... (*give*) me a ring as soon as she got home.

1 Had you noticed that there's a button .... (*miss*) on your jacket?
2 Jean offered .... (*pay*) for the lunch, but of course I insisted.
3 Maureen eventually persuaded Jo .... (*accept*) the job.
4 The opposition leader accused the prime minister of .... (*lie*).
5 I am writing .... (*complain*) about the recent programme in which ...
6 A: What do you think about the currency reform?
   B: .... (*be*) honest, I haven't really thought about it!
7 The train drivers are threatening .... (*go*) on strike unless they get more money.
8 Eastman is currently on trial. He denies .... (*kill*) a policeman during an armed robbery.
9 The charity aims .... (*raise*) money to help homeless people.
10 All her friends are telling Pauline .... (*go back*) to work.

`10`

H Vocabulary: word building

Complete each sentence with the correct form of the word in capitals.

For example:
At the moment, a lot of people are worried about the ..*economic*... situation in this country. ECONOMY

1 Bob and Martin have a very strong .... which goes back to their university days. FRIEND
2 Everybody was very .... about your speech, they all really enjoyed it! COMPLIMENT
3 Many people suspect him of lying, but there isn't any real .... PROVE
4 Please let me apologise for any .... this delay has caused you. INCONVENIENT
5 The latest tax reforms will have important .... for all those who invest money abroad. IMPLY
6 The drug should not be given to small children, as it can be .... HARM
7 The only television programmes I really like are .... about nature, history and politics. DOCUMENT

8 The police arrested the wrong person because he looked the same as the criminal. After a couple of hours they realised it was a case of .... identity. MISTAKE [8]

I Irregular verbs

Write the past tense and the past participle of the following irregular verbs.

For example:
write ...*wrote*...... ...*written*....
1 shrink ....
2 swear ....
3 burn ....
4 fit ....
[8]

J Modal verbs

Re-write the underlined part of the following sentences using a suitable modal verb.

For example:
Petra was able to walk well before her first birthday.
Petra ...*could*...... walk well before her first birthday.

1 All the flights to Milan were fully booked, so it was necessary for us to take the train.
....

2 I'm absolutely sure Jacqueline didn't phone. She would've left a message.
....

3 I was sorry to hear about your accident. I'm sure it was a very bad experience for you.
....

4 Nowadays, it is not necessary for visitors to get a visa before entering the country.
....

5 I'm afraid there are no tickets left now. It would have been a good idea for you to arrive earlier.
....

6 Guy isn't usually this late. It's possible that he has forgotten our appointment.
....

7 It's a secret! You're not allowed to tell anyone what's happened! ....

8 It was very foolish of you to ride your motorbike without a helmet. It was possible for you to be arrested.
....
[8]

K Articles

Complete the following phrases using *a*, *an*, *the* or – (no word).
1 The police stopped me for driving .... wrong way up a one-way street.
2 We've been going out a lot recently so we've decided to spend .... quiet night in.
3 There are .... number of things I need to tell you.
4 She thought she could smell burning so she raised .... alarm immediately.
5 Actions speak louder than .... words.
6 This table you sold me is impossible to put together! I think there's .... part missing.
7 The weather in some countries is .... very important factor in food production.
8 I've got .... hole in my pocket so I lost my money!
[8]

L Reported speech

The following sentences are all in reported speech. In each case, cross out the word which is incorrect or unnecessary.
1 Miss Roberts said us we could have a party if we wanted.
2 The immigration officer asked to me how long I was planning to stay in the country.
3 She said that she was very sorry, and it would never happen again.
4 Jane very kindly offered me to pay for the coffees.
5 I told to him it wouldn't be possible to change classes straightaway.
6 Everyone admired my new ring, and wanted to know how much did it cost.
7 David promised me to pay back the money as soon as he could.
8 If you want to make friends, I suggest you joining a club.
[8]

TOTAL [100]

Resource bank key

Learner-training worksheet 3

2
a where a road and a railway cross each other; British English (page 812 of the *Longman Dictionary of Contemporary English*)
b *Await* is a more formal word than *wait for*. You **wait for** something. But you **await** something (page 1605; see Usage Note).
c following closely behind someone or something; informal; *no* (page 1531)
d /kjuː/; *line* (page 1158)
e suddenly surprised; *see/hear/learn*; infinitive (page 1407)
f Meaning 2: if an animal **rears** it rises upright on its back legs (page 1178).
g your fist; page 1143 (page 1259)
h If you **succeed** in doing something, you do what you have tried or wanted to do: if you **succeed only** in doing something you fail and do the opposite of what you wanted; *in* (page 1442)
i *leap*; /liːp/; /lept/ (page 801)
j *notice sb/sth doing sth; notice sth/sb* (page 967)

Learner-training worksheet 4

1
Types of collocation: *possible answers*
a **have** breakfast / a shower / flu
b a(n) close/old/good **friend**
c **speak** quietly/fluently/well
d **think** of/about somebody
e **Once upon a** time; **one of the** highest mountains / best footballers / oldest cities in the world/country

2
b childhood sweetheart
c turned (him) down
d home town
e on
f to
g broken-hearted
h married, children; divorced; yes
i in his late fifties
j again

1A Get to know the *Students' Book*

A no
B page 148
C orange and green
D three
E dealing with problems on the telephone
F inside the front page of the *Mini-dictionary*
G purple and green
H pages 167–168
I page 160
J two
K *big* and *great*
L page 143

2A Which stress pattern?

●○
anxious
envy
science
suffer

○●
aware
depress
depressed
support
involve
involved

●○○
envious
scientist
suffering
sufferer

○●○
awareness
depression
depressing
supportive
supporter
involvement

○●○○
psychology
psychologist
anxiety

○○●○
scientific

2C How many schwas?

●○○
/ə/
happiness
confidence
genius

●○○
/ə/
jealousy
suffering
exercise

○●○○
/ə/ /ə/
continuous
certificate
political

○●○○
/ə/ /ə//ə/
dependable
traditional
development

○●○
/ə/
genetic
annoying
supportive

○●○
/ə/ /ə/
contentment
confusion
performance

○○●○
/ə/
scientific
democratic
disappointed

○○●○
/ə/ /ə/
demonstration
disappointment
politician

3A Sidney and the circus

Correct picture order: D, I, C, K, L, A, G, J, F, B, H, E

Movement verbs worksheet: *possible answers*

rush home – picture K
walk home – D
wander off – A, F
travel around – D
walk past – I
run away – G

run up to – E
walk up to – C, G
walk off – F, A
drive up to – L
run around – B
walk along – I, H

Example composition
Sidney was *walking home* from school one day eating an ice cream when he saw a poster for a circus. The advert said that the circus had been *travelling around* the country since January, and was going to be in town that evening. (**picture D**) He turned the corner and saw a big circus procession *walking along* the main street. There were jugglers, acrobats, clowns and a huge elephant. He stood and watched them as they *walked past*. (**I**) Sidney *walked up to* one of the elephants and offered him his ice cream which the elephant took in its trunk. (**C**) He then *rushed home*

to tell his parents what he had seen and ask them if they could go. They said yes. (**K**)

The next day, Sidney and his parents went to see the circus. They *drove up to* the entrance gate and someone took the tickets. (**L**) They joined the end of a queue, and while they were waiting, Sidney saw a door which said 'NO ENTRY', so he *wandered off* to have a look. (**A**) When he opened the door he realised that he was in the tiger cage. The tigers didn't look very friendly! One of the tigers jumped off his stool and *walked up to* him. He was very frightened and wanted to *run away*. (**G**) The tiger was just about to bite Sidney's head off when something lifted him up. It was the elephant he had met earlier! (**J**) The elephant put Sidney on his neck and *walked off*. (**F**)

Meanwhile Sidney's parents had realised that he was missing and were *running around* the car park looking for him. (**B**) Then they saw the elephant *walking along* with Sidney on his shoulders! (**H**) They *ran up to* the elephant, and Sidney told them what had happened. The elephant took Sidney off his shoulders and gave him back to his parents. (**E**)

3B Continuous snakes and ladders

1 was walking; called
2 phoned; was writing; finished
3 When she **got** home, her husband was watching football on television.
4 As soon as she **saw** the time, she **jumped** out of bed.
5 were waiting; rang
6 arrived; was talking; (was) laughing
7 had already gone; got
8 realised; had left
9 waited; had left; broke in
10 had been sitting; had eaten
11 The sentence is correct.
12 By the time the emergency food supplies arrived, thirty people **had died**.
13 Before the accident, he**'d** never **thought** anything like this would happen to him.
14 In sentence a, he had tried to phone her more than once / repeatedly.
In sentence b, he had tried to phone her once.
15 has been working; left
16 has been playing; started
17 has stopped; have been sitting; have already missed
18 have torn; have been fighting
19 Careful where you walk. Susie**'s broken** a vase, and Johnny's already cut himself.
20 The sentence is correct.
21 I**'ve known** him for a few months, but I**'ve** only **met** his sister once.
22 get up; am getting up
23 is playing; wants
24 I **love** hamburgers! I eat five every day, and I**'m eating** one at the moment!
25 Sentence a asks for your opinion.
Sentence b asks about what is on your mind / your mental process now.

26 Sentence a describes his general character/ behaviour.
Sentence b describes how he is behaving now
27 'll be lying
28 'll be putting
29 When I arrive at the station, my parents **will be waiting** for me.
30 In sentence a, I will start cooking dinner **before** you get home.
In sentence b, I will start cooking dinner **when** you get home.

5C Who's worked for the CIA?

Find someone who ... worksheet: *answers*

1 has written
2 has been making
3 has met
4 has learnt
5 has played / has been playing
6 has been
7 has recently broken
8 has been writing
9 has won
10 has worked / has been working

7B What's buried at the bottom of the garden?

Story card order: C, F, H, A, G, B, E, D
The completed text is as follows:
Paul stood outside number twenty-two, Rose Tree Lane, *where he had lived over twenty years ago,* and tried to see if anyone was home. The dark blue curtains in the living room were completely drawn, even though it was still mid-afternoon. There were no cars parked outside the house, and even the garage, *where he used to keep his bike out of the rain,* was completely empty.

He took a deep breath and walked up the drive to the front door, *which still had the same painted metal numbers screwed into the wood.* As he looked through the letterbox into the hallway, *where he used to sit and wait for hours for his father to get home,* long-forgotten memories came back to him. Now the hallway was dark and empty, and there were letters all over the floor. It looked as though nobody had been home for weeks. 'Did anyone still live here?' he wondered. Perhaps he should have tried to find out before he'd come. Well, it was too late now. He thought for a while, then turned and walked back down the drive.

Samantha, *who had been watching him from across the street,* hurried over to meet him. 'Well?' she asked anxiously.

'There's nobody in,' he said. 'It's now or never.'

He walked back to his car, *which he had parked round the corner out of sight,* and opened the boot. Inside were two new spades he had bought earlier that day. He handed one to Samantha, *who grabbed it with both hands,* then picked up the other and shut the boot.

'Let's make this as quick as we can,' said Paul as they hurried back to the house.

'Fine by me,' said Samantha, *whose courage was beginning to leave her.*

They walked down the side of the house and made their way to the bottom of the garden, *which was so overgrown it was like walking through a jungle.* 'It's buried just here,' said Paul, pointing to a space between two large oak trees. He immediately stuck the spade into the ground and started to dig. The rain, *which had been falling softly all day*, became heavier and heavier as they worked.

They had been digging for nearly an hour before they found what they were looking for. 'There it is!' shouted Paul as he pointed into the large hole. Samantha, *whose hands were red and sore from the digging*, threw her spade down and looked down into the hole.

'Do you mind if I ask you what you're doing in my garden?'

Paul was so surprised by the voice he nearly lost his balance and fell into the hole. Samantha looked round in astonishment and felt her stomach tighten. Standing about ten metres away was an old man in an old brown coat, *who had obviously been watching them for some time.*

8A Fame and fortune

Mark Staines knew that his job at the hamburger restaurant would never **bring him fame** and he would never make a lot of money as long as he stayed there. He did the lottery every week but never bought the **winning ticket** like the people he saw on the television news and in the newspapers.

He dreamt of **making a fortune** but his dreams never came true until he met Cynthia Palmer who worked for a modelling agency in New York.

Cynthia came into Mark's hamburger restaurant one evening and immediately noticed his good looks. 'I could **make you a star**,' she told him and he agreed to go with her to New York.

Mark did his first modelling job and became **an overnight sensation** with the public and the media. After his first photos became known, people stopped him in the street to **ask for his autograph**, which he always gave.

Within months, he was the **centre of media attention** with everything he did and everything he said reported in newspapers and magazines around the world.

He was so much **in the public eye** that he couldn't leave his house without being followed by the paparazzi.

That was when he started to hate the **loss of privacy** and felt like returning to the obscurity of the hamburger restaurant.

Finally, instead of wanting to make a lot of money, **losing his fortune** was all he could dream of.

10A Getting together

Card 1
a attraction
b Verb: attract, Adjective: attractive

Card 2
a pragmatic
b Person: pragmatist, Noun: pragmatism

Card 3
a associate
b with
c association

Card 4
a story
b watches
c well
d (wedding) anniversary
e help

Card 5
a with
b up to
c in
d to
e with

Card 6
a curious
b curiosity

Card 7
a response
b respond

Card 8
a estimated
b estimate

Card 9
a days, friends
b website
c friends
d pursuits, activities
e room

Card 10
a out
b up
c through
d up
e to

12A Reporting a crime

1 persuade/urge
2 blame
3 threaten
4 suggest
5 warn
6 assure
7 deny
8 offer
9 decide
10 order (refuse)
11 insist/deny
12 congratulate

Test one (modules 1–4)

A
1 have known; were   2 had been driving; saw
3 are taking; improves   4 woke up; was knocking
5 arrived; had left   6 hasn't rained; arrived

B
1 wants to show me his new computer   2 when James
is coming back   3 never have enough money
4 who were you talking to   5 quite a pleasant young
man   6 is usually home early enough

C
1 underpaid   2 precooked   3 anti-government
4 re-write   5 self-aware   6 postgraduate
7 non-smoking   8 oversleep

D
1 feel   2 having   3 get back   4 to disturb
5 clicking   6 not to worry   7 revising   8 be joking
9 lending   10 being followed

E (half a mark each)
● ○ ○   confident   ○ ● ○ ○   embarrassing
sensitive   ridiculous
practical   intelligence
government   dependable

○ ● ○   involvement   ○ ○ ● ○   operation
impression   sympathetic
aggressive   disappointed
ambition   undervalued

F
1 do   2 hasn't   3 isn't   4 didn't   5 don't
6 Has

G
1 along   2 on   3 about   4 around   5 from
6 out   7 up   8 down   9 over   10 under

H (incorrect words/phrases)
1 a good time   2 in the long   3 your train
4 someone a favour   5 What's   6 ridiculous!
7 get someone's   8 get to

I
1 psychological   2 enjoyable   3 dependable
4 beneficial   5 adventurous   6 criticism
7 movement   8 sensitivity

J
1 was built; weigh; have not been allowed; is visited
2 will be released; features; was shot; was described
3 are experiencing; is being built; be completed; are
advised

K
1 following   2 purchased   3 disappointed
4 refund   5 comprehend   6 discovered

L
1 the   2 –   3 a   4 an   5 –   6 The

Test two (modules 5–8)

A
1 have seen   2 had never driven   3 have been
trying   4 will have gone out   5 had been stealing
6 Have you hurt   7 Have you been waiting
8 will have been   9 had been waiting
10 haven't seen

B
1 discovery   2 celebration   3 publications
4 environmental   5 development   6 achievement
7 exploration   8 politician

C
1 dressed up; off to a great start   2 an Olympic medal;
a competition   3 progress; something possible
4 a risk; part in a demonstration   5 great; through your
notes   6 someone a challenge; a world record
7 a talk about something; a reason for something

D
1 some   2 plenty   3 any   4 many   5 any
6 much   7 enough   8 some

E (half a mark each)
1 political   2 possession   3 stamina
4 atmosphere   5 emergency   6 traditional
7 decoration   8 dedication   9 participant
10 procession   11 recommend   12 politician

F
1 spectators   2 exhausted   3 replicas   4 award
5 fancy dress   6 hurling   7 obscurity
8 abbreviation   9 soaked/soaking   10 cheered

G
Sentences 2, 3, 5 and 8 are correct. Sentences 1, 4, 6 and
7 are incorrect.

H
1 after   2 to   3 of   4 on   5 with   6 up
7 for   8 away   9 to   10 off

I
1 Although / Even though
2 Furthermore / What is more   3 Despite / In spite of
4 whereas   5 However / Nevertheless   6 although

J
1 to have won   2 eat out   3 to driving   4 to close
5 to be having   6 to have met   7 arguing
8 to pay   9 go   10 to seeing   11 not to travel
12 seeing

K
1 What on earth have you been doing?   2 What I
admire most of all is his honesty.   3 It was Beethoven
who wrote the 'Moonlight Sonata'.   4 He (really) does
mean what he says.   5 He is far more intelligent than
he looks.   6 It wasn't me who wanted to walk home,
you did!

L
1 the   2 –   3 –   4 a   5 the   6 the   7 the
8 –   9 –   10 –

Test three (modules 9–12)

A
1 I'll be teaching   2 may well be   3 will have
forgotten   4 will be serving   5 is likely to be /
might be   6 will almost certainly continue   7 I see
8 is due to arrive

B
1 shrinks   2 warn   3 refuse   4 vanished   5 arrest
6 predict

C
1 was/were   2 hadn't left; wouldn't be driving
3 would tell; knew   4 started   5 could
6 wasn't raining; was/were   7 had bought
8 wouldn't be; didn't have

D
1 a decision   2 stuck   3 wrong   4 the rules
5 a party   6 (someone) a message   7 your mind
8 shop

E
1 on   2 for   3 up   4 through   5 back   6 of
7 round   8 about   9 up   10 out

F (half a mark each)
●○○○ dictionary, supermarket, ceremony, consequences
○●○○ economy, traditional, technology, sensational
○○●○ entertaining, epidemic, engineering, education

G
1 missing   2 to pay   3 to accept   4 lying
5 to complain   6 To be   7 to go   8 killing
9 to raise   10 to go back

H
1 friendship   2 complimentary   3 proof
4 inconvenience   5 implications   6 harmful
7 documentaries   8 mistaken

I
1 shrank, shrunk   2 swore, sworn
3 burnt, burnt (this verb can also be regular)
4 hit, hit

J
1 we had to   2 Jacqueline can't have phoned.
3 It must have been   4 visitors don't have to
5 You should have arrived   6 He may have forgotten
7 You mustn't tell   8 You could have been

K
1 the   2 a   3 a   4 the   5 –   6 a   7 a   8 a

L
1 us   2 to   3 that   4 me   5 to   6 did   7 me   8 you

Questionnaire

Dear Cutting Edge teacher,

We hope you enjoyed using *Cutting Edge*. Your feedback is extremely valuable, and we should appreciate it if you would complete this questionnaire and return it to us.

■ Your name: ....

■ School address: ....

■ Average size of class: ....

■ Average age of your students: ....

■ How would you rate *Cutting Edge*?
Please circle the appropriate number 1 = very poor

                                                2 = poor

                                                3 = fair

                                                4 = good

                                                5 = very good

■ Which supplementary materials did you use *with Cutting Edge*? (Please list titles): ....

....

....

■ Did you use the *Cutting Edge* photocopiable activities in the *Teacher's Resource Book*?

....

....

■ What additional material would you like to see included in the *Cutting Edge* package?

....

....

....

Thanks very much for your help. To receive your mystery gift, please return this questionnaire to the ELT Marketing Department, Pearson Education, Edinburgh Gate, Harlow, Essex CM20 2JE, UK.

Pearson Education Limited
Edinburgh Gate
Harlow
Essex
CM20 2JE
England
and Associated Companies throughout the world

www.longman.com/cutting edge

© Pearson Education Limited 2005

Produced by Cambridge Publishing Management Ltd

Set in Congress Sans and Stone Informal

Printed in Spain by Mateu Cromo, S.A. Pinto (Madrid)

ISBN 0582 825261

Text acknowledgements
We are grateful to The Week Magazine for permission to
reproduce an adapted extract from *The Week* 15/8/98.

Photo acknowledgements
We are grateful to the following for permission to reproduce
photographs:
Bubbles Photo Library for 142 top right; J Allan Cash for 142 top
left; Greg Evans International for 142 bottom left, 154 bottom
right, 155 bottom right; Image Bank for 154 bottom left,
155 bottom left; Pictor International for 142 top middle right;
PictureBank Photo Library for 142 top middle left; Tony Stone
Images for 142 bottom middle left, 142 bottom right,
154 left, 154 top right, 155 left, 155 top right; SuperStock
for 142 bottom middle right.

Illustrated by Pavely Arts, Kathy Baxendale,
Graham Humphreys/The Art Market, Ed McLachlan.